FIJI'S TIMES

A HISTORY OF FIJI

KIM GRAVELLE

A Fiji Times project, originally published as a weekly feature series in The Fiji Times.

First published 1979
Reprinted 1980
Reprinted 1981
Reprinted 1982
Reprinted 1983
Reprinted 1986
Reprinted 1988 (Re-designed and re-typeset)
Reprinted 1991
Reprinted 1992

Printed and Published by The Fiji Times Limited, 20 Gordon Street, Suva, Fiji.
Copyright Kim Gravelle, Graphics (Pacific) Ltd.

ISBN 982-214-001-0

Produced with the grateful assistance of the Fiji Museum and the Fiji Archives.
Special thanks to Ratu Luke Vuidreketi and to Sam Berwick for assistance in checking accuracy, and to Fergus Clunie for use of material in Chapter 6, much of which came from his book 'Fijian Weapons and Warfare', a Bulletin of the Fiji Museum. I am indebted to Sr M. Stella and the Roman Catholic Archives, Suva, for material on Makogai (Chapter 41); Asesela Ravuvu for use of material from 'Fijians at War'; Dr Ahmed Ali for material in Chapters 35 and 39; the Suva Returned Soldiers' and Ex-Servicemen's Association for photographs of World War II. Photographs were willingly loaned by the Fiji Museum; the Government PRO office; and the Caines Jannif collection, used throughout the book.

CONTENTS

1   DEGEI . . . SPIRIT AND MAN AND MYSTERY

Two thousand feet up the northernmost slope of the Nakauvadra Range, just where the mission grass ends and the thick rain forest begins, there is a knee-high stone with three holes cut deep into the side.

It is called the *vatusososo*.

As Fijians have done for perhaps centuries, Uraia Nataliga, a villager from Vatukacevaceva, places a token tuft of grass into one of the holes. "It is to make the day longer" Uraia says. "And to satisfy the *vu*."

Another 800 feet up, the peak of Uluda, the sacred mountain of Nakauvadra, looms impressively against a grey sky. Near this spot, according to Fijian tradition, a chiefly voyager named Degei is said to have ruled over the cradle village, the very birthplace of the first Fijians.

In those traditions, a giant canoe named the Kaunitoni, carrying the God chiefs Lutunasobasoba and Degei, sailed from the ancient homeland and landed on the north-west coast of Viti Levu. The chiefs built their first village at Vuda ('our origin'), but abandoned it, moving inland along a mountainous ridge which stretches from Vuda to Nakauvadra.

Lutunasobasoba died on the way; Degei was lured on to Uluda, building the cradle village about five miles inland from the Ra coast near what is now Vatukacevaceva.

Uraia Nataliga believes the wad of grass pushed into the vatusososo will guarantee that he will have enough light to reach the peak and see his way safely back down again. It is a steep, difficult climb and the track near the top must be cut with a bush knife. But the purpose of his pilgrimage is to reach the *rogorogo-i-Vuda;* two great stones which villagers say were used to summon Degei from the first landing site at Vuda . . . the lali of the gods, so to speak.

Uraia, like countless other Fijians, believes in Degei as man, spirit and ancestor. In legends, Degei is an angry spirit who caused the *ualuvu levu,* the great flood which supposedly carried the first Fijians from Nakauvadra to all parts of Fiji. In legends also, Degei took the form of a snake, inhabiting a cave near the top of Uluda.

Even in the last century, Fijian warriors, guided by their priests, approached this cave on hands and knees and listened for a crash of war clubs which would indicate their success in an upcoming battle.

If Degei takes the form of a spirit, it is because he is considered the founder of a *yavusa.* A yavusa is made up of the direct descendants of a single *kalou-vu* or ancestral god, and its founder was invariably worshipped after death as a god.

When the Native Lands Commission collected information several years ago about the origin of Fijian people, a great many of those interviewed claimed to be descendants of the Nakauvadra kalou-vu. Degei's numerous sons, among them Tokairabe and Tui Lakeba, are said to have founded families that grew into the present chiefly *yavusa,* migrating to Verata, Rewa, Bau, Nayau and other parts of Fiji.

From the top of Uluda, it is possible to see as far as Vanua Levu. It is easy to imagine the spreading out of the people. "It all began here," Uraia says.

But others are less sure.

In the mid-1800's, missionary Thomas Williams spent more than a decade delving into Fijian oral history and, by 1860, wrote that he had "sought in vain for a single ray of tradition" relating to the origin of the Fijians.

Other historians of the time had a similarly poor response, including a Land Claims commissioner who spent 20 years recording Fijian ancestry: he noted 50 legends, none of which mentioned Degei, Lutunasobasoba, or Vuda. And in 1865, missionary Jesse Carey sent a letter to teachers throughout Fiji asking them to record legends or beliefs of people in their areas. The replies listed the deeds of 300 gods and ancestors . . . but again, there was no mention of Degei, Lutunasobasoba, the Kaunitoni, or Vuda.

In fact, what is now the most widely-known traditional legend in Fiji doesn't seem to have made its appearance until 1892, when a Fijian paper, Na Mata, ran a competition to trace Fijian origins. The winning entry said the people came from Thebes and travelled up the Nile to Tanganyika, eventually migrating from Africa to Fiji, led by Lutunasobasoba on the Kaunitoni.

The person who wrote it had schooled at Navuloa Mission School — where a text book in use at the time, written by missionaries, compared Fiji and Tanganyika on linguistic grounds and compared customs of Fiji with those of Thebes. The Degei / Kaunitoni legend, says one researcher (Peter France in the Journal of Pacific History) was "born of missionary parentage."

It may or may not have been Degei and Lutunasobasoba, but Uraia's ancestors — the ancestors of the Fijians — arrived more than 3000 years ago. That time period is indisputable, since pieces of pottery found in several areas of Fiji have been scientifically dated to 1500 BC.

These first voyagers sailed out of the west, moving from the south coast of Asia in successive waves from China, Indonesia, and perhaps the Philippines. They island-hopped, reaching New Guinea first and, as that became settled, moved further east.

Asia had been a melting pot of races. Whether Fijian ancestry originated there or not is still uncertain. All that is known is that Indonesia was the doorway to the Pacific.

Despite the fact that school children in Fiji have been taught for years that the Fijians originated in Tanganyika, science says otherwise. There is no evidence to indicate the Fijians came from anyhere else other than S.E. Asia. Language similarities could simply mean that people from the Asian melting pot migrated in different directions, some across the land to Tanganyika, others out into the Pacific.

One thousand years before the time of Christ, both Melanesians and Polynesians had reached the meeting ground, hard on the heels of the first Fijians, the Proto-Polynesians.

Three thousand year ago may sound like a long time, but it was late compared to the rest of the world. By the time Fiji had Fijians, Babylon was a thriving city, Egypt was already on the decline, and the first Olympic games in Athens were only 300 years away. The Vikings were just beginning to put to sea in their wooden longships. Their voyages, however, were nearly insignificant next to those of the greatest mariners in human history, the Polynesians.

Some historians believe Degei was a Polynesian, and that the Melanesians here before him, lacking a chiefly hierarchy, accepted him as a leader without a struggle. There is no evidence of Degei's cradle village now. Or of the cave which he was supposed to inhabit in the form of a snake.

Perhaps a landslide filled the cave in. Or story-tellers turned the gap between the rogorogo-i-Vuda, which in earlier times was used for offerings of tabua, into the cave of the legends.

Simon Best with 'Lapita' pottery

The volcanic plug at Vuda.

2 SEARCHING FOR SIGNS OF THE FIRST FIJIANS

"The people of Fiji, Tonga and Samoa were all one three thousand years ago. They spoke the same language; they were a single culture." Simon Best was talking as he worked, a paint brush carefully working the loose soil away from a hardened layer of stratified earth showing human habitation.

That layer of earth, at the bottom of an excavation near Tubou Village in Lakeba, was the centre of a village — about 1300 years before the time of Christ.

Mr Best is an archaeologist, one of the super-sleuths who probe beneath the soil searching for tell-tale evidence of ancient civilisation. He has been delving below Lakeba's surface since 1975, painstakingly putting together the clues that will help reconstruct the life styles of Fiji's earliest people.

In pre-historic Fiji, what did the peope eat? How did they live? Who did they interact with? Shovelful by shovelful, the earth is divulging some interesting secrets.

One of the best clues to the past is pottery: even small broken pieces (called 'sherds') can be dated quite accurately by scientific process. Pottery is in evidence at even the earliest archaeological sites.

8

In Ba, Sigatoka and in Lakeba, some sherds have been found dating back to between 1300 and 1500 BC. This earliest pottery has the same detailed designs as those found in sherds of the same period — in Samoa, Tonga and New Caledonia. Named after the site where it was first unearthed in New Caledonia, 'Lapita' pottery is one of the reasons Simon Best feels Fiji and its neighbouring islands were originally settled by one people.

Other important clues are stone adzes, shell tools and fish hooks which appear to have stemmed from a common culture. Left by their owners, 3000 years ago, they have been covered over by centuries of vegetation and soil, building the layers of earth which provide the archaeologist with a calendar of human occupation.

At the lowest level, an abundance of bird skeletons indicates man had arrived. Birds had no fear of man and could be easily caught. Higher up, the soil has been sifted through fine wire screens to reveal inhabitants about 2500 years ago became cannibalistic. Bones uncovered which were crushed, burned and chewed rules out a burial site.

Human bones, even those 2,500 years old, enable an archaeologist to determine sex, age — even how healthy those early inhabitants were. They kept fowls, and also appeared to have had plenty of fruit: in the remains of ancient cooking fires, Simon Best has recovered carbonised seeds from more than 20 different kinds of edible fruits.

One of the prizes from the Lakeba excavations has been pearl shell fish hooks, the first found outside of Polynesia from prehistoric times. Another is a flake of obsidian, a glass-like stone found in so few places in the Pacific that its origin can be traced in the laboratory: Simon thinks it will be from Tonga or New Hebrides; again it is evidence of a people who seemed to move about freely from one island to another during those times. Such treasures are priceless in helping track the paths of the earliest people.

The earliest settled site in Lakeba is against the side of a cliff, right on the flat coast line. It would have been a difficult spot to defend — so different from the hill-top fortified villages that were to follow. One of these is less than a mile away.

High up on the ridges of a rocky hill, Ulunikoro was cleared and mapped by Simon Best. It was populated 200 years later than the village site on the coast below it.

Mr Best thinks it is the largest fortified village in Fiji — perhaps one of the largest in the entire South Pacific. And this, he admits, is somewhat puzzling.

What was a village of this size doing on Lakeba 1000 years ago? Ulunikoro had miles of man-made terraces for its agricultural tenants. It had "massive defences": stone walls laboriously built and guarded by surveillance points reaching out at intervals beyond the walls. It had deep pits from which it appears people may have been hurled into the depths. At least, there were skeletal remains at the bottom.

The oral traditions of Lakeba, the tales of Daunisai and other leaders are traced back to Ulunikoro, where they started 1000 years ago. The village was vacated about 700 years ago.

Sadly, many of the stones from the historic village's walls have been

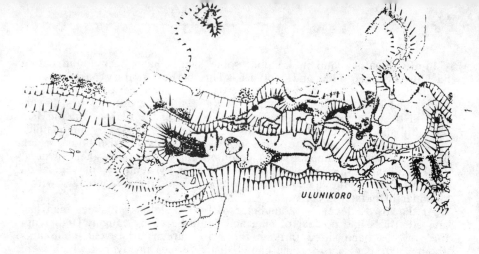

ULUNIKORO

carted away by PWD to use in Lakeba's airfield, Tubou's jetty, and other building projects.

If archaeologist Simon Best's work has been rewarding (and exhausting — it took 500 man hours just to map Ulunikoro), other archaeologists working in Fiji have made equally valuable contributions. More than 30 years ago, E.G. Gifford and his wife looked at promising sites of Viti Levu in their search for history.

One of them was Vuda. Passers-by would be unlikely to take much notice of the stony, wood-covered hill rising from a cane field . . . unless they already were aware of the story about the coming of the first Fijians.

Vuda, a few miles from Viseisei village, rises 350 feet above the bank of a small river. Its vertical stone face provides ample protection for twenty-five house platforms, the mounds still visible above the undergrowth. The uppermost five are supposedly the burekalou, the priest's quarters and the house of Lutunasobasoba himself.

Legend says the Fiji chief reached the shores near what is now Viseisei and chose Vuda for his 'yavutu'. Small as the peak was, Vuda had four temples, erected to the gods Erovunavuda, Vunayawa, Leka and Lutunasobasoba.

The ancestors of that settlement still live in villages nearby, at Viseisei, Lauwaki and Lomolomo, and claim they are the Kai Vuda, the direct descendants of Lutunasobasoba.

Gifford reached Fiji in 1947 and understandably chose Vuda as the site for one of his most painstaking digs. He wrote that Lutunasobasoba's "stone-faced platform crowns the central crag, rising as an acropolis." He understood traditions, and left a sevusevu of yaqona on Lutunasobasoba's temple, both before and after excavation.

He took the time to classify 69 different species of mollusc shells found in the ashes of the cooking fires, to better understand early life styles. And he carbon-dated the earliest artifacts he could uncover from the site. The date: 1255 to 1305 AD . . . or just about 650 years ago.

If Gifford's evidence is correct, Lutunasobasoba was a relative newcomer to Fiji, following in the canoe wakes of those who came several thousand years before him!

3   STORIES IN STONE, AGELESS MANUSCRIPTS

Primeval efforts at a written language . . . strange circular markings, perhaps the ancient symbols of sun worshippers . . . secret rites held in walled enclosures long before the first Europeans arrived . . .

Much of Fiji's earliest history is recorded in rock.

Like those brief messages of today's wall scribblers (Beware the Kung Fu King, Nadroga man wuz hia), ancient man made his marks on smooth stone surfaces, too. Possibly, some of his messages were similar: boundary warnings, and ages-old symbols of fertility. But carved into the rocks and on cave walls are unique script-like figures and magic symbols which provide one of the most exciting mystery stories of old Fiji.

Script-like engravings near Dakuniba, Vanua Levu.

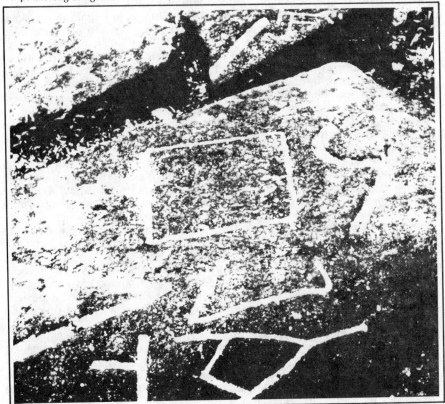

Petroglyphs — engravings in rock — are found in almost every part of the world. Early man left his art work on stone in Asia, Africa, Europe, the Americas, and in India. Researchers have tried to compare the characteristics and suggest a common origin of the people who made them.

Rock drawings have been found in almost all of Fiji's major islands. And yet, villagers treat the mysterious works with indifference, calling them simply *na vatu vola* . . . the inscribed rocks. They've always been there," villagers shrug. There is no superstition and no reverence toward them: certainly they are not *tabu*.

Some take the form of concentric circles; three or more circles inside each other. The same motif is found etched in stone in New Caledonia and the New Hebrides, Papua New Guinea, Tonga, Hawaii and the Marquesas islands. Could they, as some specialists believe, indicate sun or moon worship?

Other petroglyphs, their meaning even less decipherable, appear to be the first efforts at a written language, a jumbled sort of script without any seeming order. One of the best examples of this 'script' is near Dakuniba, in the southeast corner of Vanua Levu. Stone tools have been used to cut a pattern of geometric shapes into a number of large flat rocks. In a straight line parallel with the sea, two other boulders are similarly marked, and there are indentations nearby where primitive stone tools have been sharpened.

If the strange markings are a written language, it is a language without any apparent form, since the characters are randomly spaced and not in any line. But there is one good reason why they can't be easily dismissed as haphazard scribbling: more than 150 miles away, in a cave reached only by an underwater entrance, another series of engravings exists which is startingly similar. Cut into the limestone walls of Yasawa-i-Lau cave in the Yasawas, these petroglyphs embellish five neat, round steps which form a ladder to a shelf in the cave.

At one time, perhaps the shelf was a throne for a stone-age priest, or an idol. When copies of both the Dakuniba and Yasawa-i-Lau petroglyphs were sent to the British Museum in 1937, the experts said they could see no relationships between any known ancient or modern scripts suggesting only that they could have magical or symbolic meanings.

Other rock engravings, perhaps from more recent times, are far easier to understand. In 1883, the author of a book titled 'Camping Amongst Cannibals' described a trip into the Sigatoka Valley: He wrote that, near a village called Tawalika, ". . . there the limestone walls have been decorated . . . with representations of canoes and men, and other objects, the nature of which we could not make out. They have chipped the designs with a stone in a series of dots on the side of the cave, and have then filled in the little cavities with a light coloured clay . . ."

And on Vatulele, so badly weathered that they have nearly disappeared, cliff-side paintings above a beach on the western side depict birds, faces or marks, a canoe, a hand and other motifs. One of the birds is easily identified: a jungle fowl (called 'mangu hegwa' in the Vatulele dialect) which is a descendant of domesticated fowl brought to Fiji about 2000 years ago by early voyagers.

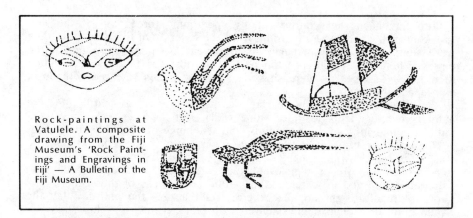

Rock-paintings at Vatulele. A composite drawing from the Fiji Museum's 'Rock Paintings and Engravings in Fiji' — A Bulletin of the Fiji Museum.

In Hawaii, there is a field of flat stones, their surfaces carved with a tapestry of concentric circles and straight, dotted lines. At Vuinadi in Vanua Levu, a boulder has been inscribed with markings so similar it is difficult to avoid reaching any 'linking' conclusions. But much more research will be necessary before such conclusions are possible.

The Fiji Museum has done much to record this country's ancestral art but there are still sites of cave drawings and stone etchings in Ovalau, Viti Levu and Vanua Levu which have not yet been visited by museum experts.

In the meantime, people can only guess at the reasons for some of the more mysterious artwork. Were they magical symbols? Or did they represent shrines of a primitive religion?

Stone and religion appeared to go hand-in-hand in Fiji's pre-contact days. Rounded stones were once anointed with yaqona, and rock walls marked the boundaries of sites used for ancient *'baki'* rites — ceremonies so secret that the punishment was death for revealing what went on.

Baki ceremonies originated in western Viti Levu. The secret rites were held annually (*'yabaki'* means year) to insure fertility, both in people and crops. Walled *'naga'* or *nanaga* sites, cleared areas hidden deep in the interior, were rumoured to exist for purposes of sorcery and orgies.

Considering that a betrayal of the rites could result in death, it is not surprising that it was 1909 before anyone attempted to explain the secrets. Then Ratu Savenaca Duratalo of Navosa, Colo West, broke the tabu. And he very nearly didn't finish writing his account.

"I began to write this on 26 January," Ratu Savenaca reported, "but was smitten with an illness which brought me nigh unto death. It has now left me . . ."

In his report, he said that the rites originated at Vuda and Nadi, and that there were four baki divisions — Rukuruku, Visina, Saqere and Buca. *Nanaga* sites were cleared and weeded until they resembled a village *rara*, and stones were placed around the clearing, one for every youth initiated into the sect. Usually, the *naga* were hidden in the midst of sacred ivi trees.

13

Ratu Savenaca said youths initially spent only three days at the site, speaking in hushed tones, learning from the elders. On the third day, they were sent back to their villages for one year "to plant yams and fatten pigs." When they re-entered the naga, this time for 14 days and nights, their heads and beards were shaved and their bodies smeared with burnt ash of candle nuts.

Ratu Savenaca, possibly fearing death, describes very little of what actually happened inside those stone walls. But the rites were connected with circumcision, warfare training, and teaching social and sexual tabus.

A detailed description of one initiation ceremony inside a *naga* enclosure was made by historian Basil Thomson. He wrote that initiates were made to approach the site on hands and knees, the eery booming of a bamboo trumpet submerged in water adding to the spookiness of the scene. ". . . here, a dreadful sight appalled them. Right across the entrance lay the naked body of a dead man, smeared with black paint . . . Above him lay another body and under this hideous arch they were made to crawl. Inside the enclosure, dead men lay in rows, smeared with blood and entrails, and over each body they had to crawl . . . "At a cry from the elder in charge of the ceremony, the 'dead men' suddenly rose up . . . and ran to wash off the blood . . . of pigs."

Women were forbidden to come near the naga sites, although there appear to be instances when this rule was relaxed, perhaps for manhood training purposes. Stone altars inside the *naga* were repeatedly bathed with *yaqona*, and a secret potion held in special *baki* pots supposedly made the novices insensible to pain.

Today, the stone fences of the naga still exist in Viti Levu, near the upper reaches of the Wainimala, Sigatoka, and Navua rivers. *Baki* rites apparently continued well into the 1800s, ending only with the eventual adoption of Christianity.

Stones used for 'baki' rites: one recorded by missionary Thomas Williams in 1860; the other a contemporary photograph from the Government PRO Office.

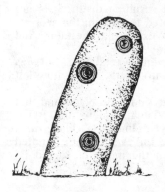

14

May 7, 1789

". . . we observed two large sailing canoes coming swiftly after us along shore, and, being apprehensive of their intentions, we rowed with some anxiety, fully sensible of our weak and defenceless state . . . Only one of the canoes gained upon us, which by three o'clock in the afternoon was not more than two miles off, when she gave over chase . . .

Whether these canoes had any hostile intention against us must remain a doubt: perhaps we might have benefited from an intercourse with them; but in our defenceless situation, to have made the experiment would have been risking too much. I imagine these to be the islands called Feejee . . ."
— From Lieutenant William Bligh
Log of the Voyage
of the Bounty's Launch

The beach at Tofua, where Norton was killed by Tongans.

William Bligh was not the first European to sight Fiji.

Almost 150 years earlier, two ships of the Dutch East Indies Company, under the command of Abel Janszoon Tasman, sailed into Fiji's north eastern section. They barely managed to slide over the treacherous Nanu-ku reefs and, in a driving rain, noted the eastern end of Vanua Levu and Cikobia before turning out to sea again. The isolated tip of southern Lau, Vatoa, had already been recorded by Capt. Cook in 1774.

But it was Lt. Bligh who made the first real European inroad to Fiji. And he did it in circumstances which became one of the world's great survival stories.

HMS Bounty, under Bligh's command, had been sent to Tahiti to collect breadfruit trees for planting in the West Indies. The Bounty's crew had found the six-month stop in Tahiti pleasant — the nights were warm, the ladies were friendly, and few of the men other than Bligh were anxious to leave. By the time the ship reached Tonga, about half the crew had decided to go back to Tahiti . . . without their captain.

When the ship was in sight of Tofua, they mutinied.

* * *

April 28, 1789
Just before sun-rising, while I was yet asleep, Mr Christian, with the master-at-arms, gunner's mate, and Thomas Burkitt, seaman, came into my cabin, seizing me, tied my hands with a cord behind my back, threatening me with instant death if I spoke or made the least noise. I, however, called as loud as I could in hopes of assistance, but they had already secured the officers who were not of their party by placing sentinels at their doors . . .

Bligh and eighteen loyal men were placed in a 23-foot open launch. They were given a 28-gallon cask of water, about seven pounds of bread per man, some rum and four cutlasses — but no fire-arms or sextant.

In his log, Bligh records that some of the 25 men aboard the Bounty (not all were mutineers; a few tried to join Bligh and were held back) "laughed at the helpless situation of the boat, being very deep, and so little room for those who were in her." Others swore "I'll be damned if he does not find his way home."

Cast off by the mutineers, they sailed for Tofua and reached the small island by nightfall. Fearing natives, they waited until morning to land.
"In the morning . . we discovered a cove with a stony beach . . . at the head of the cove, about 150 yards from the waterside, there was a cave .."

They sheltered in the cave that night, and the next day, met the islands' inhabitants, trading some clothing and buttons for a little food. But the following day, the Tofuans were not so friendly and Bligh sensed they were about to attack.

As the men retreated to the boat, one of the crew (John Norton) ran forward to free the anchor and was beaten to death with stones. For Bligh, the attack meant that there was little reason to try to reach any other part of Tonga, since he felt the Tongan's earlier good behaviour resulted from a dread of the Bounty's fire-arms.

Tahiti was the nearest place they might expect help — but they had already discovered the heavily-laden boat could not sail against the wind.

So Bligh set sail for Timor, the Dutch East Indies settlement 3600 miles away!

They were barely away from Tofua before the hardships of the journey ahead became apparent.

Sunday May 3
" . . . the weather continued severe . . . the sea ran higher than in the forenoon and the fatigues of baling, to keep the boat from filling, was exceedingly great."

Just before noon the next day they saw a "small, flat island of a moderate height" and, by mid-afternoon, they could count eight. Fiji was truly on the map!

Bligh was sailing on a course south of Moce and north of Yagasa.

Within the next 24 hours, he would pass Gau and Nairai, and note in his log that "much larger islands appeared in the SW and NNW . . ." He had seen Viti Levu and Koro, even remarking on the 'cockscomb' mountains of Korobasabasaga in Viti Levu's southern coast. And, more important, he made a chart of his path, showing the location of the islands as best he could with the limited equipment he had available.

" . . . to show where they are to be found again is the most my situation enabled me to do . . ." Bligh said in his log. And current-day navigators will tell you that this chart was amazingly accurate.

Certain that the larger islands were all inhabited, the Lieutenant kept the launch as much out to sea and out of sight as possible. On Wednesday the 6th, the same day they observed Viti Levu, one of the men hooked a fish, but it got away.

If that was bad luck, at least THEY were the ones to get away the following day. Early in the morning, just after sighting tall, rocky, partly-wooded islands (the Yasawas), they spotted two large war canoes. The chase lasted into the afternoon, and it would have been an uncomfortable experience even if Bligh already hadn't heard about the ferocity of the Fijians.

But he had. Bligh, infact, had been master of the 'Resolution', one of the two ships under Capt. Cook's command during the veteran explorer's third voyage around the world. By 1777, Capt. Cook had talked to Fijians in Tonga, and to Tongans about the Fijians, and passed his notes on to Bligh.

"Feejee and Tongataboo," wrote Capt. Cook, "engage in war against each other; and the inhabitants of the latter are often so much afraid of his enemy that they bend the body forward and cover the face with their hands, to express the sense of their own inferiority to the Feejee men . . ."

The 'Fejee men' were known cannibals, and Bligh and his 17 men must have watched those canoes like a mouse watches a hawk. The Bounty launch slipped past them, not because it was so fast, but because the canoes were sailing against the wind.

So there was no 'feast' for the Yasawans.

There wasn't much for Bligh, either: he was already handing out portions of bread which were a mere mouthful, measured by the weight of a

pistol ball they found in the boat.

Bligh had become the first westerner to really chart Fiji waters — but would he live? Even he must have had doubts during the month that was to follow.

Sunday May 17

". . . at dawn of day, I found every person complaining . . . our situation was miserable; always wet and suffering from extreme cold in the night . . . being constantly obliged to bale to keep the boat from filling was, perhaps, not to be reckoned as evil, as it gave us some exercise."

They feasted ten days later on Restoration Island on the north-east coast of Australia on clams, berries, oysters and sea birds. But the luxury of land was to be short-lived.

May 30, 1789

"Being ready for sea, I directed every person to attend prayers. At four o'clock we were preparing to embark when about 20 of the natives appeared, running and hallooing to us, on the opposite shore. They were each armed with a spear or lance, and a short weapon which they carried in their left hand; they made signs for us to come to them. On the top of the hills we saw the heads of many more . . .

Within ten days, the men were weak again, and Bligh noted "hollow and ghostly countenances."

They caught boobies, and on June 8th, a small dolphin. But the hardships of the journey were multiplied by the men's inability to move about; their clothes were rags; their bodies skin and bones; their limbs full of sores.

On June 14, 1789, within sight of the Dutch settlement at Coupang on the island of Timor, Bligh's entry reads:

"At one o'clock in the morning, after the most happy and sweet sleep that ever men enjoyed, we weighed, and continued to keep the east shore on board . . . The report of two cannon that were fired gave new life to everyone; and soon after we discovered two square-rigged vessels and a cutter at anchor to the eastward. We rowed till near daylight, when we came to a grapnel off a small fort and town which . . . was Coupang."

Bligh and his men had covered 3618 miles during a torturous 41 days, mapping a great portion of Fiji enroute. Even at the end of this almost impossible journey, with his crew reduced to skin and bones. Bligh took the time for one last task.

"I made a small jack" (Britain's flag, the 'union jack') he wrote in his log . . . "for I did not think it proper to land without leave."

5   THE CHIEFS REIGNED SUPREME

"When a Somosomo canoe visits Bau, the sail must be lowered while at a great distance, and the canoe sculled by men in a sitting posture, for to stand might cost them their lives.

. . . these men are kept outside for the first four nights, moving about in creeping posture and crying out from time to time, in the trembling voice of a shivering rat, the shout of reverence called the tama."

This is one description of Fijian lifestyles in the previous century: lifestyles which included intricate patterns of protocol and politeness, a sophisticated chiefly hierarchy — and seemingly horrifying, barbaric cruelty.

Custom and tradition varied throughout old Fiji, just as they do now. What was tradition in Bau was not necessarily tradition in Bua.

Despite these variations, it is possible to piece together a general picture of life among the Fijians several hundred years ago.

Right from birth, a Fijian's life was governed by controls of custom.

People were born into castes, villages divided into chiefly dependencies, and life and death was a result of the whims of chiefs and priestly *mataqali*, the *betes*. A chief's power depended on his ability to hold his subject people, called *qali*, together with bordering tribute-paying chiefdoms called *bati*.

The *qali* paid handsome tributes; the best of everything from their offered human sacrifices with horrifying regularity.

The *bure kalou* or 'god houses' were dedicated to deities such as Caga-walu of Bau, Batimona (who had an appetite for human brains) and Mainatavasara (whose name means he is fresh from the slaughter). It is little surprise, then, that the bete was consulted prior to any major warfare, and that it was his decision which resulted in an attack.

He would sit in the darkness of the *bure kalou*, beneath a framework of timbers decorated with intricate patterns of sinnet, a strip of white masi reaching from the peak of the roof to the corner post and ground. Trembling, seized in a fit and with eyes rolling, he would invoke the powers of the gods, whose 'message' reached him via the trail of white masi.

Religious ceremonies were also conducted under the priest's guidance to make warriors invulnerable. When someone of rank was sick, it was the bete who was called upon to seek favour of the gods and bring the sick person back to health.

Fijians even in early times are thought to have had a sophisticated knowledge of herbal medicines and were apparently skilful in surgical operations and treatment of wounds. But when these failed, the bete was consulted.

Often, he relied on 'signs' for answers to his questions. A common one was for him to violently shake a frond of dried coconuts: if all fell off, there was no hope, but if one remained, the patient might live.

Outside the burekalou, stone shrines and totem symbols were worshipped as well. Religion centred around the ancient ancestors who could take the form of a snake, shark, eel or even a grove of trees.

There were snake cults which annointed live snakes with yaqona and oils and built snake-shaped stone enclosures; sharks were tabu to eat and were given offerings of meat and yaqona at sea.

If sickness was thought to be from a 'spell', a sorcerer was summoned to work a counter-spell. This sorcerer, the *vuniduva*, traditionally used leaves and herbs to work his magic.

To make the magic work, he needed scraps of food or personal belongings from the victim — even a bit of hair — to blend in with his *draunikau*. A result of this was that most people took great care to hide or bury anything which could be used in sorcery . . . and villages stayed spotlessly clean!

Spirits were thought to be everywhere. They wandered around at night with all of the vices of men. They hid in bamboo groves, caves and haunts; they sheltered in rolled-up mats left outside at night and waylaid travellers on dark pathways.

To appease these spirits, travellers left offerings of leaves for the 'spirit owners of the land'. Other spirits could be specially paged. In the *Kalou-rere* and *Luveniwai*, fearsome spirits and dwarfs, the 'children of the water' were begged to come forth from the sea.

These little spirits were under the protection of *Dakuwaqa*, the shark god, and were invited to take possession of whoever they chose among those whose dance enticed them to land.

Spirits caused diseases like leprosy and insanity, and they crept about in human form. A villager told how *sakuka* (leprosy) entered the house gardens, fishing grounds and craftsmen went to the chief. Some of the bati were powers in their own right and could afford to be more arrogant. As warriors, their strength was needed and their allegiance could be counted on only as long as a chief seemed likely to remain in power or be victorious in war.

A *Yavusa*, the Fijian equivalent of a tribe, was broken down into five *mataqali* with distinct functions: the *turaga* or chiefly *mataqali*, from which the ruling chiefs were chosen; *sauturaga*, which supported chiefly authority; *matanivanua*, the official heralds; *bete* or priestly mataqali, and the warrior *bati*.

These chiefdoms remained small, controlling only a few miles of coastline. It wasn't until fairly recent times that confederations of yavusa gained much power.

Even the largest of these — Verata, Cakaudrove and later, Bau — were no match for the people of Beqa (who said they were *qali cuva ki lagi*; subject only to heaven) or the wild hill people of Viti Levu's interior.

But inside his own *yavusa*, a chief reigned supreme. No commoner dared stand above him, to reach over his head, even to sail past his canoe on the outrigger side. On meeting a chief, a commoner drew aside, crouched on his heels and uttered the *tama*. His house was usually large, the wooden rafters displaying a remarkable knowledge of framing and architecture, as well as scores of white cowrie shells which were a symbol of his rank.

While men of high rank wore turbans of fine white masi, the chiefs usually had their own hairdressers who spent hours shaping their hair into dramatic showpieces . . . some measuring three to five feet in circumference.

Disrespect to a chief for the smallest infractions was punishable by the loss of an ear, a finger or a nose. Or by death.

So great was a chief's power that those doomed to die passively accepted their fate, kneeling for the fatal stroke of a club.

Courts doled out punishments for theft, adultery, witchcraft, and the breaking of tabu — lesser infringements such as eating foods reserved for the chiefly, or touching chiefly possessions. It was tabu to call after fishermen on their way to sea, or for a pregnant woman to look inside the house where a newly-born child lay. In the more serious crimes, people were sometimes executed before they even knew sentence had been passed against them.

Next to the chiefs, the heralds and priests — the *matanivanua* and *bete* — held the power. A *matanivanua* was the 'go-between' the diplomat linking the chiefs with his dependencies. Since a breach of etiquette could result in war, his decisions were naturally important to the welfare of the people. Religion, sorcery and even medicine were linked together under the powers of the bete.

The priests were thought to be possessed by the gods, not only the *kalou-vu* or legendary gods, but the *kalou-yalo* or gods born as men. Through the bete the gods were summoned to provide good crops, safe voyages, and success in war.

Religion was so entangled with war and cannibalism that war gods were leaving "the prints of leper hands and toeless feet like hooves."

Leppers were isolated from the village, sometimes even being smoked over a smouldering fire to drive out the disease. More often than not, the 'cure' killed them. Others suffering a serious illness or simply old aged fare just as poorly.

The sick and the aged were held in contempt. When someone was too old to tend the gardens or do useful chores, they were strangled . . . often at their own request by their children.

Sometimes, the sick were buried alive: if it was thought that the soul had already departed, cries from the grave were ignored. In Kadavu, the seriously-ill were thrown into caves with the already-dead. Infanticide, the killing of babies, was common, particularly in times of scarcity.

Yet, for the children of chiefly families, such care was taken of an infant that it was tabu to place it on the ground or on a bed for the first eleven days, and nurses were selected from the village to coddle it day and night.

Marriage was rarely a matter of mutual attachment. Girls were given away as brides while still children, and the daughters of chiefs were betrothed in infancy.

But on those rare occasions, there were feasts, presentations of gifts from both sides, and special celebrations that varied from area to area.

In Lau, a long piece of masi joined the houses of the bride and the groom's parents, or at least a house loaned to the girl's parents for the occasion.

To make her a better marriage prospect, girls at the age of puberty received a horizontal band tatooed across their body, concealed by the tiny fringed *liku* worn by young maidens.

Only at a marriage of high rank would a meke be called for. Dance was serious business! A meke could be ordered by the chief, and it was up to the *daunivucu*, the *meke* creator, to decide its format. Sometimes, he drilled the prticipants for months to insure perfection.

Mekes were even used to propel the village into war. They were used not only for important festivals and installations of chiefs, but to show another village or province how wise and powerful the people were.

It could be both a warning ("if you want war, we are ready") and an entertainment, to say "look how smart our daunivucu is!. Mekes generated mana for the warriors, supposedly giving them power.

Warriors danced a *cibi* victory dance and the women the *wate*, so lewd that it usually ended in an orgy. A *meke ni bokola* was used to taunt the bodies destined for the ovens.

Yet, there were beautiful dances, too. In Rewa, undulating lines of dancers depicted waves breaking on the reefs and migrations of flying fox robbing the trees of fruit.

If dance was usually a serious matter the Fijians had other entertainments. Games provided much of the village amusement, with wrestling, tug-of-wars, sham fights, and throwing games using fruit, flat seeds or sticks.

One of the most popular was *'veitiqa'*, in which a number of men threw a polished hardwood knob called a 'fowl's head' to see who could achieve the greatest distance. It was customary for an old woman to push the players aside, tumbling and rolling about with a real fowl's head on a stick, until the laughter ended.

In *lutuvakatagane*, opposing groups lined up and threw oranges at each other; a man touched with the orange was out of the battle. In fact, the hard fruit were thrown with such force that players were sometimes struck unconscious.

Other games were played with such ferocity, including mock war games, that occasionally, men died. Death, among the Fijians, meant a journey to another world — the spirit land called *Bulu*.

The dead, if men of distinction, were girded in masi. It was believed their spirits departed their earthly home on the fourth night, beginning a journey along the spirit paths to the places of their ancestors. This path was a veritable gauntlet of other spirits, all making an effort to keep the newcomer from reaching Bulu.

By various means, the newcomer was forced to dodge the ghost scatterer, who attempted to stone him; Naqanaqa, the hater of bachelors, (unwedded spirits weren't welcome in Bulu) and Taleya, the dismisser, who made sure that none but the brave who had died violent deaths reached the after-world.

A chief or warrior was not expected to enjoy much comfort in Bulu without his wife or wives — so they were strangled to accompany him on his journey. The women rarely protested, but meekly sat down near the dead warrior, waiting for five or six men to gather on each side of her and slip a sinnet loop around her neck.

Thus, in warfare, if 100 fighting men were slain, nearly an equal number of women met their death in the village at the hands of relatives.

Widow strangling and cannibalism was later to strike Fiji's first missionary visitors with horror. They were quick to record the savagery of the land, but sometimes seemed to forget about the culture and finer characteristics.

When these barbaric practices were questioned, the Fijians simply replied "they are the customs of the land." These 'customs of the land' formed the backbone of religion, warfare, and everyday life.

When the war canoes returned from coastal raids, they sometimes had birds-of-the-sail dangling in the air, swinging to and fro with the movement of the sea or the flapping of the great sails.

Birds-of-the-sail, *manumanu-ni-laca*, were children hung by their feet or hands from the sail yards, a dreadful victory banner.

Consider these other terms, now thankfully obsolete:

● *vakasobu ni duru:* the 'lowerers of the post' were men killed when the corner-posts of a new temple were erected. They were often buried alive standing in the post-hole.

- *lalawa ni i sa:* 'rafter-tiers' were men eaten after the first temple rafters were erected.
- *coco:* 'grass', or the women strangled and laid on the bottom of a chief's grave to accompany him to bulu, the spirit land.
- *lago:* 'logs', or the bodies of men over which a new war canoe was launched. If there were no slain enemy for the purpose, the nearest commoners became the lago.
- *vakadradra:* 'stainer-with-blood', the bodies used to wash the decks of a war canoe with blood. Others were killed when the mast of the new canoe was first set on end.
- *botowalai:* a 'trussed frog' was a person tied in this manner in order to be baked whole.
- *batikadi:* 'teeth of the black ant', a man who creeps into houses at night to kill, often selecting children for his victims.
- *koroi:* a title given to honour those who have clubbed a person to death.

This disquieting dictionary could go on and on, but the list is adequate to show the degree to which bloodshed was a part of Fijian life. Or rather, death.

It was a time when few people lived to die of old age, and friends viewed even friends with suspicion, rarely leaving their home without a club.

In order to become a respected warrior and to gain the title of *koroi*, a man had to kill . . . if he died with an unstained club, he was doomed to pound excrement with it in 'bulu', the after-world.

To become a koroi was to be treated as a temporary chief. During four days of ceremonies, the honoured murderer was decorated with red and black dyes, clothed in folds of new masi, and sought by women who enticed him with lewd songs and dances.

In some areas, he received his honours on a platform made up of bodies of slain warriors; in others, he stood on a platform of stone with a slab of human flesh over each foot. He stood naked before a crowd of spectators while a priest or chief painted him with turmeric and clad him in masi.

He was allowed to take a new name, calling himself 'the waster' or 'the divider of land' or something equally formidable, occasionally even taking the name of the person he had killed if it was a man of rank.

Even his warclub, which traditionally remained on his shoulder during the entire four days, was honoured with a name and handled by less 'fortunate' warriors.

But the title did not always come from gallant deeds.

A koroi gained his honours with equal ceremony, even if he earned it by killing a small child of a hostile tribe, or by hiding in the mangroves and clubbing an old woman as she gathered shellfish.

Years ago, a man of Viwa gave this account of a young woman's pleading with him to save her life. Chased by a club-wielding warrior, she threw herself at his feet and cried "let me live, I'll be your wife, I'll catch fish for you, I'll be your slave . . ."

The Viwa man stepped between her and the warrior, asking him to be merciful. But the warrior was unmoved.

"I shall be koroi today," he cried, swinging his club for the stroke.

The blow probably resulted in yet more bloodshed: women and children, whenever possible, received almost sacred care and protection, for the slightest suspicion of danger — including elopement or abduction — could cause terrible tribal wars, even within the village community.

Religion called for much of the bloodshed. To appease the war gods in the *bure kalou,* human sacrifices were offered when the corner posts were first cut; when they were erected; again when the rafters were tied; when the temple was completed; and finally, when the white cowry shells, the *buli dina* were tied to the ridge pole.

The bodies were offered to the gods — and then eaten on their behalf!

Launching of the big war canoes, the drua, required similar sacrifices because they were under the protection of the war gods.

Men were killed when the mast was first set on end, to use as 'rollers' in the launching, and to wash its decks with ceremonial blood. To sail without such religious measures was to invite disaster.

When high chiefs were entertained, the resulting feast demanded bodies, usually victims of war. But if none were available, then 'low class' villagers met the demand, the warriors attacking a group of women out fishing or raiding the *vanua kaisi*, the slave lands of people who had offended a chief in times past.

Larger wars had a strict code of ethics, and there were 'gentlemen's agreements' in which heralds were sent to formally declare war, even agreeing on a time for attack.

Yet, deceit and treachery was also a way of life, and a truly clever warrior or chief was a master of deception.

The first Tui Nayau was killed during a yaqona ceremony when a small child, the assassin's daughter, smuggled a club into the house wrapped in vudi or plantain leaves. Some high chiefs customarily refused to allow weapons near them because they feared assassination — but who would suspect a small child, crying for her father at the bure's doorway?

A Rakiraki chief Waqakawai, chief Waqakawai, agreed to help a chief of Nakorovatu who was at war. The Rakiraki men were obliged to *bolebole*, a boasting ceremony in which the men display their loyalty to the allied chief.

In this boasting ceremony, men smash their clubs to the ground, testifying that they will 'cause the earth to tremble' or that 'this club will feed you . . .'

This time, they smashed it into the Nakorovatu chief's head, murdering his friends as well.

Plots, counter-plots, sneak raids and ambushes succeeded where attack and open warfare against fortified villages failed. It was not a question of cowardice, it was policy — the customs of the land.

In Fijian warfare, the tribute-paying towns changed sides anytime another power seemed more likely to be victorious, and chiefdoms secretly accepted offers from the enemy, ambushing and murdering their former allies and presenting the bodies to their new friends.

It wasn't uncommon to invite the men of a town over for a feast, a 'solevu', then murder the women and children who were left unprotected.

Or to attack a town after peace had already been agreed on.

Treachery didn't end, even in the family. There was murderous hatred between brothers of equal rank, usually ending in the untimely death of one of them. Since only one could assume a chiefly role, brother killed brother and father killed son in the interests of title.

Death often resulted from small ambushes and raids, but one murder warranted the 'pay-back' of another, and affronts to chiefs sometimes resulted in large-scale wars and massacres where hundreds of men, women and children died.

In war, any harm bestowed on the enemy was honourable. So there was nothing but praise for the *batikadi* whose special skill was to creep into enemy homes and kill defenceless women and children as they slept. The hill tribes even had what appeared to be beds for people to sleep on . . . but actually were for people to sleep under, making the work of the batikadi more difficult.

Regardless of age or sex, those who remained in a captured village were slaughtered. If their initial 'offence' had been trivial, some might be allowed to live in a condition of slavery, and women were sometimes singled out for rape.

At the end of the raid, the warriors returned dragging the bodies with them and waving streamers of masi called *boca* to indicate the number of persons each had killed.

Near the edge of the village, they danced the *cibi* victory dance and the women responded with the *wate* dance, described by one witness this way: ". . . the excitement of the women is intense. The words of the women's song may not be translated, nor the obscene gestures of the dance (in which) young virgins were compelled to take part . . ."

Warriors appeared naked in public on this occasion, standing over their victims while young girls derided the dead, jabbing at them with sticks and doing "a lewd kind of dance, making the disgraceful end of their enemies notorious . . ."

Usually-strict social restrictions broke down for the night and an orgy followed. Those women who were unmarried, widows of husbands slain in battle, or slave girls were free to show their attentions to warrior after warrior as a reward for their bravery.

However, married women never took part in these affairs. The code of conduct was so strict that the slightest look of lust could mean a club on the head, so jealously guarded were the womenfolk.

The *bokola*, those destined for the oven, were offered to the war gods through a simple ceremony of shattering the heads against the *vatu ni mena mona*, the braining stone just outside the burekalou.

Sometimes the dead were cooked immediately, portioned out by the priests with the choicest parts reserved for the chiefly. Other times, they were first set up in life-like positions, supported by sticks and spears stuck into the ground, and 're-killed' in vengeful public ceremonies.

An old chief of Gau, Cikinovu, welcomed Tanoa of Bau with a 'table fit for a king': a double line of more than 100 dead foes of Bau arranged in various postures, some sitting and some standing with a spear in their hands, supported by stakes driven into the ground at their backs.

Canoes returning from raids also had orderly displays of the dead, lashed together in sitting positions. In some areas, bodies were baked whole, trussed up like frogs and placed in the oven.

Once cooked, these *botowalai* were occasionally painted, decorated, given a wig, and paraded from village to village with warclubs tied in their hands before being finally eaten.

It was common for an old orator to mock them, asking them why they weren't so fierce now, or what kept them from swinging their club? Gruesome as this was, atrocities did not always end with the earth oven.

A particularly despised captive was subjected to *vakatotoga*, in which parts of his body — his fingers, his nose, tongue or even entire limbs — were cut off and cooked before his eyes.

At the same time, the victim was told of the "good flavour" and invited to join in the feast.

Captives were tortured to such an extent that a quick smash on the skull was preferable to being taken alive, particularly if the captive had boasted of harm he would do the enemy's leader. In Vanua Levu, these captives were first tied with bundles of dry coconut leaves, lit at each end.

For spectators, the situation was meant to be humorous. So were the cries of those placed in ovens alive.

The biggest feasts occurred at the homes of the highest chiefs, at Bau, Rewa and Somosomo, where feasting on human flesh was so common as to be nearly a weekly event.

Human flesh was usually tabu to women, but if the raids had been successful and there was plenty, women and children were allowed to join in feasting as well.

Children got an early introduction to the savage practices of their elders. Sometimes they were allowed to beat captives to death as war training, or to use them as targets for bow, arrow and spear practice.

It was into this savage land that the first sails of merchant ships came . . . and some of the crews were to be received in ways more horrifying than they could ever have imagined.

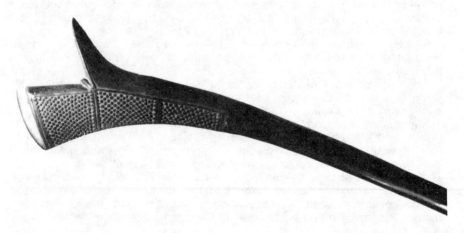

7   THE ARGO'S CARGO OF DEATH

Bukatatanoa Reef near Lakeba, about the year 1800.

The American schooner Argo slices into the reef and shudders to a halt.
    Except for one, its crew is saved — though few will live long.
    With the Argo comes not only men who are probably the first Europeans
to live among the Fijians, but one man who is to recognise a treasure
waiting to be tapped . . . sandalwood.
    With the Argo, too, is a weightless and unseen cargo of death, a sick-
ness which the Fijians will call *na lila balavu* and which will decimate
whole areas and empty villages throughout the land.

* * *

The year the Argo was wrecked, other strange things happened. Fijians
saw a comet "with three tails"; there was a total eclipse of the sun,
followed by a hurricane and tidal wave which struck the islands.

But mostly, the arrival of the Europeans is remembered because they brought the *lila*, the wasting sickness.

One of those who remembered was Lavenia, an old woman from Vatutu-va, Oneata, a village within sight of Bukatatanoa reef. Her story was included in a Report of the Commission to Inquire into the Decrease of the Native Population of Fiji, 1893:

". . . men launched a canoe and sculled towards the place and saw what appeared to be men, but they thought they must be gods, as they were biting fire (smoking) . . . a canoe Taivalata set off for Loa (a small pinnacle of land near the reef) and brought the people to shore."

A *mataqali* of Levuka people in Lakeba, whose duty was to install a new *vunivalu* of Bau, were at Oneata. The mariners were taken to Bau by the *kai Levuka*.

Soon after, "the Oneata people were affected by the wasting sickness, the lila . . . their hair dropped off . . . and no medicine was of any use".

Many were strangled "because they had been sick a long time and were offensive, and some were buried before they were dead".

Lavenia disclosed that the Levuka people offered the seamen's property to the chiefs of Bau, excluding some casks of gunpowder hidden by men of

The 'lila balavu' left hundreds of people buried in common graves.

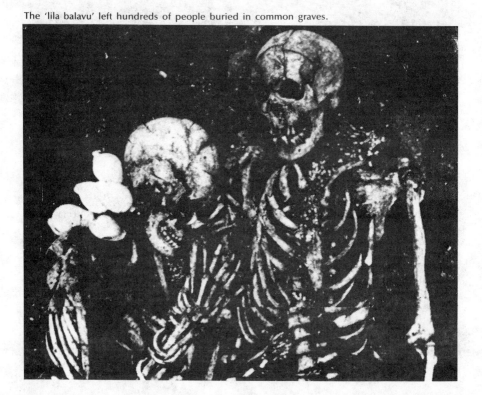

30

Oneata and used as black paint for their bodies, a sad story in itself when they got too close to the fire.

Rev. William Cross was another to describe the Argo's arrival. "Four or five shipwrecked mariners", he wrote nearly 50 years after the event, "were either killed at Oneata or Lakeba and, I fear, eaten also . . . shortly after, a dreadful distemper scouraged the natives.

"Its progress through the group was fearfully rapid and destructive; in many places it was of the greatest difficulty that persons could be found to bury the dead.

"Those who were seized died in the most excruciating agonies . . ."

One of the areas hardest hit was Bau, where hundreds of people were buried in common graves. Among those who died was Banuve, the *Vunivalu*, who was then known as 'bale i Vavalagi', the victim of the foreign disease.

In the wake of the lila, a hurricane and tidal wave struck Bau, washing people out to sea who were too sick to move.

Whole villages, including Davuilevu and Korolevu in the Toga district, were emptied by the sickness and by famine which followed it, caused by people too weak to garden, and ironically, by reckless use of food in the funeral feasts.

In the 1898 report on the decrease in population, native magistrate Ilai Motonicocoka said there were two visitations of sickness, the first from the 'Argo' and the second from the ship 'El Plumier' which followed closely behind. The first was probably Asian cholera, the second a "bloody flux" of dysentry.

The sick "reeled about and fell down, and where they fell, they lay" he wrote. "Our villages began to be empty . . . and from the time of the lila, the practice of strangling persons who had lain ill for a long time began, and it was called *yateba*".

The words of a meke, noted in the report, cheerlessly read: "the strangling rope is a noble thing . . . they fall prone, they fall with their sap still in them . . . the lila is spreading far and wide . . . many die, a few live on."

And what of the Argo's men? Apparently, only two survived both shipwreck and eventual massacre.

One of them was Oliver Slater.

Slater made his way from Oneata to Lakeba, and then voyaged to Bua Bay by canoe, where he "lived among the savages for two and twenty months".

He was rescued — quite by accident — by the derelict ship 'El Plumier' which seems to have been wandering about aimlessly in the Pacific looking for any available booty.

At Bua, its crew mutinied, seized control, and sailed for China with Slater aboard — only to have all hands imprisoned in Guam on the mutiny charge.

Again, Slater somehow managed to escape, eventually reaching Port Jackson in New South Wales.

Maybe his thirst for life was spurred on by treasure: While at Bua, he had seen groves of trees the Fijians called *yasi dina*. It was sandalwood, so highly prized and valuable in China that a shipload or two represented a fortune for the asking.

Oliver Slater confided his secret to the captain of a small schooner, and within months, they were back in Port Jackson with the first cargo of wood.

Governor King of Port Jackson had watched with interest as Slater and Capt. Aikin returned in that schooner, noting: "they failed to obtain beche-de-mer, yet . . . they acquired another of not less value, namely sandalwood, which is of such great request with the natives of India and China . . . accomplishing their object by procurring fifteen tons of sandalwood in exchange for pieces of iron at a place called by the natives Vooie . . ."

". . . should it prove abundant," King concluded, "it may hereafter be an advantageous object of commerce with China."

Fiji's sandalwood was a secret no more!

Even before Slater could prepare for a second voyage, ship after ship cleared for China . . . via Bua Bay. The 'Fair American', the 'Criterion', the 'Union', all American ships; East Indiamen from Calcutta, idle ships from Port Jackson followed each other out of the harbour for the 'Feejees'.

Once at their destination, they barted old iron, nails, beads and trinkets worth about 50 pounds for a cargo which fetched as much as 20,000 pounds on the China market.

One of the early sandalwood ships approached Koro at a time when the island was being visited by Naulivou and the leaders of Bau.

By all reports, the men from Bau were frightened, wondering if the ship was a god or sea creature. But as they gained confidence, some of the men went aboard; they purchased knives and hatchets, a pig, two geese, a cat — and a monkey.

The Bauans named the captain of the ship 'Red Face' and the vessel, the 'land ship', because it seemed to have everything aboard necessary for life. According to tradition, the monkey was a novelty, but the cat was far more useful because Bau swarmed with mice.

It is interesting to note that the ship was politely directed on its way to 'sandalwood bay'.

Another brig in the trade about the same time reported "friendly contact" with natives of Vatoa, and again Koro where they traded for fresh fruit and other foods.

Probably, most of the earlier ships were treated fairly, until they themselves broke the peace, usually by assisting one group in war against another.

As the ships arrived, so did the beachcombers, a motley assortment of men who for various reasons chose to remain on land, despite frequent threats to their lives. They were ship's deserters, men tired of the sea, convicts from New South Wales. Generally, but not always, they were the riffraff of the world's ports.

Beachcombers had become firmly implanted in Tongatabu as early as 1797, and they were described as a hive of rogues and bandits, coercing the Tongans to seize ships or attack them.

One of the sandalwood ships, the 'Jenny', stopped at Tongatabu enroute to Fiji and was swarmed with hostile Tongans. The ship "fired several swivels loaded with grape shot" into the canoes, "by way of wishing them goodbye, and leaving them to lament over their bad luck and perhaps some of their dead friends . . ."

As hostile incidents became more and more common in the islands, ship's masters became quicker on the trigger, in some cases probably inflicting damage when the 'attackers' may have been merely hordes of curious people.

At any rate, the Fijians began to be less hospitable, and life became harder for both ship's crews and beachcombers. Of those beachcombers, the first to reach Bau was a man known only as *na matai*: the craftsman. He was probably a survivor of the Argo and, in the company of a Tahitian, he reached Bau in a large canoe.

Finding that priests were respected and honoured men, 'na matai' acted out the role of a Fijian bete, even imitating the "foaming and trembling" of the priests.

He claimed to receive revelations from Nailatikau, an earlier chieftan of Bau long since dead, and Naulivou declared him to be a true priest. Na matai's charade didn't last long: he died soon after he arrived in Bau.

Ships, men, and more beachcombers continued to pour into Fiji. Oliver Slater made several journeys, sometimes acting as an interpreter for the men on other sandalwood vessels. He was killed years later, clubbed to death as he slept on a mat at Makogai. But the industry he fathered had gained its hold.

As the Fijians began to realise how valuable their wood seemed to be, the price went up: "the items of barter became axes, knives and whales teeth".

Among the ships of the East India fleet, elephant tusks were cut up to resemble tabua, the biggest of which were treasured and worth great quantities of the wood.

But eventually, even these weren't sufficient to procure a cargo. The chiefs wanted help in warfare . . . and the sandalwood ships, with their guns, were the answer. Fiji's age of musketry had begun — and the beachcombers were to show them the value of this formidable weapon.

Charlie Savage

8 STEEL MUSKETS AND SILVER DOLLARS

It was a June night in 1808 when the American brig 'Eliza' hit the reef near Nairai. Where, a few years earlier, the wreck of the Argo had inflicted Fiji with the 'wasting sickness', the Eliza brought something equally formidable.

Muskets . . . and Charlie Savage.

There was something else, too. Hurriedly salvaged from the wreck were thousands of Spanish silver dollars, the eventual tale of which would induce still more beachcombers to jump ship in the Fijis.

The Eliza's last major port had been Buenos Aires, where it had traded whale oil for Spanish silver. It had been working out of Port Jackson and was probably on the way back to New South Wales when it stopped in Tongatabu. Here, two shipwrecked sailors joined the ship: John Husk and Charlie Savage.

They hadn't even cleared Tonga before there was trouble.

About 140 canoes filled with armed men encircled the ship, but, on Charlie Savage's advice, the Eliza's master, Capt. Correy, pointed a pistol at the chief's head. The canoes turned back.

A few days later, the Eliza hit Mocea Reef near Nairai.

In a narrative describing the adventure, crewman Samuel Patterson wrote "we . . . cut away the rigging and the masts went over the side; which as they fell broke our whaleboat in pieces, but we got the long-boat over and put the money in it to the amount of 34,000 dollars . . ."

John Husk drowned, attempting to swim from the long-boat back to the wreck.

The rest reached Nairai, about nine miles distant, to find a reception of club and spear-wielding Fijians "in great numbers".

All of the ship's survivors were immediately stripped of their clothes and all their possessions. Patterson noting "they took the papers (letters and his seamen's papers) and rolled them up and put them thro' the holes in the rims of their ears".

"I was left naked," he said, "but all around us were in the same condition."

Charlie Savage had learned a little Tongan and some Fijian in Tongatabu, and could put forward a reasonable argument. After about a week, Capt. Correy, Savage and three others were allowed to take the long-boat in search of the ship 'Jenny' which they knew to be in Fiji waters.

They took with them about 6000 Spanish dollars they had been able to recover from the people of Nairai — but left Patterson and at least one other behind.

Poor Patterson. Yet, he managed to keep his sense of humour in an awkward situation. At Nairai, the villagers would "come and feel my legs, and tell me 'peppalanga sar percolar en deeni' " (papalagi sa bokola dina), meaning they considered him ready for the oven.

And at Batiki, where he journeyed with a chief from the island after collecting more of the Spanish dollars, he made another grave mistake. The chief, in biting a 'kutu' plucked from his hair, choked.

"One of the scampering rogues . . . made his escape from the grinders (down) the chief's throat," Patterson wrote. But when he laughed at the incident, the enraged chief nearly split the visitor's head with a club.

Eventually, Patterson made it to Bua Bay, still holding on to the silver he had collected at Nairai. So did Capt. Correy and the four others, but only after a repeat of their Nairai experience.

They first reached "Ambow" (Bau), where they had again been stripped, and were detained a further three weeks before setting out once more in search of the Jenny.

This time, the silver dollars remained behind, the Bauans deciding that coconuts would be of more use than the strange pieces of shiny metal.

There are conflicting stories, but it is doubtful if this portion of the Eliza's silver was ever recovered. Some Fijians believe it is still buried near Bau, on the mainland to the west.

Capt Correy and four men finally reached Sandalwood Bay, as Bua Bay was already being called, and the Jenny.

Almost immediately, Correy teamed up with a man named William Lockerby. With some of the Jenny's boat crew, they sailed for Nairai in two long-boats, only to find the rest of the Eliza men had gone to Batiki with "the greatest part of the money".

They still managed to recover a further $9000, but not without an effort: the Nairai people, obviously getting curious about the value these white men placed in the coins, attempted to seize the long-boat with the money. Lockerby and Correy were thrown into the water, but managed to climb back aboard, making their escape after firing muskets and a swivel gun.

The Jenny was having difficulties gathering sandalwood. Two other ships had reached Vanua Levu before her, and competition for the wood was fierce. The "gentlemen of Botany Bay" had even tried to seize the Jenny and run the American boat on shore.

But the Jenny's Capt Dorr was suspicious about the sailor's unusual friendliness. He plied them with rum, found out their intentions, and "broke some bones" as the Botany Bay men left the ship.

The two ships from New South Wales eventually left, but sandalwood was already getting scarce. William Lockerby, however, had made friends with the Tui Bua, whose name was Rawaike, and the Tui Bua told him there was more sandalwood a short distance away, at Wailea.

The Jenny quickly filled with cargo. But while Lockerby and six of the boat crew were loading at Wailea, a storm carried the Jenny out to sea. With a broken mast, the ship was unable to return . . . and abandoned the men on ashore.

Hesitantly, very hesitantly, Lockerby and the six approached the Tui Bua. But the old chief welcomed them, and for the next nine weeks they lived under his guidance and care.

It is interesting to note that Lockerby was given the privileges of chiefly rank, even being fed by hand (since it was tabu for chiefs to touch their own food), but the boat's crew were treated as commoners.

During this time, Lockerby kept a journal which is easily the best historical description of events during Fiji's sandalwood era. The journal also provides some valuable insight:

". . . on this island," he wrote, "there are four persons who call themselves kings (Tui Bua, Tui Macuata, Tui Cakau, Tui Dama) . . . the one under whose protection I lived was considered the most powerful, being able to bring into the field three thousand men . . ."

He noted that "the women are remarkably handsome, and have all that delicacy of form and softness of voice and manners which distinguish females . . .in every part of the civilised world".

At Bua, he "adopted their manner and customs as much as possible and went naked with only a belt made from the bark of a tree around my waist . . . my body was sometimes painted black, sometimes white . . ."

During this time, the fortunes of the Tui Bua had soared. With the sudden prosperity brought by the sandalwood trade (the Tui Bua had even been given a wooden house by the merchants of Botany Bay), rival chiefs became jealous. Neighbouring *qali* were after more of the spoils, and even far-off Bau was among the dissatisfied.

Realizing attack was imminent, Rawaike had a fort built at Bua, apparently the first time one had ever been needed.

Lockerby and the boat crew were busy in making the boat left by the Jenny sea-worthy, planning to sail out of Fiji at the first opportunity.

Just before it was ready for launching, they saw a sail: it was the brig 'Favourite' after sandalwood, and it sailed straight into the bay.

The ship's captain agreed to give Lockerby and his men passage, once a cargo was loaded. And the wily Tui Bua agreed to provide a cargo — as long as the ship's crew helped him in his fight in the expected battle.

In the lull before the storm, Lockerby and a few men from the 'Favourite' made a quick trip to Wailea to scout for wood: unfortunately, they ran into a fleet of about 150 canoes from Bau which were on their way to attack a Bua allie, Tavea.

They were captured and held on the canoes, Lockerby being detained in the canoe of "the chief island of Ambow", and, during the next three days, were unwilling spectators on the attack of Tavea.

"Each day," Lockerby wrote, "about twenty prisoners (were taken) and at night they (the Bauans) hauled up their canoes, and there they cooked and eat the bodies of their prisoners . . .

"The natives by chance went into a long point of mangroves that projected from the island, where they discovered the retreat of about 350 old men, women and children."

All were massacred.

"I saw two men bring down at one time five (captives). Each of them had a pole, at the ends of which were hanging two children. No quarters were given to any but a boy about ten years old, who was remarkably deformed in his limbs and body; he, they said, was a Callow . . ."

The Bauan canoes and fleet from Tacilevu then made ready to attack Bua — but two European ships, the Favourite and a recent arrival, the General Wellesley, were in the way.

Lockerby barely reached the ships alive, jumping from the Bau canoe after an abortive rescue attempt by a canoe full of armed sailors.

Bau's fleet turned back, in despair of being able to attack the King of Myemboo" (Bua) if the ships helped in its defence.

Tui Bua sought peace with his former vassals. "Several chiefs," said Lockerby, "who had revolted from the king came to adjust matters with him and with them brought all their property (*soro*). This the good old king returned, only retaining some of the hogs from the Callow; and later pardoned them . . .

But two chiefs, among them Valevatu of Tacilevu, refused peace.

The Tui Bua again asked for help, and Lockerby, with sixteen sailors from the Favourite and General Wellesley, joined a force of nearly 2000 warriors in the attack of Tacilevu.

In the resulting massacre, two hundred men, women and children were slain.

Wrote Lockerby: "When I agreed with the king to attack the natives of Tacilevu, I got him to promise me that none of the women and children . . . should be killed. Although the king might have been inclined to save them, yet it was not in his power."

Soon after, the General Wellesley and the Favourite, now with full cargoes, sailed.

They took with them, not only Lockerby, but Samuel Patterson and as much of the Eliza's silver dollars as had been recovered. But they did not take Charlie Salvage.

Charlie Salvage had reached Bau, and shortly after, had managed to collect the stores of muskets and ammunition from the wreck of the Eliza.

The Vunivalu of Bau, Naulivou, was quick to realise the advantage muskets would give him in warfare. He made Charlie Savage his personal warrior — *Koroi na Vunivalu* — and the warrior from Sweden was to wreak havoc on Bau's enemies until the creeks ran red with blood.

Massacre at Wailea. Illustration from Capt. Dillon's own journal.

9   A MASSACRE ENDS THE SANDALWOOD ERA

Charlie Savage stood in a canoe in the middle of the Rewa River, firing at close range from a stack of pre-loaded muskets.

The balls pierced the arrow-proof reed fence, and the astonished people of Kasavu piled up bodies of the slain and sheltered behind them, until the stream next to the village ran red with blood.

It was Charlie Savage's first opportunity to show his host, Naulivou, the Vunivalu of Bau, how effective his musketry was.

It was the first of many such opportunities. Verata fell next, and Bau's war chief quickly made Savage his personal warrior, the *Koroi na Vunivalu*, second in power only to himself.

Charlie Savage reached Fiji in the ship Eliza, which was wrecked near Nairai. Not too much is known about him, except that he was Swedish and his real name may have been Kalle Svenson.

While he was still at Nairai, a canoe voyaging from Lakeba to Bau stopped at the island. The Tui Lawaki, the chief of Nairai, was asked to part with Savage as a gift to Bau — to be the "Vunivalu's white man."

Charlie took with him four muskets and some ammunition, and may have returned to Nairai later in Bauan canoes for more.

Naulivou wasted little time, and attacked Kasavu almost immediately. It was an easy victory. The Kasavu people had never seen a musket, and those that were not felled by shots fled to the clubs of the Bau army.

The conquered were required to present young women to the king, but at Savage's request, the ladies were handed over to him as his reward.

At Verata, the scene was the same. Until the arrival of the musket, Verata had been able to withstand Bau's frequent attacks. But not this time.

The Swede had a set pattern of attack. He moved in close, singling out chiefs for the first shots. Once a chief fell, the warriors usually lost all will to fight, some even beating the ground with their hands or throwing their clubs in the air at the loss of their leader.

In a siege on Nakelo, Savage had the Bauans plait a basket of sinnet large enough to hold him and thick enough to turn arrows. With a small slit for the musket, he was lifted into the trees overlooking the wall of the fort, firing at his leisure. The town fell.

The fame of Savage and the power of Bau spread. At one point, even the Tui Nayau "borrowed" Savage and his muskets to help him take a neighbouring island. The Tui Nayau told of how the Koroi na Vunivalu shot down the people as they waved spears on the beach, without missing his aim, until they fled in dismay, "believing the gods had come".

As Bau's power spread, so did its army of white men. Before Bau attacked Verata, Savage warned four shipmates there to join him at the chiefly island. And a year or so later, he persuaded others to jump ship at Sandalwood Bay and come to Bau.

The promise of an "easy" life and multiple wives was too much to resist, and Bau soon had 20 "kaivavalagi" among its ranks. Some were ex-convicts, some deserters, some lured to the area by the tales of Eliza's silver dollars. And certainly, life at sea wasn't any too pleasant. A good example was the sandalwood boat General Wellesley which, coming from Malaya, lost her first and second mate and two score seamen to illness during the nine-month voyage.

Charlie Savage was to live at Bau for five years. He, and the other beachcombers, had the run of the town and as many women as they wanted. Paddy Connel, who was later to desert Bau for Rewa, had "100 wives."

Generally, these were women of a low social status. But Savage's numerous wives were of high rank, as befitting a man titled and second to the Vunivalu.

Kapua, a chieftainess and daughter of the Roko Tui Bau, was his principal wife; another was a daughter of the Tui Lomaloma. Because his wives were of chiefly rank, any son born to Savage would have been a vasu and would have held almost unlimited power. As a political safeguard, the Bauans made sure his sons were stillborn, although a few daughters were allowed to live.

The beachcombers had a strange code of ethics. They didn't mind killing neighbouring villagers for the good of Bau, but they disapproved of cannibalism and widow-strangling. For a time, these practices had to be conducted secretly to avoid upsetting the kai vavalagi. One of the men, however, known only as Peter, was slightly more heathen, becoming tattooed and "addicted to cannibalism."

All dressed like Fijians, wearing only bark loinclothes and painting their skins so as to be less conspicuous targets in warfare.

Derrick says the beachcombers had "the morals of the poultry yard." Fergus Clunie, in Fijian Weapons and Warfare, is far more hospitable: "These men lived closer to, and probably understood and sympathised with, the Fijians more than any other foreigners living in Fiji have done since."

Despite this "easy life, the beachcombers continually fought among themselves, and some died. They also forgot their manners in the company of the chiefs, and three were clubbed to death in a rage by Bauan men before the chiefs could intervene.

When sandalwood ships came, the coconut grapevine usually got the word to Bau and the beachcombers were only too pleased to lend a hand, taking their pay in muskets, ammunition, and the one thing they couldn't get, rum.

One of those ships was Hunter, an East Indiaman under Captain Robson, which reached Wailea in February 1813.

Hunter had had a difficult time — there was almost no sandalwood left, and the Wailea chief Vunisa demanded help in his wars before he would allow the boat's crews ashore.

At first, Captain Robson wouldn't agree to the request, but when no cargo was loaded, he finally gave in. Twenty armed men in three boats, with a small cannon, followed more than forty Wailean canoes in a successful raid up the Dreketi River.

But, four months later, the ship was still half empty, and the Waileans, pressed for the promised cargo, were becoming less friendly.

Savage and 11 of his Bau companions had arrived to help Hunter and its tender, Elizabeth, to load sandalwood . . . except there was nothing to load. Vunisa said there was no more wood, and an angry Captain Robson vowed vengeance.

Just before this, two large canoes from Bau, with several hundred warriors, came to fetch Savage and the other 11 "white Bauans" — and their wives — back.

Probably urged on by Savage, the Bau party agreed to assist Captain Robson in his raid on Wailea.

On landing, the Europeans, under the command of the ship's first officer Mr Norman, began to break up into bands of three and four.

Savage, with the master of Elizabeth, Peter Dillon, seven other Europeans and two Bauan chiefs, gave chase to a few Wailean warriors, burning houses as they went.

Behind them, thousands of Wailean warriors silently moved in behind, cutting them off from the ship and the Bauan fleet.

It was a perfect ambush.

The Waileans surged forward, reaching the stragglers first. Of these, few had a chance to fire twice. The people of Wailea had been with the men of

Hunter before as allies — and knew that reloading the flintlocks was a painfully slow process.

Ten men, including Dilon and Savage, turned back to find "on reaching the path where we were to descend . . . infuriated savages stood in the thousands on each side of the path, brandishing their weapons with their faces and bodies smeared over with the blood of our companions."

Norman staggered a few yards and fell, a spear passing through his body.

Six men managed to half run, half clamber to the top of a steep rocky crag nearby — Charlie Savage, Peter Dillon, Thomas Dafny, a man named Luis (both survivors of Eliza), Martin Bushart and William Wilson.

Dafny had "four arrows stuck in his back; the point of a spear pierced his shoulder." Nevertheless, he was kept re-loading the muskets as the other five fired in alternate volleys to fend off a mass attack.

Dillon was later to write: "From our elevated situation, we had a clear view of the landing place, the boats at anchor, the two Bau canoes, and the ship."

The men watched as the remainder of the Bau warriors (about 40 had been killed) set sail for their island.

They also watched as the Waileans prepared cooking ovens for the men on the rock.

Meanwhile, Captain Robson had taken eight captives, who were aboard Hunter. Savage managed to convince the men surrounding the rock to allow Dafny to go unharmed to the ship, to ask for a ransom and captives in exchange for their lives.

Dafny made it to the ship, but in the lull which followed, Charlie Savage and Luis decided to climb down from the rock as well, Savage being sure he could bargain for the group's safety.

Luis was immediately clubbed to death; Savage was grabbed by the legs and drowned in a nearby pool — thus preserving his skull for a yaqona bowl.

On the rock, the remaining three — Bushart, Dillon and Wilson — watched as both were cut up and placed in ovens.

The attack on the rock began again; two men reloading and one firing, in which Bushart missed only once in 28 shots.

But by nightfall, the powder was running out and the situation seemed hopeless. "We determined, as soon as it was dark, to place the muzzles of our muskets to our hearts . . . to avoid the danger of falling alive into their hands," Dillon wrote.

Instead, just at nightfall, a Wailean priest brought the eight hostages to the rock, and the three men instantly seized him, putting the muzzle of a musket against each ear and one at the back of the *bete's* head.

Led by the *bete*, who fearfully shouted out not to harm his captors, this strange parade walked through the warriors to the beach and a boat waiting to take them to Hunter.

The next day, after an unsuccessful effort to reclaim the bones of some of the ship's men, Hunter and Elizabeth sailed for China.

It was the end, not only of Charlie Savage, but of the sandalwood trade as well. With one exception, it would be five years before any other ships were to visit . . . this time in search of a new cargo, beche-de-mer.

One of the earliest photographs of Bau in existence.

10   BAU BEFORE CAKOBAU

Bau . . .

Twenty acres of land, a tiny dot of an island . . . a tiny dot which, in the early 1800s, was already pushing and squeezing against the powerful states of Verata and Rewa.

By 1808, the warrior chief Naulivou, muskets, and Charlie Savage had tipped the scales and Bau was the political centre of the Fijian universe.

But Bau's rise to power began long, long before the musket . . .

* * *

The island was once occupied by the Delaikorolevu people: the Butoni who lived in the lower areas, and the 'Dwellers on the hill' who were to become known as the Levuka people.

Bau was called Ulu-ni-vuaka, the pig's head, and the eventual Bauans lived on the coast nearby.

Sometime in the mid-1700s, Nailatikau attacked Ulu-ni-vuaka, and the Butoni and Levuka people were defeated. After presenting a *soro*, they were allowed to live, providing they became the fishermen for Nailatikau and the Bauans.

But the Levuka and Butoni men made a mistake which was to cost them their homeland. Years ago, Inoke Wagaqete told historian Lorimer Fison about it: He said the Levuka men speared a great fish "such as had never been seen before". Rather than present it to the Bauans, they cooked it on the reef, and those who ate it were sworn to secrecy.

But a boy took one of the fish's ribs and made a bow, and when the Bauans saw the strange bow and asked about it, the boy told all.

The Levuka people would have been killed for their insult, but a Bauan priest intervened, and Nailatikau ordered them banished from Bau, as soon as canoes could be outfitted to carry them.

At the same time, according to the story teller, the Tui Nayau, the paramount chief of Lakeba, had ordered a huge tapa cloth to be made, and this great piece of white masi was spread on the beach of Lakeba to dry before being painted. His daughter, Adi Lagi, was instructed to keep watch so that it wouldn't be ruined by rain — but she fell asleep.

Rain came, the masi was ruined, and the Tui Nayau beat his daughter so severely that she left home, floating to sea on a raft.

Adi Lagi drifted to Kaba, where the chief of a soon-to-be banished Levuka people found her.

This chief carried her to Bau, rolled up in a sail, and hid her until the canoes were ready to sail.

It is possible the return of a chieftain's daughter may have offered the prospect of a warm welcome to an otherwise homeless people.

At any rate, despite misgivings when no land appeared for several days, the Butoni and the Levuka people sailed in the direction she pointed.

At Koro, the Butoni men quit the voyage. But the 'Kai Levuka' sailed on, past Cicia and on to the Lau Group, where they reported "seeing all the earth" before reaching Tui Nayau's Kingdom.

Lakeba was in mourning. The feast for the dead — for Adi Lagi — had already been held when the Tui Nayau was told that his daughter still lived.

The joyous father had a strip of masi unrolled stretching from the canoes to the village, and presented feasts and land to the seafarers.

The Levuka people had found a home: at Lakeba, they continued to speak Bauan, and were soon to be given a unique responsibility — the periodic installation of the Vunivalu of Bau.

The installation of the Vunivalu and other customs of Bau before the arrival of the missionaries is described in a long paper written in the early 1900s by Deve Toganivalu, the Roko Tui Bua.

Deve Toganivalu's paper gives a remarkable insight into the ways of early Bau, customs which would have been followed even during Nauli-vou's time and the years of the beachcombers.

Extracts of that paper are presented with only slight changes here.

The chiefs of Bau install the chief of the Yavusa Ratu clan to be their principal chief and he is Roko Tui Bau; the high chief second in rank is the head of the Tui Kaba clan; his installation title is Vunivalu or Tui Levuka.

At the installation of the Roko Tui Bau, a matanivanua (herald) goes outside by the rows of houses, announcing to the various parts of the town that the Roko Tui Bau's yaqona is about to be made.

At that time, it is strictly prohibited for anyone to sing out, the children are prohibited from crying and it is forbidden for any canoe to be poled along in the water; they are to remain still and be absolutely silent.

All the chiefs who are in the house take off their turbans and arm ornaments.

After drinking the yaqona, the Roko Tui Bau remains in the temple, Navatanitawake, for four days, during which time the various clans prepare the feast and presentation of property.

When they at Bau have selected one to be Vunivalu, they report to the Levuka people who live at Lakeba that they may come and install him. They were the natives of the island of Bau in the olden time, and live on Lakeba still, speaking the Bauan language.

When the drinking ceremony for the Vunivalu is finished, their chief, called Dau ni Lakeba, stands up and takes a turban of masi and ties it on his shoulder, ending the ceremony.

Toganivalu also tells us about marriage and death in Bau, and of the respect given to the chiefs.

If a girl was born and she had a cousin, their relatives would decide that they should be husband and wife. And when the time has arrived when they have slept together, the woman then goes to her mother and tells her to provide her with a large skirt dress, as she has slept with her husband.

The dress of a girl is not the same as the dress of a woman who has known a man . . .

The relatives of the man first go and spread mats for them in their marriage house, and when they have spread the mats, then the woman is taken by her relatives to the marriage house together with her property.

Then the shaving is done, and the hair of the woman's head is completely shaved off (with kai shells or shark's teeth).

If any other man has seduced the woman before she has slept with her husband, the man will direct his relatives to prepare the food badly, the yam to be broken about and the pigs disfigured in a certain way, that the woman's relations may know that she has been seduced by another man.

When the food is brought forward and the woman's relations see how it is spoiled, they will understand the meaning of it and be ashamed.

When a canoe sailed to Bau knowing of a chiefly death, they would hoist on the mast property and whale's teeth and when about to lower sails at Bau, all the property was thrown into the water as 'iloloku ni mate' for the chief. The people on land would swim out for that property and it became theirs.

When a commoner speaks to a chief, he will keep pronouncing 'saka' in all his sentences. He will always speak to the chief as if he were speaking to many people.

If a commoner is sitting on a threshold of his house, and a chief comes along, he will slide down and 'tama'. It is unlawful to be sitting on the threshold of another person's house.

Except for high chiefs, it was also 'tabu' to pole a canoe to Bau with the bows empty; for the outriggers to be turned toward the town when poling past, or even to use a frond of the fan palm for an umbrella.

When boys and girls were growing up, they went quite naked. But when they reached 13 or 14 years, boys were dressed with the 'masi' and girls in the 'liku'. The children of chiefs generally remained naked, until they were 16 to 18 years of age.

The principal work at Bau was sailing in the sacred canoes; they were in the habit of sailing away to the islands of Lomaiviti to collect tribute, a cargo of yams, taro, madrai and other property.

This was Bau in its prime, and many of the customs survive today. Nailatikau was succeeded by his son, Banuve, who in thirty years strengthened not only the political empire but the physical one: he was a natural 'engineer' and he reclaimed tidal lands to increase the island's size; built stone seawalls to halt erosion, and made other improvements to the kingdom.

Banuve died from the 'wasting sickness' which reached Fiji with the Argo, and the warrior chief Naulivou came into power.

Naulivou had conquered all of the islands of the Lomaiviti Group — Levuka, Gau, Koro and Nairai, Batiki and Wakaya.

The coastal people of north-eastern Viti Levu all the way to the mouth of the Ba River paid tribute; so did clans as far away as Somosomo, Moala and Lakeba.

Bau was truly "on top of the hill".

But things were to change.

Bau's neighbours got firearms, too, and the arms race was on!

The little island kingdom had been first with the musket: now it devised plans for its own ship and cannon . . .

11 BOLA-I-TAMANA GETS A MUSKET

Bola-i-Tamana traded his sister for a musket.

He wasn't the only one. Within the next few years, young girls, barrels of beche-de-mer, and eventually even land were to be given in exchange for guns.

The frantic scurry for firearms swept along the coasts of the Rewa, Macuata, Cakaudrove and the Bua areas with the speed of a musket ball.

It was suddenly a matter of life and death to the Fijians. Failure to have firearms once warlike neighbours had them was certain catastrophe.

And the muskets poured in. They quickly became the common article of trade aboard the beche-de-mer ships, whose captains were only too happy to part with inferior, trade-store muskets for barrels of smoked *dri*.

For nearly a decade after the collapse of the sandalwood trade, few ships sailed for the "Feejees". But with the discovery of another cash cargo for the China market — the sea-slug known as beche-de-mer — the merchant ships returned.

This time, almost all of them bartered in firearms.

The trade was in full swing by the end of the 1820s, and "a common musket, worth two or three dollars" was payment for 12 to 15 hogsheads of the "sea slug".

Firearms, and the powder and shot to go with them, were so sought-after that chiefs refused any other offers, even from the relatively few traders who attempted to barter with other items.

So it was not surprising to find a beachcomber on Wainunu in Vanua Levu buying "a young girl for two muskets" or, years later, for the British Consul Pritchard to be concerned at the sale of young women for "from one to five muskets".

One of the first Fijians to own a musket was Bola-i-Tamana, a chief of Dama in Bua Bay. When he saw a demonstration of the "*dakai ni tamata*," the bow-of-men, he instantly bartered one of his sisters for the weapon.

But the captain got the poorest part of the bargain, because the wily girl slipped over the side at night and disappeared into the bush.

Bola-i-Tamana had what he wanted. A fearless warrior, he quickly attacked and sacked villages in Macuata, Makogai and neighbouring Vuya. How successful a marksman he was will be never be known, but the flintlock must certainly have boosted his morale and helped to scatter his opponents. His name was feared throughout Vanua Levu and Cakaudrove.

In an attack on Taveuni, Bola-i-Tamana was caught by the Cakaudrove people as he was being ferried across the Somosomo Straits, a "landsman who could do nothing in water," and the attackers were killed.

Some thought the ferocious warrior had eluded them again . . . until he was recognised among the "heaped-up dead" by a shark tattooed on his thighs.

Samuel Patterson, one of the Eliza's survivors, tells how Fijians were so frightened of firearms that they would "pull and at the same instant drop the piece on the ground, and spring from it, that it might not kick them over, or turn its thunder against them."

Some held them at arms lengths; others gave a yell, fired in the air, and disappeared!

When lead ran out, they filled the barrels with stones and another new addition to their environment — broken bottles.

They believed that the more powder they used, the greater the effect. The cheap trade-store weapons often blew up in their faces.

So, while firearms were prized possessions, they may not have done a lot of damage. At least, not initially. When things got right down to the crunch, it was the hand-to-hand weapons Fijians had used for centuries that won the battle.

Throwing clubs, carried in the warrior's waistband, were launched with such complete accuracy that birds and flying-fox were easy prey. The fact that some throwing clubs have been retained by collectors — with as many as 50 marks carved into the handles for human prey — shows their deadly accuracy.

Spears, too, were thrown with such accuracy that it is a wonder the Fijians even bothered with firearms.

A seaman from the beche-de-mer ship Glide reported this demonstration by a Macuata chief aboard the vessel in 1831: ". . . a coconut was placed upon the windlass and this chief, standing near the tafferel, grasped a spear and at a distance of about sixty feet . . . drove it directly through the middle of the nut."

Spears were known to pass right through their victims, and those that only scratched were sometimes just as lethal, bearing stingray tail spikes or barbs dipped in poison.

Still, the demand for firearms continued.

By the end of the 1820s, beachcomber Will Cary said "most of the chiefs had muskets, and many of them were skilled shots."

Ten years later, British and American ships had supplied Bau and Macuata with huge stocks of firearms — the Vunivalu of Bau being upset that he had a stockpile of "only two hundred kegs of powder."

Survivors of the ship Glide reported casks of powder taken from their ship, stacked on the floor of a bure "in the centre of which a fire was kindled, and (a man) sat on a keg of powder before the fire, composedly smoking his pipe . . ."

The new weapons changed at least one aspect of war: Traditionally, in club-and-spear warfare, a chief was so well guarded that he was relatively safe. Furthermore, some were regarded as gods and were purposely missed as targets. But the musket was less personal, and its muzzle pointed at chiefs as well as commoners.

Others to be effected were the "invulnerables," the *vodi* who, in long ceremonies before the priests, were told they could come to no harm. Believing this, they were incredibly daring and usually victorious. Spears they had sometimes been able to dodge. Musket balls they couldn't.

The result, as pointed out by Derrick (A History of Fiji), was that the character of warfare changed. Small wars were discouraged and warfare became more serious.

And that's how, during the year 1834, two ships were attacked by the Fijians in separate incidents in an attempt to seize cannon.

In that year, Bau and its ally, Viwa, attacked Somosomo, and a captain of the French ship L'Amiable Josephine agreed to carry the rading party to Somosomo and back, in return for a cargo of beche-de-mer.

The men of Somosomo easily beat off the attack, and a disgruntled mob of Viwa and Bau men began the return trip home.

It was an unhappy day — unless there was another way of saving their pride. Such as having their own ship and cannon.

The Vunivalu of Bau, Ratu Navuaka, urged two chiefs of Viwa — Namosimalua and Varani — to seize the ship. They did, although Varani was later to claim that he had been nearly strangled by the Bauans until he agreed to the plan.

L'Amiable Josephine's captain, des Bureaux, and most of the crew were massacred. It wasn't the first time the ship had witnessed bloodshed, since Captain de Bureaux a few days earlier had allowed a captured warrior from Somosomo to be cooked and eaten aboard the vessel.

Just enough sailors were left alive to help the Fijians to sail their new prize. Almost immediately, the ship was turned toward Naselai in the Rewa River, a town which has resisted previous attacks, and the ship's cannon were put to use. Naselai fell.

But the jubilant party's joy was short-lived. On the way back to Bau, the ship ran aground near Kaba, and L'Amiable Josephine settled slowly into the sand forever.

A month later, another ship was to fall victim to a similar attack.

It was the Charles Doggett from Salem, and unbeknown to its captain and crew, it was considered a perfect present for the chief of Rewa, Qaraniqio.

Veidovi, who was Qaraniqio's brother and a *vasu* to Kadavu, had agreed to pilot the brig to Kadavu and to assist in collecting a cargo of beche-de-mer.

The captain, fortunately for him, also hired Paddy Connel, a beachcomber who had been living at Rewa.

The ship reached Ono Island but Paddy, wise to the ways of the land, could sense that something was wrong. He warned the captain to be on his guard.

At Ono, most of the crew went ashore to work in the *vata* house, the small shed on the beach where beche-de-mer was cured.

Veidovi then came back to the vessel, pleading with the captain to come ashore and urging him to bring medicine for a sick chieftain there.

The captain prepared to go ashore, but Paddy told him quietly that "to go on shore was as much as his life was worth." The firt mate was sent ashore, instead.

From the ship, Paddy Connel and the captain watched as the vata house was set alight. The men inside were clubbed as they ran from the flames.

Paddy, the captain, and the few remaining crew fired cannons but saved no lives except their own. One man, miraculously, swam to the ship. Ten were killed, including the first mate and a young boy who had almost reached the ship's boat before they were struck down by throwing clubs.

With the anchor up and the ship ready to sail, Paddy was told to try to bargain with the Kadavu people for the seamen's bodies.

"Seven were brought down to the shore, much mutilated" he said in a court hearing, when Veidovi was brought to justice six years later . . .

" . . . and this had been in consideration for a musket."

Rev. Cargill: the church tried
to erase him from memory.

12 CARGILL AND CROSS BRING THE CROSS

"On the morning of the 12th October 1835, the 5th day after our departure from Vavau, we sighted Lakeba.

". . . as we drew near to the landing place, nearly 200 men, some armed with muskets, others were bayonets fastened to long sticks; some with clubs & spears, others with bow & arrows: having their faces painted, some jet black, others red . . . and all nearly naked, were standing about 100ft distance from the place at which we stepped on shore."

The first European missionaries to Fiji — the Wesleyans David Cargill and William Cross — had arrived.

* * *

It is little wonder that the Fijians were "astonished, and seemed not to know what to think of us," Lakeba was off the path of the trading ships, and the missionaries were accompanied by their wives — probably the first white women the Fijians had ever seen.

Using a mixture of Tongan and Fijian which they had learned in Tongatapu, they asked to see 'the king', and were shown into a settlement surrounded by a stone wall and a moat nearly 100 feet wide.

Considering they'd been informed in Tonga that Lakeba was civilized and had been for many years," the greeting by armed men on the beach and the heavily-fortified village must have been a shock.

Surrounded by "the king . . . and many of the chiefs and principal men," Cargill and Cross explained the purpose of their visit and were welcomed by a clapping of hands.

Their reception went off without a hitch. The Tui Nayau promised them not only safety, but land for their houses and a mission.

The missionaries and their families spent the first night in a canoe house. Mosquitoes pestered them and crowds of curious Fijians gathered in the shadows, but things certainly could have been worse.

In three days, the villagers built them houses, and on the very first Sunday, just a week after their arrival, Brothers Cargill and Cross held their first service.

It was attended by "about 70 Tonguese and as many Feejeans" . . . among them, the Tui Nayau.

Three Tahitian missionaries had actually beat the Wesleyans to Fiji five years earlier, but the Tui Nayau wasn't impressed, and sent them on to Oneata. They never learned Fijian, and spent years waiting for a ship to take them home . . . which never came.

Hanea and Atai, of the London Missionary Society, Tahiti, died at Oneata years later, still waiting.

Cargill and Cross reached Lakeba with a delegation of Tongans and a message from King George of Tonga that they be looked-after, and that's the main reason their arrival went so smoothly. There were already a lot of Tongans in the Lau Group; so many that Tongan was spoken almost as much as Fijian.

Within a few weeks, the "congregation consisted of about 200 persons — Tonguese and Feejeans, who listened with deep attention while Bro. Cross read the first chapter of Genesis in the Feejean language and preached in the Tonguese."

And within a few months, they had classrooms with about 100 pupils learning to read and write.

Extracts from David Cargill's diary about this time read: "Bro. Cross and I united in marriage six couples . . . spent the afternoon in preparing (to be printed) a part of St. Matthew in the Feejean language . . ."

The two had already made enormous progress in simplifying written Fijian. Even before they left Tonga, they had produced a four-page primer called 'A Vosa Vaka Viji I Manda' which had adopted single letters to express combined sounds — such as 'c' for 'th'. During the next few years, they would shape and simplify the written language even more, giving it the form it has today.

It might seem that the two mission families, with their early success, would be living in relative comfort. They weren't.

Cargill and Cross barely tolerated each other. To make things more difficult, the Tui Nayau refused to accept Christianity, sometimes even attacking and threatening those who did. The chief said it would be an insult to Bau to accept it until Tanoa had *lotued* first.

During November and December, just after the Wesleyan's arrival, storms lashed the Lau group. "Our frail house rocked to and fro in the tempest," Cargill wrote. "The Feejeeans were in great terror and through the medium of the chief Priest, frequently consulted their god of wind."

This priest, the bete, responded by saying the winds were punishment because the gods were angry that missionaries were on the land.

Again, in 1837 when dysentery ravaged the villagers, the bete claimed it was useless to offer pigs to the gods — because they had already 'fled from the country'.

Some that had become Christian fearfully retreated to their old beliefs.

A bete's dislike of missionaries was understandable, since belief in their teachings undermined his traditional powers.

High chiefs feared a weakening of their powers as well: the missionaries taught pacifism and a single god; a ruling chief held his power by war and the *mana* of many gods.

By 1838, Cargill had written London asking for help. "What are two missionaries among so many?" he pleaded. "Some suppose the population to amount to 200,000."

He got help. Within the year, Brothers Hunt, Jaggar and Calvert arrived, bringing with them Fiji's first printing press. Soon after, the missionaries agreed that Bau and Rewa were the political centres of the islands. Despite the enormous amount of work Cargill had spent on a dictionary and grammar of Lauan Fijian, it was decided written texts should henceforth be in Bauan.

After almost four years at Lakeba, Cargill and Cross were to begin anew on Viti Levu. Rev. Cross had been so sick that for several months, he planned to leave Fiji, but nevertheless made plans for a mission at Bau.

If their work had sometimes been frustrating at Lakeba, it was horrifying in Rewa.

The missionaries were witness to cannibal feasts and killings which must have been an unimaginable torment to men of the cloth.

Cargill reported "20 dead bodies of men, women and children were brought to Rewa as a present to the Tui Dreketi from Tanoa . . . the children amused themselves by sporting with and mutilating the body of a little girl."

Somehow, the missionaries stayed alive, perhaps because the Fijians weren't quite sure how strong their mana was. But, though high chiefs tolerated them, they were tormented by others who delighted in upsetting them.

Thus, Cargill writes: "This morning . . . near the front fence of the Mission . . . we found a human head in our garden, placed with the intention of annoying us."

It was a scene to be repeated many times. When Father Breheret and the Roman Catholic mission arrived a few years after, they were ignored and allowed to live in such poverty that, at the end of a year, few still retained even their clothes.

The Marists had their gardens destroyed and what little they owned robbed, and when they were reduced to starvation, they were offered presents of cooked meat — which cruelly turned out to be human flesh.

Rev. Cross was turned away at Bau, not by Tanoa who seemed willing to receive a missionary, but by a powerful young Bau chief, Tanoa's son Seru.

Still, there were some noteworthy signs of success: By 1840, Viwa was a Christian settlement, and even had a chapel built by Namosimalua himself.

The notorious Varani, the chieftain who had seized the French brig L'Amiable Josephine and murdered most of its crew, had been converted.

So had Ravulo, the chief of Suva.

Lakeba followed a few years later, when Rev. Calvert (who replaced Cross and Cargill at that post) reported the Tui Nayau had, in 1849, 'lotued'.

There were many setbacks. The Tui Cakau was one of the first high chiefs to accept Christian beliefs. But when his son Rabici was lost at sea, six of the young prince's wives were strangled and buried a few yards from the Somosomo mission house of Revs. Lyth and Hunt.

A story with a happier ending occurred at Bau.

Mrs Lyth and Mrs Calvert were alone in the mission house at Viwa when told that 14 women were about to be put to death as a feast for visiting Butoni people.

The two women raced to Bau in canoes, already listening to the sound of death drums which meant the slaughter had begun. They stormed into the sacred temple where no woman had ever been, right up to Tanoa himself. Stunned by their appearance, the aging chief halted the murders.

Nine had already been killed, but five women were set free — an amazing victory considering women were considered powerless in Fijian affairs.

More missionaries arrived, but those had come earliest were dying or already dead. William Cross, after years of illness, died in Somosomo in 1842. Rev. Hunt, who had translated the New Testament into Bauan, died at Viwa six years later.

Cargill, like Cross, died before he was 35 . . . but his death has a particularly tragic side to it.

By 1840, he was a wrecked man. His wife and two children had died and been buried at Rewa. He was drinking too much brandy, and the other

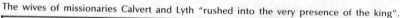

The wives of missionaries Calvert and Lyth "rushed into the very presence of the king".

missionaries agreed he should be sent back to London.

Cargill went to London, but in less than two years, he re-married and was back in Tonga. And that was a disaster. The Tonga he remembered as pious and churchly had reverted to its old ways.

On a Tuesday afternoon in April, 1843, Rev. Cargill calmly sat down in his study with a bottle of laudanum — which in tiny quantities was used as a medicine, but was highly poisonous — poured out a quantity of it, and drank it! He remained in his study and continued writing until he died.

Most tragic of all is that, despite all he had accomplished, the Wesleyan Church, because of its views on suicide, effectively erased him from memory.

His grave was left unmarked. When another missionary died in Va'vau years later, the church erected a marker reading "Here lie the mortal remains of The Rev. Francis A. Wilson . . . being the first Wesleyan Missionary to die on the Tongan field."

Albert J. Schultz, who edited a newly-released book on the life of Cargill (The Diaries and Correspondence of David Cargill, 1832-1843, Pacific History Series No. 10), from which much of this source material came, feels that Cargill suffered not only from memories of horror and the death of his wife, but from the effects of dengue fever which left him psychotically depressed.

But Cross and Cargill had made their impact.

One of the best examples of their work was Namosimalua.

According to an account by Rev. Cross, the warrior chief had laid siege to Macuata on instructions from Bau, forcing the inhabitants of the fortified town to exist without water for days.

On the eighth day, a Macuata man was sent out to plead for water and to urge Namosimalua to spare their lives.

Cross said that Namosimalua remembered "if thine enemy hunger, feed him; if he thirst, give him drink" . . . and allowed the Macuata people to fill their drinking vessels.

Namosimalua ended the seige without taking a life, much to the disgust of Seru of Bau, who "was indignant at such a way of conducting a war."

"This had a most extraordinary effect," the Reverend wrote. "The people declared it was a new thing for Fiji . . ."

Tanoa, Vunivalu of Bau.

13   SERU THE CENTIPEDE AND TANOA'S RETURN

Tanoa, the Vunivalu of Bau, sat at the head of the council.

He was accepting presents of 'tabua' from the high chiefs of Rewa, Viwa and Bau — most of whom were pleading for their lives.

His own brother was among those presenting gifts. Tanoa ridiculed him, telling him "I am still strong, but you are a lame, fat pig who can do nothing but sit and sleep."

After five years in exile, Tanoa had returned triumphantly to the most powerful position in the land.

But it was not Tanoa who had won the victory. It was his young son, Seru.

* * *

Ratu Seru almost hadn't been born.

His mother, Adi Savusavu, had been so ill while carrying him that Tanoa said she should "pierce the child" before it caused her death.

A priest intervened, saying the child must live . . . and that it would be a chief who would rule Bau.

Adi Savusavu never regained her strength and died when Seru was three or four months old. But by this time, he was strong enough to survive.

In the years to come, Tanoa was to appreciate the priest's wise decision.

Even before he had become the Vunivalu, the short, heavily-bearded man under the masi turban was becoming unpopular.

He had too many wives of high rank and too much wealth and property to avoid causing jealousy. The tribute he demanded from Bau and neighbouring dominions was tyrannical.

Among those who slowly simmered, biding their time, were his two brothers, Ratu Navuaka and Ratu Caucau, and another Bau chief, Ratu Mara.

They offered Namosimalua of Viwa a present of six tabua and a young girl, a niece of·Tanoa's — if he would kill the Vunivalu!

While Tanoa was away at Nairai, Namosimalua decided the time was ripe.

He and the Bau chiefs set sail, arriving just after dusk around a point from the village where Tanoa was staying.

The Bauans were eager to complete the task, but Namosimalua urged them to wait until morning. Then, he secretly sent a messenger to warn the Vunivalu of his danger.

At sunrise, they saw Tanoa's canoe far out to sea, speedily retreating to Somosomo.

Namosimalua, in an angry rage which only he knew was false, made immediate plans to return to Bau, outfit canoes to go to Somosomo, and capture the escaped chieftain.

If the Bau chiefs were unhappy that Tanoa had escaped, they at least had something to look forward to. At Bau, they began the redistribution of all of Tanoa's wives and property.

Then, two large *drua*, the Roiroi and the Lemaki, were made ready to sail to Cakaudrove. Just before leaving, Tanoa's sons — Seru and Tubuanakoro — were sent for.

Tubuanakoro arrived first . . . and was killed. Seru was saved by the Roko Tui Bau, who called him as he passed by, saying "Seru, come here and prepare my *yaqona* . . ." and kept him inside the temple until the canoes sailed.

It was an understandable gesture, since Seru's mother, Adi Savusavu, was the sister of the Roko Tui Bau.

In Somosomo, things went poorly, even with the aid of L'Amiable Josephine (see chapter 11). The Somosomo chiefs refused to deliver Tanoa into their hands, and insulted the Bauans before pushing them back to sea.

Tanoa was to remain in Somosomo, still collecting tributes from the Lauans and still living in style, for more than three years.

At Bau, Tanoa's brother, Navuaka, the Tui Veikoso, was invested Vunivalu, a puppet figure for the other chiefs.

Ratu Seru somehow stayed alive. Namosimalua wanted him slain, but the chiefs decided Seru was harmless. The youth busied himself with games and seemed totally unconcerned about politics or the fate of his father.

But they were wrong.

His games were not so simple, and he secretly was paving the way for Tanoa's return, buying allegiance from neighbouring states with gifts and promises.

Once, he was nearly caught. The Bauan chiefs heard that Seru had given *tabua* to Tudrau, the chief of Dravo, and they demanded a reason. Tudrau covered well, saying they were foolish to think there was a plot, and that he had simply begged the whale teeth from the boy.

Tanoa, too, was biding time and getting closer to Bau. After three years in Somosomo, he moved to Rewa where he was a *vasu* and could count on protection. During his journey there, he was guarded by a fleet of canoes from Cakaudrove and by Lakeba's Tongan chiefs Tubou and Lajiki, who had formed a strong alliance with Tanoa.

Seru, still seemingly unconcerned, began providing food for the Lasakau people and offering them property if they became his allies and made war on the rebel Bau chiefs.

It was 1837 — five years after the rebel chiefs had taken command of Bau — when Seru decided all was ready.

In the dead of night, the people of Lasakau erected a war fence between their town and the rest of Bau. As dawn broke, a deadly barrage of musket balls, spears and flaming arrows was unleashed. Bau began to burn.

As the Bauans fled their burning town and started swimming to the mainland, the Lasakau people began to launch canoes to kill them at sea. Seru prevented, it saying *Sa ca ko Bau edaidai* — Bau is bad (destroyed) today; it has had enough!

Ratu Seru had just earned new names. One was Cikinovu, meaning centipede, because the centipede crawls about with indifference until it is sure of its prey, and then bites severely.

But another name was to have much more impact: Cakobau.

Seru Cakobau was only 17. During the seige of Bau, his young wife, already carrying her first child, was kept hidden in a hole dug beneath a Lasakau house to shelter her from musket shot.

Bau was still smouldering when Seru sailed to Somosomo to report that Bau was burned. The Cakaudrove people, in a fleet of fifty canoes, followed him back to the island to make a feast which would herald the triumphant return of Tanoa from Rewa.

The chiefs of Bau were now scattered to inland towns, and Tanoa sent a message to them, demanding they slay the rebels who had plotted against him and bring their bodies to him.

In September, just one month after the seige, Tanoa called a meeting. It was attended by his brother Navuaka, whom the rebels had made Vunivalu during his exile, and by other high chiefs — the Roko Tui Dreketi who was titled the King of Rewa, Roko Tui Veikau, and Namosimalua.

Those at the meeting were uneasy, certain that Tanoa's intention was to kill any who were still alive who had aided the rebel cause.

Namosimalua must have been the most uncomfortable to all.

A missionary living in Rewa at this time, Rev. William Cross, was able to describe the events that followed. He said the Roko Tui Bau opened the session by presenting three whale's teeth to Tanoa as a peace offering, assuring him that he knew nothing of the designs of his enemies, and asking that he and his people might live.

The Vunivalu received the offering, telling him "You and I are friends . . . don't you know? I have been driven from my land, but my anger is now over and my enemies are punished. They are dead . . ."

The Roko Tui Dreketi then presented 39 canoes to Tanoa, also begging forgiveness. "If Bau be at peace," said the Roko Tui Dreketi, "we shall all be at peace, and all will be well; if Bau be at war, we shall be at war, and all will be ill."

Tanoa's brother spoke next. "Your enemies brought your title to me, but I did not seek it, nor did I take any part against you . . . be gracious, and let me live."

Tanoa is said to have held his brother, weeping and laughing, assuring him that no harm would come, but also deriding him for being "a large pig which has grown too fat to walk about."

During all this, Namosimalua crept silently away.

Tanoa asked who instigated the plot. The chiefs said they didn't know. Tanoa replied "the man who was the cause of it (Namosimalua) has just retired, no doubt to dream up some other evil. Tomorrow, he will be tried."

The following day, he was, and the Viwa chief made no effort to hide his guilt. It was true, he said, that he had agreed to kill the Vunivalu for six whale's teeth and a woman.

According to Rev. Cross, Tanoa said: "That is good, I like you for speaking the truth. You will live."

The chiefs of Bau were amazed. But only Tanoa and Namosimalua knew the real reason — that the Vunivalu had survived because of Namosimalua's warning at Nairai.

When Tanoa had said "my enemies are punished . . . they are dead," he was referring to one in particular: Ratu Mara.

Mara was a statesman, one of the few chieftains of the time who was noted for taking towns by open assault. He was a skilled seaman and ferocious in battle. But a price had been set on his head.

Ratu Mara was taking refuge at Namata when the town's chief, to gain favour with Bau, agreed to his assassination. Suddenly surrounded by Namata people who attacked with hatchets, clubs and knives, Ratu Mara was reduced to biting his enemies before he finally succumbed.

The body was taken to Seru Cakobau.

It is perhaps best the warrior died where he did. Another rebel leader, captured alive, is recorded as having been "taken into the presence of young Seru, who commanded his guards to cut out the tongue of the offender, which he devoured raw, talking and joking at the same time with the mutilated chief, who begged in vain for a speedy death."

From this time onwards, it would be Seru Cakobau who controlled the politics of Bau. But Tanoa held the honorary title and remained Vunivalu for another 15 years!

In 1839, two years after Tanoa's return to Bau, a missionary described him as "about 70 and forbidding in aspect . . . his head, face, beard and breast are generally daubed with an earth which produces a jet black colour."

'Old Snuff'

Beachcombers called him 'old Snuff' because of a funny wheeze the aging Vunivalu had when he spoke. But he lived in comparative splendour.

Rev. Cargill said Tanoa's house "surpasses, in magnitude and grandeur, anything that I have seen in these seas. It is one hundred and thirty feet long and forty-two feet wide, with massive columns in the centre, and strong, curious workmanship in every part . . ."

The missionary added one other note:

"His son Seru is not by any means prepossessing in his appearance and manners. He will probably be his father's successor in the government of Bau."

The good reverend had no idea how right he would be.

The four ships of the United States Exploring Expedition reached Fiji in May 1840.

During the three months they spent in Fiji waters, they surveyed almost all of the important islands and reefs, sent shore parties far into the interior, and collected data on everything from tides to hot spring temperatures.

The result was not only the first accurate chart of the group, but an important record of events of the time, written by the expedition's leader, Commodore Charles Wilkes.

For Wilkes and the many scientists aboard, the expedition came close to being a total success . . . until the ships reached Malolo.

As Wilkes wrote in his journal: "I was congratulating myself that I had now finished my last station of the survey . . . when it was reported to me that three of the ship's boats were in sight.

" . . . on the first sight I got of them I found that their colours were half-mast and union down. I need not describe the dread that came over me . . ."

American sailors in Levuka, 1840.

The sloops-of-war Vincennes and Peacock, followed by the brig Porpoise and the tender Flying Fish, anchored at Levuka as their base of operations.

Vincennes was the flagship of Commodore Wilkes, but the Flying Fish was the most important ship there. It was filled with zoologists, geologists, botanists and artists needed to illustrate their findings.

Levuka was already a cosmopolitan centre of sorts. There were 40 houses and 12 Europeans "who were all married to native women and generally had huge families."

Crowds gathered on the shore and applauded as the sailors, dressed all in white, climbed the rigging to furl the sails.

David Whippy, described as "the principal man among the whites, and much looked up to by the chiefs", boarded the Vincennes to act as interpreter. With him came the Tui Levuka, who "was a well-made-man, strong and athletic, entirely naked with the exception of a scanty *malo*, with long ends of white tapa hanging down before and behind, and a turban of white fleecy tapa." This chieftain promised to help in any way he could.

The scientists set up their camp, including instrument-filled tents and an observatory, on a site about 30ft above the beach.

At the same time, Wilkes wrote out a list of instructions to officers who would be on their own during exploration of various parts of the group. They were to avoid landing unless the land was uninhabited. And "no natives must be suffered to come alongside or near your boats without your boarding nettings being up . . . and your arms and howitzers ready to repel attack."

If the Commodore seemed suspicious, it was with good reason.

The Americans had heard bizarre stories of savagery in the islands. Just after the fleet arrived, beachcomber Paddy Connel, who had been a witness to the massacre of ten of the Charles Doggett's crew, told Wilkes the story of the tragedy.

After hearing the story, the Commodore decided Veidovi must be captured and punished. But it was going to be up to Captain Hudson, commander of the Peacock which was already at Rewa, to do it.

In Ovalau, Wilkes awaited the arrival of Tanoa, the 'King of Bau', summoned by Tui Levuka's messenger.

On the morning of the 12th, eight days after the fleet reached Levuka, the wait ended.

" . . . the canoe of Tanoa, the King of Ambau, was discovered rounding the southern point of the island; it had a magnificent appearance, with its immense sail of white mats; the pennants streaming from its yard denoting it at once as belonging to some great chief."

Tanoa, his face dubbed with oil and black paint, soon was seated on the deck of the Vincennes, where he signed an agreement safeguarding treatment of overseas ships — one of the principal reasons of the exploration's visit to Fiji.

He was given a tour of the ship, a demonstration of the vessel's cannons, and a look at the observatory on shore . . . which he was convinced was for "looking at the great spirit."

Seru, too, was taken aboard the Vincennes.

Wilkes wrote that he was "young and frisky" and that the firing of the guns seemed to take his fancy much." He also noted that " . . . the reputation he bears is pretty well founded. He on one occasion had sent word to one of the islands, Koro, for the chief to have a quantity of coconut oil ready for him . . . Seru went to the island and (when he found the chief did not have it ready) struck him on the head and killed him on the spot. This is only one of many instances of the exercise of arbitrary authority over their vassals."

Within a month, not only Tanoa, but Tui Dreketi of Rewa, Tui Bua, Tui Kilakila of Cakaudrove and Tui Macuata had all signed the agreement on ship's safety.

In the meantime, Captain Hudson had the problem of Veidovi to think about.

He tried a subtle invitation to Veidovi to get him to visit the Peacock. Veidovi didn't turn up, naturally. Even the Tui Dreketi, Kania, had gone into hiding when the ship dropped anchor at Rewa.

But with the help of a well-travelled Fijian, Cokanauto or Mr Phillips as he liked to be called, the Tui Dreketi and his wife, along with Kania's brother Qaraniqio, agreed to come on board.

They were treated to an exhibition of fireworks, which made the Tui Dreketi "tremble like a leaf". And, when seventy or eighty Rewans were seated aboard, they were "immediately informed, through the interpreter Paddy Connel that they were prisoners, and that the object was to obtain Veidovi, the murderer of the crew of the Charles Doggett, some eight years before."

Adi Dreketi asked if they were all to be put to death, and Cokanauto was so frightened he could not speak or even light a cigar that was given to him.

But Captain Hudson assured that he meant them no harm. He said that, since all means of obtaining Veidovi had failed, he would detain them until the man was captured.

"The king and chiefs," Hudson reported, "when they had recovered themselves a little, acknowledged that our demand was a just one . . ."

Qaraniqio agreed to go quietly to Rewa and take Veidovi by surprise, and was released. While he was away, the hostages were entertained by a stage show put on by the sailors — apparently such a good one that the captives were soon relaxed and applauding.

Veidovi, probably aware that to refuse Qaraniqio's request meant death, came to the ship and was given an instant trial. He bragged of his exploits — and was put in irons.

The warrior chieftain stood on the deck, his arms in mannacles, as the Tui Dreketi "kissed the prisoner's forehead, touched noses, and turned away — whilst the common people crawled up to him and kissed his feet. None but Qaraniqio was unmoved."

During the next month, the United States Exploring Expedition criss-crossed the Koro Sea, circled Vanua Levu and Taveuni, and continued making charts and taking scientific measurements.

At Somosomo, Wilkes found the Tui Cakau "sitting plaiting his sennit, surrounded by his wives and family . . . such cheerfulness as reigns among them is quite remarkable."

The Tui Nayau, on the other hand, struck him as being "a corpulent, nasty-looking fellow (who) lives in the midst of all kinds of excesses."

When the Peacock reached Bua, the district was at war. The aging chiefs Tui Bua and Tui Muru had quarrelled and their towns — Tiliva and Vaturau — were barricaded and ready for battle.

Captain Hudson decided to bring the rival chiefs together aboard ship, and they "were kept out of sight of each other, until they had been made to understand the object in view. When brought together, they were soon reconciled and solemnly promised to forget all that had passed."

But the day the Peacock made ready to sail from Macuata, Captain Hudson learned that war had begun again in earnest.

The ship's crew learned it in a rather striking manner. A canoe came alongside the Peacock, bringing a "skull yet warm from the fire, much scorched" as a curio for the scientists. But the crew was more horrified to see its vender still nibbling on an eye, removed minutes before. Wilkes wrote "Previous to this occurrence, no one in the squadron could say that he had been an eye-witness to cannibalism . . ."

Fortunately, a nicer sight awaited them at Ovalau. Wilkes and his men had just seated themselves on stone walls to see a club dance performed by the Levuka people when:

"Suddenly we heard shouts of loud laughter in the open space beyond, and saw moving towards its centre a clown. His body was entirely covered with green and dried leaves and vines bound round in every way; on his

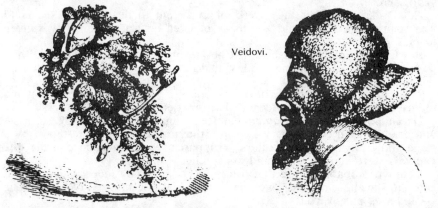

Veidovi.

head he wore a mask somewhat resembling a bear's head, painted black on one side and orange on the other; in one hand he carried a large club, on one side in the other, one of the short ones, to which our men had given the name of 'Handy Billy'."

The men were soon to see clubs again in a far less comical situation. At Malolo, Wilkes was congratulating himself on nearing completion of the job when he saw the ship's boat returning, their flags at half-mast.

He stood on deck as crewmen delivered the bodies of Lieutenant Joseph Underwood and his nephew — Midshipmen Wilkes Henry.

The two had been part of a survey party working between Malolo and Malolo-Lai-Lai. They had captured a Fijian to hold as hostage while they went ashore to barter for food.

But the captive escaped and one of the boat's crew fired a musket shot over his head. A chieftain on shore cried out that his son was killed, and the Malolo people — with apparent good reason — took up the battle.

Underwood and Henry tried to fight their way out, but both were felled by throwing clubs.

Wilkes ordered the cutters of the Vincennes and Peacock to circle the island, destroy all canoes, and prevent anyone from leaving.

Then he sailed for an island about ten miles from Malolo to bury the two officers. Their flag-draped bodies were lowered into the ground in a grove of fig trees as 20 sailors stood at attention.

After that, he attacked Malolo.

It was not to be an easy victory. At Solevu, the people of Malolo sheltered behind war ditches, moats, and a walled fort. They had firearms and ammunition, and shouted "lako mai" (come) as the sailors approached, flourishing their weapons.

Wilkes commented that the women and children were as actively engaged as the men, firing muskets and arrows. He also noted "the expertness with which these people dodge a shot at the flash of a gun."

But the Americans used rockets, the remains of their fireworks displays, to set the thatched roofs of the fortification on fire.

The people fled into the hail of bullets from the sailors.

"The island, which but a few hours before had been one of the loveliest spots in creation," Wilkes wrote, "was now entirely laid waste, showing the place of the massacre, the ruined town, and the devastated plantations."

" . . . the sound of distant wailings was heard, which gradually drew nearer. About 40 men appeared, crouching on their hands and knees, and occasionally stopping to utter piteous moans and wailings. When within 30 feet of us, they stopped, and an old man, their leader, in the most piteous manner, begged pardon, supplicating forgiveness . . .

". . . two great chiefs of the island, and all their best warriors had been killed, all their provisions destroyed, and their houses burned. They acknowledged a loss of fifty-seven killed."

Commodore Wilkes was later tried, on arriving back in America, for acting in a cruel, merciless and tyrannical manner, but was cleared of the charges.

He claimed that he had punished the Fijians in the only way understood, "requiring of them their own forms of submission, and their own modes of acknowledging defeat."

"On taking our final departure from these islands," he wrote, "all of us felt great pleasure.

"Veidovi alone manifested his feelings by shedding tears at the last view of his native land."

15   WARS, WARS, WARS!

The 1840s, from beginning to end, had one thing in common: Wars.

Villages were burned, people were slaughtered, and in retaliation, raiding parties burned more villages and slaughtered more people.

Bau was the cause of much of it, the 'root of war', and the island empire was continually in battle throughout the decade. Sometimes, it was involved in two or three wars at once.

But it wasn't just Bau.

There was warfare from one end of Fiji to the other, an epidemic of bloodshed.

A Macuata chieftain, Gigi of Galoa island, raided the Yasawas in 1840. On his way there, he stopped at Yadua for food. But there wasn't any. A hurricane a few weeks earlier had levelled the gardens and the Yadua people lost everything.

So Gigi and his warriors killed most of the people, taking them for food instead.

In turn, Gigi and about 90 others were massacred a year later when Varani attacked Galoa.

And so it went; the methods of war differed, from the sneak raids of guerilla bands to the full-fledged *i valu ni tu* which demanded a gentlemanly announcement of attack — but the results were the same.

Macuata and Bua were so devastated by wars that there was no time for planting and little reason to rebuild villages.

The coastline was marked by one smouldering village or plantation after another, until it was practically deserted and those who remained alive were destitute.

At Lau, payments of tribute to avoid war had reduced the Tui Nayau to misery. The Tongans took half his food, the Bauans the rest.

In Ra, every pinnacle and peak was turned into a fortress as protection against other coastal clans and the marauding hill people. And the hill people, safely sheltered in caves with walled-entrances, ventured out in stinging attacks on other hill tribes and the prosperous coast.

At Korotiki, a pinnacle near what is now Nanukuloa, Rabaraba fought off the Natotoka warriors by rolling stones down on the enemy. Huge boulders laboriously carried up by hand were held back by vines which could be cut by a single knife stroke.

Navatu, a lofty cone a few miles west of Rakiraki, was another natural fortress, a rock so steep and protected that the attacking Saivou and Nalawa warriors had a hopeless task. Once the gardens at the foot of the rock gave out and the attackers grew hungry, the siege was over. For awhile.

With the exception of the Nadi people, who were strong enough and inaccessible enough to make even Bau hesitate, no place was safe.

Tiny islands with small populations suffered most. They were a convenient crop for wayfaring warriors, a 'garden' of war.

So it is not surprising that, when the people of Wakaya were attacked and could no longer hold out against the assault, more than 100 of them threw themselves off a high cliff.

It was preferable to the treatment in store if they were captured alive.

By the 1840s, some pretty sophisticated fortifications and war devices had evolved, designed to stand up against new weapons, including musketry.

Limestone caves and rocky crags were fine for the *Kai Colo*, but the major centres east of Rewa were building engineered forts.

Towns were surrounded by water-filled moats and inside these, there were high walls, sturdy gates, earth-filled ditches and a gauntlet of protected passageways.

Muddy waters of the moat held surprises, too. Along the bottom, an arsenal of upturned stakes and spikes, some just below the waterline, awaited anyone foolish enough to attempt to cross.

Entrances to forts were styled after a fish trap, wide at the mouth but narrowing so that only one man, bent double, could pass through at one time.

Sharp spikes stuck into the ground made it difficult to force the gate, particularly when they were hardened in fire and soaked in poison.

In fact, the Fijians found lots of uses for sharpened bamboo. One of them was the *lovosa*, a thinly-covered pit, the bottom of which was filled with spikes of bamboo which impaled a falling victim.

Another was the *tabua*, a camouflaged pair of crossed and sharpened bamboo blades which worked like scissors. Hidden in pathways, the blades cut deeply into both sides of the foot. When the wounded man fell, there were more tabua to slash his hands and wrists.

War, Fiji-style, was getting a little nasty, and the islands were getting battle-scarred. But nowhere was the result of war so obvious as it was in the Rewa delta.

From the air, even today, the area surrounding the lower reaches of the Rewa River is tattooed with hundreds of circular trenches, the remains of moats and ring-ditch forts built during countless confrontations.

Unfortunately, no matter how strong the fortifications were, there was no defence against treachery from within . . .

A classic example of this was the massacre of the Namena people.

Namena had been a Bau ally, but it changed sides and backed Tui Cakau during a Bau-Somosomo war that began in 1840.

When Namena tried to get Namosimalua and Varani of Viwa to join its ranks, Varani swore his support . . . and then told Seru Cakobau of his plan to trap the Namena people.

Ratu Seru was delighted. He was particularly happy because Bau had already failed in an effort to subdue Verata, of which Namena was a part.

As a little incentive, Seru promised one of his daughters for Varani's wife, if Namena could be destroyed.

Varani's biggest problem was to trick Namosimalua, who was unlikely to go along with the plot.

He started a rumour, saying Bau was angry with Viwa and had decided to destroy it.

Namosimalua ignored the story.

Varani then let it be known that Namosimalua's wife, during a recent trip to Bau, had been bedded by a young Bauan chief.

Namosimalua decided it was better to seek out the man who injured his reputation, rather than wage war on Bau.

But Varani didn't give up easy. Bau, he said, hadn't bothered to buy pigs for an offering to their gods . . . because they intended to use the bodies of Viwa people instead.

This time, Namosimalua broke down. He agreed to assist Namena, and urged that Viwa prepare for war against Bau.

Cakobau, aware of all that was going on, began to assemble a force to go to Viwa. Varani sent for his new allies, and 12 Namena canoes with about 140 warriors came to his aid.

The Namena people were in the net, and Varani and Seru worked out the details of a plan which was devastatingly cunning and treacherous.

Reverend William Cross, an early witness to one of Fiji's most horrific wars, tells the rest of the story:

It was arranged that Seru should attack Viwa with a large force, which was to be divided into three companies. The strongest, with Seru at its head, was to land at a part of the island most distant from the town, and the others to be posted so as to cut off those who might attempt to escape. Varani met the party that was to attack the town, and pretended to oppose their landing. After a few muskets had been fired on both sides, Varani explained his whole design to his men, many of whom had known nothing of it till that moment.

Seru did the same to his warriors, warning them not to kill any Viwa men, as they were their friends, nor to touch anything belonging to the Missionary, but to assist Varani to kill the Macoi warriors (the Namenans). During the firing, some of the Bau people pretended to be shot, and the news was immediately taken to the town that an enemy had fallen: the Macoi people, who were to die in a few moments, clapped their hands and rattled their spears for joy.

The drum was beating, to indicate success on the Viwa side, and all was joy in the town, when Varani and his party rushed in with the Bau people close after them, and fell on their surprised victims like so many wolves. In the space of a few minutes about one hundred of them were massacred. A few were shot, others were cut to pieces with hatchets, others had their brains dashed out with fearful clubs . . . Many of them fell within a few paces of the Mission house, and some closely by the door.

It was a new sort of treachery, and the Viwans' recent contact with Christianity made it even unpopular. But by the time the deceit was revealed, it was too late to stop.

The warfare in the group took an incredible toll of lives. In the above attack, besides the dead Namena warriors, Rev. Cross noted that 80 women were strangled to accompany their men to the spirit land.

The costs of averting war were nearly as disastrous.

Tui Kilakila of Somosomo sought Cakobau's help in punishing the Natewa people, who had gained enough strength to rebel from Somosomo's authority.

Cakobau agreed to assist, and a few months later arrived with 3000 warriors and a fleet of 66 double canoes and 16 outriggers.

As a prize for their assistance, the Bauans received 40 huge bales of cloth, 70 turtles, 38,000 yams . . . and "yaqona from Rabi in five canoes which, when piled, formed a wall thirty-five feet long and seven high."

The feasting and celebrations at Somosomo lasted several days, during which time processions of warriors displayed their weapons and boasted of their prowess.

On the fourth day, more than 150 canoes with nearly 5000 men, including Tui Kilakila's own warriors, reached the Natewa stronghold, a fortified hilltop with an entrance guarded by "frightful precipices on either side."

A witness at the time said the resulting war was brisk — but ineffective.

Eventually, a few Natewans ventured out too far and were killed, and Cakobau called his men off, saying they would take the town the next day.

But the next day, there was nothing to take. The Natewa people had fled during the night (as Cakobau probably intended) with all their property.

They presented a *soro* to Cakobau, saying they were certain he would prove merciful, but that Tui Kilakila would have them killed, and it was accepted: six representatives brought whales teeth and baskets of earth, crawling on their knees to Cakobau to signify their full surrender.

A soro was humuliating. Sometimes an entire town was made to crawl on hands and knees, begging for mercy. The town was invariabliy burned; the crops, livestock and property collected as spoils of war. The defeated, if not outright slaves, became subjects of the victors, tribute prayers, sometimes forfeiting use of their land for years.

But as humiliating as a soro was, the real victim in this case was Tui Kilakila.

By the time the Bauans left, they had stripped his gardens, carried off the best of his property, and taken not only his canoes, but the carpenters who built them.

Cakobau had very neatly gained a new province, Natewa, while trimming a powerful rival down to size.

The 1840's belonged to an arrogant Bau. But one of the worst massacres of Fijian history was not of Bau's doing.

It was the siege of a village named Suva . . .

It began with a stolen pig.

It developed into a slaughter of four hundred people — one of the most savage massacres in Fiji's history.

Then, the siege of Suva erupted into Fiji's longest and most devastating war, a war which was to last for 12 long years.

This is the story of what happened in Suva in 1843. The details of the tragedy were collected by a Suva historian, Colman Wall, in 1919 — while there were still people alive who could recount the disaster.

* * *

Suva in 1843 was a growing, busy village, its bures and temples surrounded by a moat where the Thurston Gardens are today.

At the front entrance to the town, the temple of Ro Vonu (the turtle) towered above everything else, and near it, underneath the *nokonoko* trees, was the sacred temple of Na Leka, the dwarf.

Most of the village was protected by an earth wall inside the moat, but a number of bures were also scattered on the rising ground known as Na Buabua, the present site of Government House.

They'd been living there for about twenty years, ever since they abandoned Uluvatu, a citadel on top of the steep rock cliff rising straight up from Walu Bay.

In the early 1900s, when Colman Wall was gathering information about the siege of Suva, there were still conical house mounds on top of Uluvatu and traces of moat which completed the rock's defences.

On the landward side of the bluff, so well-hidden that the entrance was almost invisible, was a cave which was used as refuge for women and children during times of war. Another cave on the cliff-side was used for burials, and the flat land on top housed the *bure-ni-sa*, the warrior's clubhouse, and the houses of the 'Kai Walu' fishermen.

Uluvatu was abandoned about 1820, supposedly because its chief, Tabakaucoro, had married "a great Bauan lady" who was not interested in climbing hills.

Tabakaucoro was relatively powerful. He controlled a court of carpenters and fishermen and about 1000 warriors, and he was a *vasu* to Bau, putting Suva under its protection. Since Bau was the paramount power in central and eastern Fiji, the Suva chief probably paid little heed to the expansion of Rewa — despite the fact that Rewa had conquered Beqa and Kadavu and controlled so much of the southern coast of Viti Levu that even Nadroga was known as the *yala yala* (boundary) *ko Rewa*.

What's more, Bau and Rewa were on friendly terms. But a struggle between the two states was growing closer. Suva was to provide the spark.

In 1841, Qaraniqio of Rewa paid a friendly visit to Nadroga and on his way back, he stopped at Suva, landing on the beach of what is now Nasese. Only Bau canoes were permitted to pass in front of the town with sails hoisted and flags flying, and the Rewa chiefs avoided the indignity of having to lower their masts by anchoring before they reached it.

On entering Suva, Qaraniqio noticed a large pig, and ordered his men to put it on board his canoe.

But the pig belonged to Tabakaucoro and the Suva people became quite hostile in protecting it. Qaraniqio was informally hustled back into his canoe, and he and his men sailed around the point, anchoring in Laucala Bay.

Just before dawn, when the Suva *batikadi* were scouting the bush surrounding their town, one of them discovered the sleeping camp and drove a spear through the chest of a Rewan, killing him on the spot.

Qaraniqio and the others, fearing an ambush, fled, but the insult was done. A few months later, Qaraniqio attacked Suva . . . but the attack was a failure.

Cakobau learned the purpose of the Rewan fleet and warned Tabakaucoro to "look after his war fences."

By the time the Rewa canoes reached Suva, the town was prepared, and the only casualties were some of the Rewans themselves, who were cooked and eaten.

Nothing could prevent war, now.

Rewa was determined to get revenge, and if Qaraniqio knew an assault on Suva would bring it into a full-scale war with Bau, he would at least get rid of a powerful Bauan ally first.

To do it, Rewa began a slow process of buying off Suva's allies.

It was 1843 before Rewa was ready to move. Banuve and Qaraniqio had a secret weapon — the Lomaivuna clan from the Waimanu River.

They also had an assault force which included Burebasaga, Naselai, Nakelo, Lokia and other villages eager to share in the plunder.

The forthcoming attack was by this time no secret, and Bau decided to take action. Tui Sauwaqa, the *Mata ki Burebasaga* of Bau, was sent to Banuve to remind him of the friendship between the two states, and that custom forbade either one from attacking an ally of the other without approval first.

The Rewan chiefs said the gathering army was only to punish some rebel towns in Kadavu.

Tabakaucoro was also aware of what was happening, but when he asked his neighbouring clans for assistance, they gave evasive answers.

Just at this time, the Lomaivuna warriors arrived on their 'visit' to Suva. Both groups had fought before and weren't exactly good friends, but custom demanded that guests be received hospitably, with feasts given in their honour. Tabakaucoro probably also hoped they would help in the upcoming battle.

While the Lomaivuna warriors were being entertained, Rewa advanced. They had with them, not only a brass cannon plundered from a French ship, but the warriors of Kalabu, Vuniveilakou, Tamavua and the Vuna clan on the Waimanu — all former allies of Suva who had been bought off with a promise of spoils.

The attack began in the late afternoon, when the women (who formed the chief part of the spoils) were back from the plantations.

Again, Suva was prepared. Rewa's canon did little damage and the town was so well fortified it might have withstood the siege . . . until the Lomaivuna men, the secret plot of Qaraniqio, set the town on fire.

Within minutes, Suva was a mass of flames. Its warriors stood back to back, one side holding out against the Lomaivuna, the others driving a wedge into the attacking Rewans.

They stood in a ring, dying.

Tabakaucoro, holding the opposite side of the town, saw that everything was lost. In a last desperate rush, he and his warriors broke through the enemy ranks, pushing them far enough back so that the women and children could escape. It was thick forest all around, the women knew the bush well, and by nightfall, they were well-hidden in the dense 'Vu-ni-ivi' — the area at the bottom of Marks Street and Edinburgh Drive.

For the Rewans, it would have been an ideal time to strike; they outnumbered the remaining Suva warriors five-to-one, but with the barricades down, they looted the town instead.

During the night, the Suva people re-grouped at their deserted fortress of Uluvatu, the men replacing war fences and the women gathering food from the nearest plantations.

The following day, the beleaguered band of survivors watched as Rewa canoes crept into Walu Bay and the canoes of Suva's former allies blocked the mouth of Tamavua River.

That was on the cliff side. On the landward side, the Lomaivuna camp and hostile Tamavua and Noco people sealed off any chance of escape.

Rewa didn't hurry the attack. The Suva people weren't going anywhere, so they feasted instead . . . on the plantations, the turtle ponds, and *bokola*.

On the summit of the cliff above Walu Bay, the thinned ranks of the Suva people held a counsel.

There were about 400 women and children taking refuge on the hill, and Ratu Naieba wanted to make an attempt to take them through the hostile country which lay between Uluvatu and Colo, the upper reaches of the Tamavua River where Wailoku is now.

Another leader, Tukevunadawa, said that as long as so many young women were cooped up in the fortress, there was no hope of the siege ending and no hope of escape.

There was not much food, either, and Suva men were weak from wounds and fatigue.

On the morning of April 9, 1843, a herald named Korotatibi set out with a *soro* of a whale's tooth and a chieftain's daughter, a maiden anointed with oil and the most attractive girl available.

The herald and the girl left the cave of refuge and passed through the Suva warriors, sullen with defeat, crossing what is now the western end of Reservoir Road.

Less than half-a-mile from the fort, they met the hostile chiefs, including one named Ca-mai-sala. Qaraniqio was still with the Rewa canoes in Walu Bay.

The chiefs had watched the coming of the embassy and had already made up their minds: They did not want to attack desperate men defending their last stronghold. The soro was accepted.

According to Fijian custom, the lives of the Suva people were safe. And it did not take long for them to quit their fort. Women, children and warriors — 500 of them — marched in a thin line through the hostile ranks.

What happened next should never have happened.

The soro had been accepted and the people were spared. But, near what is now Suva Reservoir, a Rewan chief named Kovelevu seized a woman who was carrying a child, and when she struggled to get free, he clubbed her.

The woman's husband grabbed a weapon . . . and the battle was on again.

Tabakaucoro and a few others were forced down the steep slope towards the river.

Colman Wall's description of the rest of the slaughter reads: " . . . by far the greatest number of the women and children who had escaped death from club or spear in the running fight were hemmed around at Na Ca (the place of evil)."

Behind them, the steep precipitous cliff falls down sheer for a hundred feet to the low bank of the Tamavua River. Then followed one of the darkest tragedies in Fiji history. The women stood crowded together on the top of the bluff, and died with the stoic fatalism of their race; for a brief time nothing was heard but the thud of the club . . .

"To the credit of the Fijian race, this massacre has no parallel in their history . . . there is happily no other instance on record of the slaughter of a crowd of defenceless women after an armistice had been granted."

From the time the first woman fell until the last victim at Na Ca was clubbed, four hundred were killed.

Tabakaucoro and a few followers made their way to the hilltop overlooking the present cemetery. He was so exhausted that he couldn't climb the rise, and was carried up by a woman named Ganiwaiwai.

Just before dark, he watched as the Rewa canoes, filled with bodies, returned home to the feast.

All that were left of the Suva people slowly made their way across the Tamavua River, following the hill track to Colo and Vunibua on the Waidina River, and found refuge near Vunidawa.

The siege of Suva was over. But for Rewa, the trouble was just beginning.

Rewa had earned the bitter enmity of Bau by sacking Suva. It was an unprecedented breach of custom, and the smaller Rewa allies which had taken part in the execution fled the area.

The Lomaivuna people crept to isolated spots on the Waimanu River; the people of Veisari sheltered at Wai Vuso, and others went as far as Beqa.

For more than a year, the shores of Suva harbour were empty.

But Cakobau was not to forget.

He made a trip to Lau, partly to postpone the war until the time was ripe, and partly to make sure that the Lauans were allies. And then Bau declared war on Rewa.

It would last longer than even Cakobau imagined.

17   BAU AND REWA BEGIN THE 11-YEAR WAR

On a June morning in 1845, Cakobau's war canoe Ra Marama and the Bauan fleet entered the Rewa River, supposedly to witness the formal surrender of Rewa and its allies.

Rewa and Bau had been at war for two years, and Banuve, the Roko Tui Dreketi, King of Rewa, had agreed to Cakobau's offer of peace.

That wasn't the real reason the Bau canoes were there.

As Banuve came on board, his head was split by an axe blow . . . from Cakobau himself.

The Bau-Rewa war wasn't ending. It was only beginning.

★ ★ ★

A chief of Rewa.

It had begun after Rewa's attack on Suva, an insult difficult for Bau to ignore. It was further aggravated when one of Tanoa's wives was unfaithful and fled to Rewa, to become the wife of a Rewa chief, a no-no by any custom.

By late 1843, the two greatest kingdoms in Fiji were at war.

It was a strange sort of war, because the two giants had been on friendly terms for so long. They were linked by marriages, and leaders of each place were *vasu* to the other.

Raivalita, Cakobau's half-brother, was Vasu Levu to Rewa, Cokanauto or Mr Phillips, the brother of Banuve, joined forces with Bau. And Qaraniqio, brother and a loyal supporter of the Roko Tui Dreketi, had been a childhood playmate of Cakobau's.

Cakobau had spent much of his boyhood in Rewa, and he and Qaraniqio taunted each other continually about what they would do when they were older, one saying "I will destroy your fortress," and the other saying "and I will eat you".

For a while, both powers managed to avoid each other in open battle.

Kidnappings, guerilla raids and skirmishes near border towns kept them content. A plot to assassinate both the Rewan king and Qaraniqio failed. So did a Rewa plan to kill Cakobau, who learned just in time that Raivalita had agreed to kill him, providing Rewa became a tributary of Bau when he had taken Cakobau's place.

Raivalita was knocked to the ground with a club and buried alive. Cakobau ignored his cries from the grave.

A Rewa missionary, Rev Thomas Jaggar, described some of the day-by-day events of the war:

January 13. Several of the allies of Rewa were cut off to-day . . . and while yet in concealment the enemy found them out, and killed thirty of them.

January 22. This day the chiefs and people of Rewa and their dependencies went to prepare a town by throwing up mounds and building fences; when a kingdom of some importance, which had been subject to Rewa, rose up against them as an enemy. Seventeen men were killed and the others put to flight . . .

February 15. The enemy made a powerful attack this day on a town two or three miles distant . . . they burnt more than one town and approached near to us, so that we could see the smoke of their muskets when fired . . . the king and a select few were at the time drinking yaqona at the gate of our premises: they were, however, soon dispersed, and great confusion followed; for there is nothing like order amongst them on such occasions.

May 13. Two boys went today to catch eels: they were discovered by the enemy, clubbed, and carried away. A foraging party also this morning killed a man belonging to the enemy.

And so it went, a bitter and drawn-out process.

Villages which had sided with Rewa at the beginning of the conflict began changing sides.

Rewa was weakening. Its gardens were destroyed or lost to deserted allies and food was getting scarce. Bau's forces hemmed Rewa in on three sides. The river was on the fourth. Only Nakelo, a strong Rewa ally, separated the two armies.

But then, the Tui Nakelo was bought off with the promise of Cakobau's sister.

It was the final straw. Banuve was ready for peace. He sent a high Rewa chief to Bau to negotiate the price, and the Rewa chief was given a good one — if he would help Cakobau destroy Rewa and kill the king!

On that June morning, the Bauans sailed into the mouth of the Rewa, while Bau's allies placed themselves in different positions around the town.

The Ra Marama, with Cakobau and other leading chiefs, moved opposite the king's house in an effort to save the queen of Rewa, a Bau lady of rank.

One of the Bau chiefs called to her, to come over the river in a small canoe and bring her children with her.

She did . . . but with her came her husband, Banuve.

When the Roko Tui Dreketi stepped into the canoe, the Bau chiefs shouted at him to go back, but the king, believing Cakobau had come in peace, would not. He said he was coming with his family, and the Bauans could do what they liked. Someone fired a musket at him, but missed. Another threw a spear.

Unarmed, the king boarded the giant canoe and Cakobau ordered one of his brothers to club him. The brother refused, saying he couldn't strike so great a chief.

Banuve pleaded for his life, but Cakobau told him his insults had been too great. Snatching a club with an axe-head lashed to it, he "clave his skull to the jaw, splashing his wife and children with blood". No sooner had he fallen, then columns of smoke rose from Rewa as the traitors inside the fortifications set fire to the houses.

Roko Tui Dreketi was taken to Bau, but because of his rank, he suffered a different fate from most war victims. He was *buried*.

Rewa was destroyed. With rebels inside the walls and the Bauans outside, between three and four hundred of the people were massacred.

Among them were three of Qaraniqio's children. But Qaraniqio wasn't with them. He had been away when the attack began and, returning to see Rewa in flames, he escaped in a canoe to Vuniveitakau on the Samabula River, and then fled to Colo-i-Suva.

Cokanauto, who had been pro-Bauan, was made king of Rewa, a puppet figure for Bau to manipulate, and he ruled his kingdom from Nukui.

Qaraniqio remained in the hills, waiting for a chance to strike. Tui Nakelo, the treacherous chieftain who had burned Rewa on the promise of Cakobau's sister, never got his lady. She was given to Gavidi, the chief of Lasakau, instead, and Tui Nakelo was so angry he turned his support to Qaraniqio.

The two joined forces and rebuilt Rewa, in defiance of Bau.

But the team was short-lived. Tui Nakelo was assassinated by a 'friendly' village bought out by Cakobau, who then proceeded to destroy Nakelo's allies. He invaded the Kuku villages, and when Nakelo rushed to the defence, Bau's army fled in a mock retreat. The Nakelo people returned home in triumph . . . only to find that about 800 Bauans had been secretly landed at night.

Rewa, just rebuilt, was destroyed again in 1847. Cakobau sent a messenger to Qaraniqio, saying he was angry "only with Nakelo for rebuilding your town." He said he must burn Rewa again as a matter of policy and kill the commoners, after which Qaraniqio would be bothered no longer and could "occupy the site of your father's house."

Cakobau suggested that Qaraniqio take refuge at Nukulau during the siege.

Qaraniqio and his forces abandoned the town, not to the island Cakobau suggested, but to a hill top (in Nasinu where Valelevu is now) where he could watch the Bau canoes surrounding Nukulau to cut off his escape.

"De ni vuaka" (pig's dung) he is supposed to have said. "Cakobau takes me for a fool".

Qaraniqio stayed up in the mountains. Cakobau repeatedly sent presents of turtles, tabua and other goods to the mountaineers in exchange for the Rewan's life. The mountain men ate the turtles and kept the presents — but refused to betray their friend.

For several years, Bau remained unchallenged. Then, in 1850, Cakobau declared war on all Christians. Dama (in Vanua Levu) and Viwa were attacked, but Cakobau thoughtfully issued orders that the missionaries themselves were not to be harmed, since he feared foreign intervention.

Christianity was becoming a nuisance to him. The missionaries continually thwarted him, even though he allowed them to live within sight of Bau and to convert his subjects. They denounced the customs which he practised and crowed over any of his courtesies as surrendering to their teaching. More important, mission stations were refuge to chiefs and warriors who fled to their sanctuary whenever war turned against them.

Harmed or not, the missionaries fought back. They got protection from a Tongan chief who, with 300 men, was on a visit to Bau. This chief sent a canoe to guard the missionaries and some of its crew were killed by Bau's allies, the Tailevu people.

The Tongans were about to become involved in the war, and a British warship, H.M.S. Calliope, anchored at Bua to protect the Christians. Cakobau wisely quit the plan. He'd already seen an example of a modern warship's firepower.

A year earlier, Captain Erskine had entertained the Bauan leader with a demonstation of HMS Havannah's cannons.

The missionary Calvert had been on board, and Cakobau had told him: "This makes me tremble. Should I offend these people they have but to bring their ship to Bau, when, having found me out with their spy-glasses, my head would fall at the first shot."

The demonstration gave Cakobau a new ambition. The kings of Hawaii and Tonga had ships of their own. He wanted his own, too.

Cakobau ordered a ship from America, agreeing to pay 1000 piculs of beche-de-mer for it, and, when it failed to arrive after a few months, he ordered another from Australia.

Both reached Fiji about the same time, but the Bauan opted for the American boat, a new ship of 76 tons, appropriately named the *Cakobau*.

Paying for it was another matter. He ordered a tax of beche-de-mer throughout his dominions, and sent messengers from island to island to drop off bags which were to be filled with the cured 'fish'.

But when he himself reached the islands, sailing in luxury in what the Cakobau's master called 'picknicking', there were empty bags or none at all. The bags were left to rot, or burned before the messenger's eyes.

In desperation, Cakobau took nearly ten thousand fighting men, one of the largest armies ever assembled, to Macuata to collect 'dri'. He set them an example by fishing with his own hands, but the men worked grudgingly and slowly. Finally, after sending the Cakobau to New Caledonia with more men, enough beche-de-mer was collected for a partial payment, and the Americans gave him the ship in disgust.

The ship was his, but at a colossal cost in popularity.

For Bau, things began to take a turn for the worse. Cokanauto, Bau's puppet king of Rewa, died from home-made liquor and the Rewa chiefs ended Bau's reign by eating him.

Qaraniqio came out of hiding, returned to Rewa, and in a single night, turned Rewa back into a fortress again, taunting Cakobau to do what he might. Years of guerilla warfare, when he had a price on his head, had not weakened his spirit or his taste for revenge. He swore Bau's chief would someday cook for him — or be eaten.

Bau attacked Rewa again and again, but failed. Qaraniqio began gaining a foothold in Bau's border villages, whose people were angry over such things as the beche-de-mer tax. Within weeks, Bau was circled in a ring of revolt. Tui Levuka and Ovalau had declared its independence. Qaraniqio was strong again, and there was another rebel chief raising hell with Bau — Cakobau's own cousin, Ratu Mara.

But he also had some unexpected allies . . . the Tongans.

The great Bau-Rewa war had been going on for nine long years when Tanoa, senile and pitiful, died.

Cakobau, already styling himself 'Tui Viti', officially became the Vunivalu and King of Bau.

Huge gifts from Tui Kilakila and chiefs of other dependencies bolstered his fading authority, but it was not a very bright future facing the king.

Rewa had grown strong again, some of Bau's allies had defected and were nibbling at its sides, and, to make matters worse, the Europeans had entered the war.

Except for a few veteran beachcombers, the *Kai Valagi* had remained neutral in the affair.

Ratu Seru Cakobau, 'Tui Viti'.

But then Levuka was burned to the ground, supposedly on Cakobau's instructions. Their attitude changed a little.

The sparks which set Levuka on fire actually had begun in August, 1853. A Levuka boat, the 'Wave', was seized by the people of Malake, off the Ra coast, and some of Ovalau's traders set off for Ra to "secure justice".

The Tui Levuka, with 40 warriors, went with them. Fourteen of Malake's people were killed and 13 women carried back to Levuka.

Malake was under the protection of Bau, and the traders were warned there would be reprisals. When the town was set alight by an unknown arsonist a month later, Cakobau was held responsible.

He, in turn, said it was not his doing. In fact, Cakobau sailed to Levuka right after the fire to express his sympathy, but was ignored.

A witness to the visit said "it was a visit terrible to the once-formidable chief . . . not a soul spoke to him. He courted a friendly recognition; but it was withheld, and the king then marched past the corps with all the dignity and pride of a conquering general. The Levuka chief would not consent to see him and a mountaineer, had he not been prevented by the whites, would have killed him . . ."

The whole of Ovalau, traders, coastal villages and hill people, were now against Cakobau.

Qaraniqio didn't waste any time in taking advantage of his new Ovalau allies. With the Tui Levuka and the Europeans, they organised a League pledged to blockade Bau. No ship was to be allowed to approach Bau, no tribute-bearing canoes filled with food, no ammunition.

Varani, the Viwa chief who got his name ('France') from the capture of a French brig years earlier, was still loyal to Cakobau.

In a heroic move, he decided to go to Ovalau's mountaineers, the Lovoni people, in person and get their help in destroying both the Tui Levuka and the blockade.

With six others, he landed on a deserted beach of Ovalau at night. By dawn, he reached Lovoni and its chieftain, Koroicava.

It was a courageous thing to do, and Varani nearly carried it off. The tabua had been presented and all was going well, when a messenger from Tui Levuka, who had heard of the visit, offered a prize for his death.

Varani and five others were clubbed as they returned unarmed from their bath. The sixth, who escaped into the bush, said Varani had wrestled a club away from an assailant, and then flung it away to prove Christian teachings.

His death was a blow to Cakobau.

There were others. At Kaba, the long peninsula separating Bau and Rewa, 500 of Cakobau's own men rebelled and joined Qaraniqio. They had with them his largest canoe, his biggest stockpile of ammunition, and the sails for his new ship, the 'Cakobau'.

To make matters worse, one of Bau's leading figureheads who had been in exile for months had returned. His name was Ratu Mara Kapaiwai. And he, like Qaraniqio, was intent on overthrowing the Vunivalu!

Ratu Mara was Cakobau's first cousin. He was *Vasu Levu* to Lau and wealthy. He was also very popular.

Ratu Mara had been banished to Lasakau after getting into a little mischief with an already-married Bauan girl. When a tabua was presented to Gavidi calling for Mara's death because of the incident, Mara decided to avoid any embarrassing incidents and leave for Lau.

From there, he sailed to Tonga, apparently the first of his rank to sail to Tonga in a canoe manned by Fijians. He got a cool reception from King George — he wasn't even allowed to set foot on shore for two days. But in time, he and King George became inseparable, with Ratu Mara acting as his personal protector.

When the Houma people of Tonga formed a plot to murder their king, King George heard about it. He went to Houma anyway, guarded by Mara and a few others.

The Tongans took note of "a huge warrior sitting on the war fence, his face fully blackened, his streamers of tapa blown out by the wind . . . and dressed in a manner foreign to the Tongans, with a great battle axe glistening in the sun . . ." They gave up their plan.

When Mara left Tonga, the king ordered Ma'afu and other high chiefs to accompany him back to Fiji.

His sins were forgiven and Mara was allowed to return to Bau, but when Cakobau ordered the chieftain to go to Lau and collect beche-de-mer to help pay for the ship 'Cakobau', he was indignant.

He went instead to Rewa and offered his support to the Roko Tui Dreketi, and then joined the gathering of dissatisfied Bauans at Kaba.

Bau, by this time, was truly in trouble. The blockade set up by the Europeans was so effective there was little food or ammunition.

There had been a major fire, apparently an accident, and much of Bau had burned, including the re-built temple dedicated to the war god, Cagawalu.

Koroi Ravulo, one of Bau's more influential chiefs, joined the rebel forces, setting up defences at Sawakasa on the Tailevu coast. This meant Bau had a war on two fronts: Kaba on one side, which Qaraniqio and Mara continued to strengthen, and Ravulo on the other. Koroi Ravulo was strong enough that, when a chief of Namena near Sawakasa attempted to aid Bau, the rebel bribed 500 warriors to stay home.

Despite fires, the blockade and a dwindling army, Cakobau decided to attack Kaba.

When he was organising his army, a hurricane levelled Bau, or at least, all that was left of it after the fire.

It also smashed Kaba and tore down the war fences. For some strange reason, Cakobau didn't attack.

By the time the gods were consulted and the boasting ceremonies completed, a week had passed, and Kaba's war fences were repaired. Behind them was a contingent of Europeans who realised Kaba was the last defence before Levuka.

Bau's troops attacked, but after a few hours or random shooting and shouting, they were suddenly seized with panic and fled to their canoes.

Of 2000 warriors who reached Cautata (a few miles from Kaba), most remained concealed behind trees, well out of range of musket shot.

Cakobau was sick, worn out, and covered with sores. His dominion had nearly collapsed. An American ship, the Dragon, broke the blockade and sold him ammunition, but Bau was already on the defensive. Qaraniqio and Mara were moving closer.

His only hope now lay with King George.

The Tongan ruler stopped at Bau in November, 1853, on his way to Sydney, Cakobau quickly offered him the canoe Ra Marama if he would crush Kaba and help end the rebellion. King George was evasive, but promised to return to Bau when he could.

Cakobau bided his time as the ring tightened around him.

A few months later, a letter reached him from King George. It warned him that the U.S. Commercial Agent in Levuka, John Brown Williams, had written to Sydney's newspapers appealing to civilized nations to destroy Bau, which was guilty of "savagery and oppression". This could be done, said Williams, "by a warship in the time it takes to smoke a cigar".

King George wrote: "I expect to visit you with the Tongan friends to bring away my canoe" and added "It is good you should be humble . . . I wish, Thakombau, you would *lotu*."

The king ended the letter by saying ". . . it will be well for you, Thakombau, to think wisely in these days."

Tired and smarting from constant defeat in war, Cakobau yielded to King George's advice.

On Sunday, April 30, 1854, the Rogorogo valu, the death drum which usually summoned men to a cannibal feast, called Christians to a service at which the Vunivalu would *lotu*. Temples were spoiled and the sacred nokonoko trees chopped down.

Cakobau's decision caused more desertions from Bau. He was so unpopular few spoke to him. He sat in his house, alone.

Cakobau may have turned Christian, but he wasn't to part with his chiefly powers. When Rev. Waterhouse drew up a nine-point plan, which would have established a council of chiefs and abolished the rank of Vunivalu and practice of polygamy, Cakobau calmly told the missionary "I was born a chief and I will die a chief."

Qaraniqio, too, was weakening. Suffering from dysentery, he had nevertheless offered to end the war by a duel. He was brought aboard the ship 'Dragon' for the first face-to-face meeting with Cakobau in years, and he said "it is shameful that so many are being killed; let you or me die."

Cakobau had replied "We are not dogs that we should bite one another. We are both chiefs. Let us fight like chiefs."

But, within months, Cakobau was asking for peace — and Qaraniqio refused. His wounds were too deep — the Bauan had killed not only his brother, but his three children and heirs.

Now, Qaraniqio had no reason for peace. Kaba was a hive of warriors, all well-supplied with food and arms.

But before they could strike, Qaraniqio died. Hours before his death, Adi Civo of Rewa noticed a taro weeping, foretelling the tragedy. The Rewan leader was too weak to speak and died without naming a successor to carry on the war. A missionary, Rev Moore, gave him medicine for dysentery just before his death and was blamed for poisoning him: he and his family barely escaped with their lives.

After 11 years of bloodshed, Rewa was ready for peace. So was Cakobau.

The rebels on Kaba weren't. Heathen chiefs everywhere had joined Mara; it was no longer a Bau-Rewa war, it was Christians versus non-Christians.

Mara prepared his forces. There was nothing to prevent success . . . until word reached him that the Tongan fleet had just anchored at Moturiki.

Two thousand Tongan warriors in 40 canoes, many of them collected from Lakeba and all supplied with firearms, had come to mediate. They saved Cakobau from certain death.

King George and Ratu Mara were old friends. But the Tongan chief also held Cakobau in high regard. He probably would have collected his promised canoe and kept out of the affair.

But Mara's rebels changed all that. They killed a Tongan chief, Tawake, who had gone to Ovalau to deliver a letter from Tonga's Wesleyan mission to the priests at Levuka.

King George volunteered his support to Cakobau. On April 7, 1855, the Tongan fleet, now bolstered by 1000 of Cakobau's forces, bore down on the promontory. It must have been an incredible sight.

As they reached the point, the rebels united in a volley of musket fire which would have turned back the usual Fijian siege.

Kaba's priests had already predicted that the Tongans would "throw away their muskets in flight" and there would be none left alive to work the sails. The Kaba rebels were actually looking forward to the coming assault.

But to their astonishment, the Tongans didn't stop for the musket fire. They left their wounded to women to look after, and kept on coming.

Instead of hiding behind trees, they advanced in the open. It was a strange way of battle to the Fijians. They fled!

King George commanded the assault in person, and he had intended to stop at the first defences, surround Kaba, and starve the rebels into surrender. But the warriors of Va'vau ignored his orders and stormed ahead.

Later, they said they were looking for the defences — but didn't see them.

Fourteen Tongans were killed. Two hundred of Kaba's fighters fell, and another 200 were taken prisoner. This, too, was new: both Cakobau and King George had said they wanted prisoners, not bodies.

Cakobau, in his honour of triumph, was remarkably merciful: all 200 were spared. He asked that Koroi Ravulo alone be killed, but King George reminded him of his new faith.

Ratu Mara, who knew the Tongan's method of battle, wisely escaped when he saw the fleet approaching. He reached Ovalau and, with the Tui Levuka, continued to stir up revolt . . . until he was captured, taken to Bau, and publicly hanged.

Ratu Mara Kapaiwai, who came so close to being Vunivalu and King of Bau, was buried on Bau's hill.

The great war had ended. With the fall of Kaba, Cakobau's religion became the people's religion and whole districts *lotued*.

There would never be another Fijian war like it.

War canoes portrayed by J. Glen Wilson, aboard HMS Herald, 1856.

19   RA MARAMA AND THE WAR CANOES

A Canoe named Ra Marama changed the course of Fiji's history.

King George, of Tonga, came to Fiji to collect it . . . and saved Cakobau and Bau in the process.

After the battle of Kaba, the two great heads of state, King George and Ratu Cakobau, sailed to Rewa, Kadavu and Ovalau on the huge *drua*.

Forty other canoes followed in their wake.

It was not the biggest procession of Fiji's navy, but it was an impressive one.

Ra Marama was 100ft long and carried, besides its two dignified gentle-man, a contingent of 140 chiefs and attendants.

It was certainly a canoe fit for a king — although "canoe" is hardly the word to use for a vessel with a thousand square feet of deck space, a 60ft mast, and two sleek hulls which would slice through the seas faster than a merchant ship.

In fact, Fiji's canoes were superior to any in Melanesia, and they'd been luring the Tongans here for years.

* * *

The Tongans began making occasional trips to Fiji as early as the 13th Century, but it was probably the late 1700s before the "canoe trade" developed. They offered tapa or their services in war in exchange for huge logs of vesi which were to become canoe hulls.

By the early 1800s, they had even given up their own Tongan designs in favour of Fiji's, with Rev Cargill noting "the shape of the canoe, the manner of lashing it together . . . are all Feejean. This is creditable to the skill of Feejean mechanics."

At Fulaga and Kabara, at Koro and the Natewa Peninsula, colonies of Tongans worked on the canoes. It took four or five years to complete one.

Hulls were made of split logs lashed to frames with sinnet, then caulked with gum from the breadfruit tree. Sails, huge mats of voivoi, came from Kadavu, Macuata, and even the Yasawas.

Many of the big canoes returned to Tonga with their owners and craftsmen. Others were built for or traded to Fijian chiefs.

One of the largest to remain here was the Rusa-i-Vanua, built in Fulaga. It was 118ft long.

When Commodore Wilkes, of the US Exploring Expedition, reached Fiji, he watched the Tongan chiefs Lajiki and Tubou Totai, with 500 followers, sailing huge *drua* on their way to Bau. Tubou "told me he and his brothers had been residing several years in the Feejees . . . employed building canoes on some of the eastern islands, and that it generally took them seven years from the time they left Tonga to finish them and return."

Ra Marama was built in Somosomo and completed about 1853. It was presented to Bau by the Somosomo people as tribute, and a beachcomber, "Cannibal Jack" Jackson, was aboard it when it sailed from Taveuni to Bau. He described its now-notorious launching ceremony this way:

Cakobau inquired if there had been any human sacrifices to ensure and propitiate the gods for the success, smart sailing, and durability of the canoe. They said, that during the seven years she was building, several people had been killed and eaten on the spot, but that no late sacrifices had been made. He said he wondered at Lala ko Lovoni's scrupulousness in not hauling the canoe over the bodies of slaves as rollers, but said that he did not wonder much, when he came to consider that he had been living under the dictates of "bete ni lotu Bolatagane" (English missionaries).

In lowering the mast, the heel slipped and caught one man and killed him, and two were slightly wounded, which accident Cakobau immediately attributed to the wrath of the gods, and despatched Gavidi off in secrecy for a canoe-load of victims. Ten bodies had been killed by Gavidi that morning, but on account of the accident, Cakobau said there had not been sufficient sacrifices. Gavidi soon returned with 11 bodies of persons who he had fallen in with in a canoe and killed them all, making in all 21 human sacrifices.

Fiji canoe fleets, including the large, plank-built *camakau* outriggers and *tabilai* fighting canoes, sometimes numbered 150 or more.

There were some monumental sea battles.

Ratu Deve Toganivalu, one of Fiji's earliest historians, recounts several sea battles during the Bau-Rewa war in which Cakobau's war canoes numbered 200. He wrote that, when they sailed out to battle, "Laucala Bay was absolutely crowded with canoes."

In one of them, a number of Rewan canoes were seen returning home from Kadavu, unaware that their kingdom had just fallen into the hands of Bau.

Cakobau sent three large *drua* outside the reef — the Tui Nayau, Kabalavu and Lemaki — with orders to ram the Rewans. By the time the Lemaki had reached two of the canoes, their crews had jumped overboard and begun swimming to windward.

The Tui Nayau rammed one of the Rewan druas and sank it, and the Bauans slaughtered the crew as they tried to swim to safety.

The Kabalavu chased another all the way to Beqa, smashing it as it neared shore. This was their best battle technique, since the giant *drua* and even smaller *camakau* had four or five feet of solid timber at their bows to use as rams.

The Rewans suffered again soon after, when the Bulumakau and Bukanivanua came inside Laucala Bay after sailing from Kadavu.

Again, Cakobau sailed out to attack. He personally commanded the Lewayada, accompanied by the Tawaibula and Lekau.

According to Toganivalu, "the Tawaibula and the Lekau ran into the Bulumakau and its crew were all killed; many also of the crew of the Tawaibula died. The Lewayada, on which Ratu Cakobau embarked, chased the other Rewa canoe, the Bukanivanua . . . which was swift and went aground." The crew fled and Cakobau gained another addition to his fleet.

There were large "naval engagements" in which the big canoes fought side-by-side, some even using war fences to shield the crew.

Outriggers were fast and carried large number of fighting men, too. Their only weakness was that they were vulnerable to small sailing canoes which swept past the windward side.

A stroke of the hatchet at the mast stay brought mast and rigging down on top of the men, and those who survived the falling mast were easy victims when they bobbed to the surface.

When a canoe was sunk, there were few survivors.

But on one of those Rewan canoes returning from Kadavu, a very lucky man told his story to Rev Waterhouse. The Reverend wrote that the canoes . . ."who knew not that the king's youngest brother had been driven to Nukui, were unexpectedly attacked by a Bau canoe, and nearly 30 men, women and children were shot, clubbed or speared to death. One got free in a curious way. When the two canoes struck, the mast of that from Kadavu fell, and the poor fellows were entangled in the sail, and clubbed.

"The (Bauans) threw the sail into the water, and having taken what things they more particularly wanted from the canoe, permitted it to drift away to sea; thinking, perhaps, that they had better escape as soon as possible, as it was evening. One man, however, managed to conceal himself in the sail, and when it was thrown overboard floated away with it. Some of the enemy again wished the sail to be secured, others opposed it. He heard them talking about it and knew, if they again obtained the sail, he would be discovered and killed. He said that he was almost dead with fright, but that he prayed to his little god, and he saved him . . .

When the enemy were out of sight, he swam to the canoe, which was afloat, although filled with water. He then called out to know if any of his friends were yet alive; after some time had elapsed, he saw two men swimming towards the canoe . . . They then got ashore, climbed some nut trees, and made a sail from some of the leaves, and were able to reach Beqa and were saved."

Canoes were speedy and silent, and they were used in a variety of ways. One trick was to let a large craft drift ashore as if it was abandoned, the warriors hidden beneath its rounding sides until some unfortunate victims on shore waded out to claim it.

In peaceful times, the drua made remarkable voyages, with chieftains sailing between the Lau Group, Yasawas, Cakaudrove, Viti Levu and Kadavu without any apparent fear or worry.

Their navigation methods are only now beginning to be studied, and when they travelled for long distances out of sight of other islands, they must have relied on prevailing winds, star navigation — and luck — to reach their destination.

But, when there was war, it was not uncommon to see drua and big outriggers carrying cannon, a development supposedly introduced into Fiji by Ma'afu.

Ra Marama was one of these: it had two cannons mounted on its foredecks.

That elegant war canoe, with Cakobau and King George aboard, passed through the Rewa delta entertaining high chiefs on its decks, the same chiefs who, a month earlier, had been sworn enemies. At the end of the cruise, the two great leaders parted company, and the gunboat "Cakobau" which had caused its owner nothing but trouble, and the Ra Marama proceeded on to Tonga.

The Tongans had saved Cakobau from certain death, and they weren't likely to forget it. King George had returned to his islands, but others, including Ma'afu, were so permanently entrenched that a new power struggle was developing.

Before long, Cakobau would realize he had merely exchanged one menace for another.

20   TWO AMERICANS

In the years before Cession, there were two Americans who did a lot to change the way of life in Fiji.

One was a good man who was just a little bit bad. The other was a bad man who was just a little bit good. But no one can deny that David Whippy and John Brown Williams made an unforgettable impact here.

★ ★ ★

Levuka about 1860.

Whippy was from Nantucket, the port from which most of America's whaling fleet sailed. He was the son of a sea captain and he dutifully went to sea at the age of 16, serving as mate under an older brother.

Life at sea was bearable, but his brother wasn't. Whippy ran away when the ship reached Peru, staying hidden in Callao's twisting streets until the ship left.

Eventually, he joined a brig bound for the 'Feejees'. It was the 'Calder', under the command of Peter Dillon, the man who had made such a miraculous escape from Wailea ten years earlier. (Chapter No. 9)

David Whippy's job on shore was to supervise work in the curing sheds for the beche-de-mer, and he would be absent from the ship for weeks while the vessel went to other parts of the islands collecting cargo.

He quickly learned Fijian, and the job wasn't difficult — except that the ship never returned! Some men might have been a little upset at the situation, but Whippy wasn't. He made friends with the Tui Levuka, a friendship which was to last for 20 years, and under his protection he began making himself a home on Ovalau.

Within a year, he was *Mata ki Bau*, the Tui Levuka's official messenger to Bau.

On one of these trips to Bau, Whippy met an old friend, William Cary.

Cary was the sole survivor of the 'Oneo' a Nantucket whaling ship wrecked on Vatoa in the southern Lau group in 1825. He had hidden in a crevice for three days as the rest of Oneo's 22 crewmen were massacred.

Finally, he could stand it no longer and climbed out into the daylight, waiting to be killed. Instead, he was taken to a chieftain who "made me understand I was now his son".

Chieftain and 'son' eventually sailed to Lakeba, and then to Bau, where Cary was due for a surprise . . .

"Soon after our arrival here I saw a canoe coming from Ambau, in which was a white man. As they came alongside our canoe the white man reached out his hand and addressed me by name. I was dumb with astonishment. At last he said "don't you know David Whippy?" "Yes", I answered, "I formerly knew him well. He was a townsman of mine and an old playmate." "Well", said he, "I am that David Whippy."

The two Nantucket men must have had quite a reunion. Whippy told Cary that he had left the brig Calder some 13 months before, and that he "had no desire to leave the island, as he was a particular favourite of the king and chiefs."

He said there were two other Europeans living with him, all valued by the Tui Levuka "as the village had previously been troubled by raiding mountaineers," the Lovoni.

William Cary and Whippy crossed paths several times during the next year. Both bartered for trade goods by helping visiting ships collect beche-de-mer. Later, Cary was to write that, while they were both at "Labooca", war was declared "against one of the villages on the island of Thawcan-drover (Cakaudrove) and David and I were invited to join the expedition."

"David, dressed like a native, led our party. He got shelter behind a stump, singled out one of their chief warriors, fired and shot him through the head. As soon as their chief fell the enemy fled for the woods and mountains. Then we rushed forward, broke down their bamboo fence and entered the village.

"We killed all who had not made their escape, plundered the town, set it on fire, then marched back to Navatu, singing songs of victory. Here we were paid for our services with hogs, turtle, fishing nets and whales teeth."

David Whippy, the man who was to become the most respected member of the early traders and the very founder of Levuka town, was a soldier-of-fortune.

But it is difficult to be too critical. He was living in very violent times and life was cheap. Cary's account of their expedition to Vanua Levu is the only one which mars his record.

Everywhere else he went, he made friends. As more and more ships arrived, all making Levuka the first port of call, Whippy made sure that the villagers received proper payment for their goods . . . axes and knives made out of reasonable steel, rather than makeshift tools cast from pig iron.

He had a reputation for being able to heal the sick and, after a particularly successful effort of treating one old man, 150 people from the man's village arrived by canoe for a similar treatment.

Captains of visiting ships all asked for "Whippy". When the US Exploring Expedition arrived in 1840, Commodore Wilkes met David within minutes of dropping anchor, telling him he had heard of him years earlier. Whippy was translater aboard the American ships during their stay, and his accounts of Fiji and its customs became a major part of Wilke's famous 'Narrative'.

David became America's vice-consul here soon after the Commodore's return to the States, and Wilkes added: "Ovalau is the principal residence of the white men in the group, to whose general deportment and good conduct I must bear testimony."

Levuka was growing. Whippy was certainly doing his part . . . first with the assistance of Tulia, who bore his first child (David), and then with a woman from Natokalau and another from Koro, (Dorcas), who convinced him they should be formally married.

By the 1840s, Levuka was a prosperous little settlement of traders, and the firm of Whippy, Simpson and Cusick was building sailing cutters for all of them.

But by 1844, there were problems.

One of the less-scrupulous traders, Charles Pickering of Rewa, broke the European's rule of "non-involvement" and assisted Qaraniqio in the Bau-Rewa war. When his schooner was wrecked on Cicia, Cakobau sent a party to capture him — but some of Levuka's traders reached him first and carried him to safety.

Cakobau was so angry he gave the Europeans and their families three days to leave Levuka.

Everything that couldn't be carried was abandoned, including the just-built hull of Whippy's 70-ton schooner.

For the next five years, the traders lived at Solevu Bay on the tip of Vanua Levu, a mangrove swamp which claimed 16 lives from dysentery before Cakobau, in 1849, relented and let them return to Levuka.

Their houses were gone, the schooner's hull destroyed, and Whippy's friend, the Tui Levuka had been killed in a Lovoni raid.

They started all over again, building houses and trade stores and a school which opened with 80 pupils — most of them the "fruit salad" off-spring of the Europeans.

Whippy remained leader and spokesman. But, as US vice-consul, he had some new tasks as well. One was his appointment as arbitrator in claims against Cakobau made by the American Consul, John Brown Williams. American war ships came and went, each captain dismissing Whippy's modest appraisals in favour of a claim which spiralled ever higher.

Historian Stan Brown has this to stay of David Whippy in his book 'Men from Under the Sky': he "was one of the few early arrivals who tried to understand the Fijians and probably the first one that Fijians understood."

They might have understood Whippy. They certainly never understood John Brown Williams!

Williams had been the American Consul in New Zealand until the British took over. But with the British came duties on rum and tobacco and a ban on firearms, putting an end to a lucrative trade.

Instead, he was appointed US Commercial Agent to Fiji and he arrived in February, 1846. Within weeks, he was doing a land-office business . . . but it wasn't exactly for America.

Williams began buying land, always putting his name along with several 'associates' on the deed. He bought Nukulau Island for $30, Laucala Point for $50, and then a tract on the coast of Namosi, paid for in trade goods.

By the time he was officially the American Consul, he was able to register all the land titles in his name only — by the simple process of erasing and scratching out the names of his associates!

His first official duty was a letter of protest written to Cakobau after an American ship which had gone on the reef near Ovalau was plundered by coastal villagers. Tactless, he threatened Cakobau (who knew nothing of the event) by saying "severe punishment will be inflicted upon the chiefs and people. No leniency will be shown."

John Brown Williams was losing ground with the high chiefs quickly, and with Cakobau faster still . . . particularly after he began selling arms to Bau's enemies, Cokanauto and Qaraniqio.

As an agent of the US Government, Williams had no right to be taking sides in a local war. But then, Rewa was giving him political insight: land in exchange for arms.

America's consulate at Nukulau was fast becoming a paying proposition. Williams celebrated with a party on July 4, America's independence day, and it got off with a bang. During a cannon salute to amuse visitors, one of the cannons exploded. Besides tearing off the arm of the American negro who fired it, trade store and consulate caught fire and burned to the ground.

The Fijians who were at Nukulau saved what they could, but, in Fijian style, kept what they had saved.

Williams claimed compensation for items "stolen", which he valued at $5000. It was the first of the American claims which were to plague Fiji for 20 years.

After the fire at Nukulau, Williams moved Consul and trade-store to Laucala. Once again, his house was burned down.

When Qaraniqio died, the Rewa people burned the mission house nearby (they thought the missionary had poisoned him), and, just for good measure, set fire to William's house as well.

There were claims for more losses. At first, the payment sought was 100 bags of beche-de-mer. But as the years went by and no payment was received, it escalated a little . . . to $43,000.

True, the claims now included losses suffered from the Levuka fire and from pillaged American ships, but the Consul's own personal claims accounted for half of it.

Four times in William's life in Fiji, American men-of-war stopped at the islands and each time, the captains reviewed and judged the validity of the claims.

Each time, they decided Cakobau, as 'Tui Viti' must be held responsible. Each time, Cakobau promised faithfully to pay, then forgot about it again after the navy ships left.

During one of those visits, Commander Boutwell of the USS John Adams summoned Cakobau aboard ship. Ratu Vakula of Vutia was with him. He later told a Lands Commission inquiry: "I remember going on board a man-of-war at Laucala . . . we were told to touch the end of a pen, which we did. Williams then said, "You have confirmed Laucala . . ."

Commander Boutwell then ordered payment of $12,000 to Williams, a new house, and title to lands at Nukulau and Laucala which were being disputed, along with the rest of the claims for $43,000.

When Cakobau hesitated, he was told to sign it — or be carried away to America. He signed.

John Brown Williams died in 1860, before he received any part of the claim money. His one apparent act of charity was to give land to a Wesleyan mission (Mataisuva) whose members were trying to see him removed from Fiji.

But the legacy of John Brown Williams — the American claims — would be the biggest reason behind Fiji's decision to become a British colony.

It was an amazing non-achievement for an American commercial agent.

Ma'afu and wife. An "able chief and a caged lion".

21 MA'AFU AND THE TONGAN TAKE-OVER

A red and white flag flew over most of the Lau Group . . . Ma'afu's flag.

Parliament sat at Lakeba, under Ma'afu's leadership. He had already developed a sophisticated system of land-leasing, taxes, courts, uniformed police and even public works.

By 1869, the Tongan held the allegiance of half of Fiji, including Vanua Levu, and his position was so strong that it looked like the other half would soon follow . . .

The Tongans began their take-over of the Lau Group long before Ma'afu arrived. They'd been arriving for decades: ousted chiefs from Tonga's civil wars, and then adventure-hungry warriors after the wars ceased, all sailing west.

The Fijians paid a heavy price as hosts. The Tongans arrived with no leaders and no discipline. They took everything they could and gave little in return. They robbed gardens, and plundered villages, and sold their services as mercenaries to chiefs who would regret, later, ever hiring them.

Chiefs became servants, and even the Tui Nayau was powerless to ward off his arrogant and costly visitors.

Then, King George came. Taufa'ahau, the first King of a united Tonga, arrived quite by accident — his canoe was blown off course during a voyage from Samoa to Ha'apai.

What he saw in Fiji came as a shock: colonies of malcontents living a riotous existence, a potential army of invasion which could turn back and menace Tonga just as easily as it had pushed its way into Lau.

Taufa'ahau didn't waste any time. He sent over one of his kinsmen, a young prince named Enele Ma'afuotu'itoga, who in Fiji would become known simply as Ma'afu.

It was a smart move for a lot of reasons. One was that Ma'afu had just as much right to Tonga's throne as Taufa'ahau had, so it was convenient to get him out of the way. The other was that Ma'afu was a natural leader and warrior who was happiest on the battle field, a perfect choice to control the errant Tongans.

He arrived in 1848, a 22-year-old with just enough soldiers to establish his authority. Within a few months, the "terrible Tongans" were completely under his control. So was the aging and weak Tui Nayau.

Ma'afu made Lomaloma (Vanua Balavu) his headquarters — after assisting the under-dog in a local war, and then easing the victors out the back door. It was a good technique, and he would use it again, each time with the same success.

What the Tongan prince couldn't take with manpower, he took with religion, and as a self-proclaimed 'missionary', his methods were a little suspect. He invaded Matuku in 1853, conquered the island after a three-month effort, and then forced the survivors to become Christian.

It was a strange way of doing business: looting, burning and killing to teach people religion. His missionary zeal earned him expulsion from the Wesleyan Church, but it didn't matter.

Ma'afu decided Christianity was a reasonable excuse for kingdom-building, and he took Moala the same way he took Matuku.

Totoya followed, the rightful chiefs being replaced "after Christianity" with Tongans, or at least subservient Fijian chiefs.

Whenever he made a conquest, the land was divided into individual holdings under Tongan control, rather than being left in the Fijian communal system of land ownership.

When the Tui Cakau visited Tui Nayau to barter for one of the large Lauan canoes, Tui Nayau didn't have one to offer.

But Ma'afu did. In return, Tui Cakau gave him sovereignty over Vanua Balavu and all the islands of northern Lau, extending south to Moce.

Within five years of his arrival, Ma'afu had fought, bought and evangelised his way to power over an immense amount of area.

About this time, Cakobau was losing ground to Ratu Mara, and Ma'afu prepared to help the Kaba rebels put an end to Bau's reign forever!

King George intervened, and Ma'afu, out of duty to his king, was forced to help restore power to the very man he planned to overthrow.

Cakobau was safe again, at least temporarily. But not fooled. He watched as Ma'afu's power grew, and as the Tongan parcelled out more and more of the kingdom . . . and then watched bitterly and helplessly as the Tongans, in 1859, attacked Macuata — Bau's ally — and chased the Tui Macuata into exile.

The Tongan raiders were led by two brutal terrorists named Semisi Fifita and Wainiqolo, whose reputations for cruelty became village legend.

They swept up the Macuata coast, burning and murdering as they went, and they chased Ritova, the Tui Macuata, all the way to Taveuni. In his place, they installed Bete, the son of the former chief of Macuata, and a favourite with the Tui Bua.

Tui Bua was pleased — until he realised the price for Tongan assistance. It was the same old story . . . and now Ma'afu held authority in Vanua Levu as well as Lau.

Bau was next.

Ma'afu began making plans for the attack, and as an opening move, he sent a force to occupy Beqa, while the Tui Bua took Ra.

The pincers probably would have closed, Bau would have fallen, and Ma'afu would have become the Supreme Chief of Fiji — if the British hadn't stepped in.

Britain's Consul, William Pritchard, arrived in September, 1858. He set up an office in an unfurnished house in Levuka, and within a week was besieged with more than 20 complaints from British subjects. But none of these were important enough to keep him from working on his pet project.

Pritchard was convinced Fiji should be annexed to England . . . before the Americans, the French, or the Tongans got it.

The Consul was quick to recognise Ma'afu's ambitions. In fact, they were already well-known: a Tongan empire which would include not only Fiji, but everything between New Hebrides and Samoa.

And the Americans were still after their claims for $45,000. Another warship, the USS Vandalia, was pressing Cakobau for immediate payment.

Exhausted from the pressures of both Tongans and Americans, Cakobau agreed to Pritchard's request. He signed an agreement offering to cede Fiji to Britain!

It was October 12, 1858. Pritchard had been in Fiji just eight weeks before he left for London with Cakobau's offer. While he was gone, Ma'afu raised more hell than ever. A British take-over would put an end to his dreams, and he had to move quickly.

By the time the Consul returned, a frightened Cakobau hurriedly explained the Tongan's doings, and said, since Fiji was on the verge of cession and "almost British", Tongan aggression was an act against the Queen.

At the same time, Ma'afu paid a visit to Pritchard, too, saying it was time to "get rid of that old savage".

The two rivals were both pressing for the advantage, and Pritchard coolly solved the problem (for a while) by called a meeting of chiefs.

It was the very first Great Council of Chiefs ever held. Some were rivals of Cakobau's and some, outright enemies. But they feared Ma'afu's power and they were jealous of his success.

In England, the Crown had been dubious about Cakobau's offer of cession. Was he actually King of Fiji, and were the 200,000 acres of land he offered in payment for the American claims really his?

Pritchard's meeting of the First Council of Chiefs at least strengthened the offer. The chiefs gave their support to Cakobau, the lesser of two evils, and ratified the provision for the land.

Ma'afu was at the meeting. So was a British warship, HMS Elk, which was anchored a few hundred yards from the consulate. The Tongan was removed to the privacy of the ship, and then told to give up all his claims in Fiji.

The resulting argument apparently lasted five hours, but in the end, he did. He signed an agreement which read, in part, "I, Ma'afu, chief of Tonga, definitely state that I am here solely to manage and control the Tonguese in Fiji, that all Tonguese claims in Fiji are hereby renounced." It must have been a bitter pill to swallow.

More setbacks followed. Ritova was restored to his former chiefdom and a British ship ordered that no Tongans were to set foot on Macuata for at least one year.

Then, Semisi Fifita was dragged aboard a French vessel, the Cornelie, charged with flogging and maltreating Roman Catholics in the Yasawas, and sentenced to hard labour in the French settlements of New Caledonia. He was never seen in Fiji again.

Ma'afu's empire was collapsing, bit by bit. He had countered the British insults by submitting a claim, on behalf of King George, for $60,000 for Tonga's help at Kaba — which was ignored.

King George, Cakobau's former ally, probably never expected to get money from the Kaba claim, but he was looking with interest at Fiji.

After all, Ma'afu still had the support of half the group. It shouldn't be too difficult to help him get the rest.

Taufa'ahau began preparing for an invasion, but other Tongan chiefs opposed it so strongly that the King backed down. For months, rumours of a Tongan attack grew and grew, until Pritchard himself boarded a ship for Tonga, to dissuade King George from giving support to Ma'afu.

When the Consul got there, in April, 1862, he found not only King George waiting, but Ma'afu as well. To Pritchard's amazement, it was Ma'afu who got the rebuff, and King George signed an agreement that Tonga would not make war on Fiji until the question of cession to Britain was decided.

That decision came three months later. The British said no.

London had sent Colonel Smythe to Fiji to report on the proposed plan for cession, and the Colonel took back an unfavourable report.

Cakobau, he said, was only one chief among many and didn't have the authority to offer Fiji to England. The land he offered to the Crown was not his.

Colonel Smythe also stated that Fiji was too isolated, that its waters were difficult to navigate, that cotton being grown on a trial basis would "never be more than marginal", and that England was already suffering embarrassment and expense from a Maori war and would find it difficult to administer "yet another savage race".

The decision was a disappointment to Cakobau, who feared renewed Tongan aggression.

It was also a disappointment to the European traders and settlers, who had flocked to Fiji, two thousand of them between 1861 and 1869, at the prospect of British protection.

They wanted a government — any sort of government — which would put an end to warfare, offer security, and settle disputes.

They proposed a confederacy of native kingdoms, and in 1865, the idea was accepted.

Fiji's first constitution was drawn up and signed by seven "independent chiefs of Fiji", representing the 'states' of Bau, Lakeba, Rewa, Bua, Cakaudrove, Macuata and Naduri. Each state was to be self-supporting, although it would form part of the General Assembly, the over-all legislative body.

Cakobau was elected president for two years in a row. The third year, Ma'afu sought the seat, the Fijian chiefs refused to be governed by a Tongan and withdrew.

The confederacy collapsed!

It didn't bother Ma'afu. He went ahead and organised his own government, the Confederation of North and East Fiji, 'Na Tovata ko Natokalau kei Viti'. Lau, Cakaudrove and Bua were united with a European adviser (the U.S. vice-Consul Swanston) and Tui Cakau as President.

Ma'afu gave himself the title of Tui Lau, then neatly pushed the Tui Cakau aside two years later, in 1869, to claim the presidency.

The confederation was very successful. Ma'afu banned all land sales, an idea he got from King George, but instigated land leases on very favourable terms. He offered protection and good government to the planters and they came in droves. A large trading firm moved to Lomaloma, making an area independent from the Levuka merchants.

Ma'afu's confederation was strong and healthy, and for the next four years, it flourished.

Cakobau's had collapsed. A coronation ceremony in 1867, complete with a $4 tinsel crown, invested Cakobau as 'Tui Viti' in his second attempt at government, but the British wouldn't recognise it, and when demands were made for poll and land taxes, neither would anyone else.

The Tongan was pointed out as the obvious choice to be King of Fiji. Ma'afu and Cakobau would continue their duel for power until 1871.

Only then would one of them be truly named 'Tui Viti'.

Thomas Baker.

Governor Thurston and Nawawabalavu, the chief who killed the missionary.

22   REV BAKER, MISSIONARY TO THE INTERIOR

Reverend Baker, Missionary to the Interior, sat down at Dawarau and wrote a letter to his wife.

". . . I find we are about midway across the land, and I have resolved to go all the way now I am so far in . . . we start early in the morning for Navosa. I anticipate no difficulty except at this place. If they do not lotu, I do not believe that they will venture to kill me . . . there is no fighting anywhere now, so I feel the coast is clear. Kiss the children for me — all of them . . ."

But the coast wasn't clear. Rev Thomas Baker was about to become the only missionary to be killed by the Fijians.

* * *

At least once before during his eight years in Fiji, the Reverend had been a little apprehensive about his chances. There was the time in 1862, just three years after his arrival, when he had been returning to his mission station at Tiliva, Bua, and his canoe was overtaken by a Macuata raiding party.

The missionary's crew tactfully remained silent while the Macuatans, fresh from murdering the chief Bete, pulled alongside and abused them.

"I thought Fiji had not yet stained its shores with a missionary blood," he wrote later. "Am I to be the first?"

Now, it was 1867. He was stationed at Davuilevu on the Rewa Circuit — and he was setting out to cross Viti Levu via the upper reaches of the Sigatoka Valley, a rugged area where no man of the cross had ever been before.

He had ventured into the bush from Davuilevu a number of times, urging the villages of Naitasiri, Viria, Dawarau and those along the banks of the Wainimala to *lotu*.

But an encounter with the hill people could be different. While villages on the coast were following Cakobau in accepting Christianity, the hill people didn't like Cakobau, *or* Christianity, *or* coastal people in general.

So when Baker, a well-respected minister named Setareki Seileka, and eight students from Davuilevu pushed the mission boat out into the river that Saturday morning, July 13, they must have been a little curious about the future.

It is probable that, initially, only Baker had plans for crossing all the way to Vuda. The minister Setareki would (and did) dutifully follow the missionary anywhere without thought of danger, but the students reportedly urged Baker to turn back once the mission boat had gone as far up the Rewa River as it could.

The reverend decided a decision would be made at Dawarau. They would turn back if there seemed to be a good reason . . .

On the way to Dawarau, they stopped nights at villages and at plantation houses which were beginning to spring up in the delta. The mission boat was left at Navunimoli, on the Wailevu River, with instructions for its return to Davuilevu if the party continued on west.

Waqaliqali, the chieftain of Dawarau, had only recently become Christian, and he was proud of an opportunity to show it. The band of 10 were treated like royalty, and instead of staying one night, they stayed three.

Rev. Baker inquired about the Navosa tribes whose territory was another 20 miles inland to the west. He heard nothing to cause him to change his mind.

Besides Baker and Setareki Seileka, the party included six students and two teachers — Sisa Tuilekutu, Josefata Tabuakarawa, Taniela Batirerega, Nemani Raqio, Nafitalai Torau, Setareki Nadu, Aisea Nasekali and Josefata Nagata.

Before departing, Baker gave Waqaliqali a tabua, asking the chief to conduct them to the Navosa area himself. Waqaliqali accepted the gift and agreed, but in the morning backed out, saying it was too dangerous. He *did* send two guides.

Despite this warning, the reverend had made up his mind. He requested that the letters he had written be dispatched, including the fateful one to his wife which said "I have only decided this evening to go . . . when you get this I shall be at or near Vuda . . ."

The axe reportedly used to kill Rev. Baker, killed during a contemporary mass of Reconciliation.

Saturday evening, just one week after leaving Davuilevu, they trudged up the path to Nagagadelevatu, 3000 ft above sea level, in the high plateau above the Sigatoka Valley.

Compared to their reception at Dawarau, Nagagadelevatu wasn't going to be any picnic.

Even after Setareki presented a tabua to its chief, Nawawabalavu gave them a cold reception. There was no feasting as there had been in the last village. In fact, they weren't even offered food.

Nawawabalavu told them he hated Christianity, but said he would show them the way to Vuda the next day.

Setareki held a prayer service that evening. Some of the people came.

That night, while the rest of the party slept, Setareki looked out of the house and saw lights moving toward the village.

He wasn't to know the meaning of it — especially that the visitors were bringing another tabua to 'press down' the powers of the first . . . a tabua asking for the death of the mission party.

In the morning, a crisp sunny Sunday, Baker also noticed something to arouse his suspicions. He pulled away from the doorway and said, "Lads, let us be quick or we shall be killed." Nawawabalavu came to the door just then, and told them to follow him at once, saying "people are coming who will kill you."

They left, moving out of the village in a thin line. At the head of the column was the chief, then Baker, then one of the Vatusila men from the village, carrying on his shoulder one of the steel battle axes from America.

Setareki, the two teachers and six students followed.

They had not gone more than 100 yards when the last in line looked back and saw armed men, their bodies covered in black paint, running silently toward them. He bolted into the thick grass.

The one ahead of him was lucky enough to be carrying a tin box on his shoulders, and the glancing blow of a club was absorbed by the metal. He was knocked into the bushes — alive.

Their names were Aisea Nasekali and Josefata Nagata, and they snaked through the grass into the edge of the ravine, half-running, half-falling to the river below. At night, they made their way down river and eventually reached Rewa and Davuilevu.

They were the only ones.

Rev Baker was struck from behind with the steel axe. As he lay dying, Setareki is said to have stooped to kiss his fallen leader before receiving his own death blow.

The two guides sent by Waqaliqali, kept back at Nagagadelevatu, later said the bodies of the murdered men were piled up, but that Baker's was carried to Nadrau.

There, the chief refused to have anything to do with it, and it was carried back to Cubue where it was cooked. As was customary when the victim was someone of rank, portions were sent to various parts of the district.

One authority, Rev. Small, who researched the incident carefully, said that the chief of Nubutautau, Nawawabalavu's nephew, had personally come to Nagagadelevatu to safeguard the mission party's journey, arriving too late to save them. He was so enraged he tried to kill the *Mata-ni-vanua* who offered him a piece of flesh.

But why were they attacked in the first place?

There's a long-standing myth that Baker removed a comb from Nawawabalavu's hair, which would have been a gross insult. The story is unlikely, because Baker had been in Fiji or years, spoke the language fluently, and is reported to have had "a knowledge of native customs and habits which was unique".

Far more likely is the story that Nawawabalavu accepted a tabua from a chief of Naitasiri, pressing down the first and demanding the death of men who spread "Cakobau's religion".

The hill people were suspicious of religion, feeling it had something to do with subservience to Cakobau, who was by then a Christian.

It is significant that, in 1903, the Naitasiri people presented a tabua to the Wesleyan Church — a soro of atonement for their guilt. That tabua, with Rev Baker's bible, is still at Davuilevu.

Mrs Baker received the reverend's letter on July 23, ten days after his departure, saying he anticipated no difficulties. The next day, she was told he had been killed and eaten.

When the acting British Consul, John Thurston, heard the report in Ovalau a few days later, he visited Cakobau. The king's 'coronation' in 1867 hadn't been recognised by the British Government, but since he claimed to be the supreme chief of Viti Levu, Thurston said it was up to him to bring the murderers to justice.

Time passed, and nothing happened. Thurston continued his demands, each time getting angrier and angrier.

Finally, after prodding by a British warship, the HMS Brisk, Cakobau reluctantly organised an expedition into the mountains. His hesitation stemmed from common sense; the hill people weren't under his dominion, and they could be mean as hell!

On April 2, 1868, nearly a year after the incident, Cakobau staged a two-pronged attack on Navosa. He personally led the troops who moved down from the north coast. Two of his sons, accompanied by Thurston, moved up from the south.

Cakobau's column almost reached Nabutautau before an ambush forced them back, killing 13. The southern column got as far as Dawarau valley and then the Namosi contingent deserted and the rest were attacked. Sixty-one were killed and 15 wounded.

The retreat was particularly damaging to Cakobau, whose weakness in controlling his 'subjects' was all too apparent.

Cakobau decided on an unusual solution. He sent a circular to Australia, calling for mercenary settlers!

The Military Settlers who agreed to "faithfully serve and defend King Cakobau until the subjugation for the rebellious and cannibal tribes release them from active service" were to be paid in free land.

They would be able to select any land they chose from the conquered districts, with size depending on their rank; field officers would get 2000 acres, rank and file 400.

They were to come equipped with their own rifle, revolver, bowie-knife, and 500 rounds of ball cartridges.

The only problem was that the Australian press got hold of the circular and published it . . . and the British Government quickly let it be known that any British subject who took advantage of the offer would be fined or imprisoned.

That ended the punitive expeditions. The deaths of Baker, Setareki and the others went without retribution.

And that was fortunate. If Cakobau's plan for Military Settlers had been accepted, there would have been 'subjugation' of people and villages which were in no way connected with the Baker deaths, or even the least bit hostile.

23   THE TRADE IN 'BLACK IVORY'

"It was dark as the inside of a lump of coal, but led by the skipper, we worked our way along in silence.

When we got quite close, we spread out all along the road, behind the houses, right round them, and then laid down until the word came to rush in and do the work.

There was no movement at all in the place, the poor devils were in their houses fast asleep (except for) some of them asleep round the fire.

By and by, the boss came along, crawling on his belly like a great ugly lizard, and gave us word to catch the men round the fire first, and when they sung out and made a row, to rush the houses and stop the rest from getting away, but to do no shooting . . . we rushed upon them, and before they knew what was up, they were lashed quite safe.

Of course they sung out like anything to their friends in the houses, who tried to get out and escape to the bush, but the men we left at the doors kept them in till we came up to help.

"Keep them in. Keep every mother's son of the black devils in" shouted the skipper, running about quite wild with a pistol in each hand. "Don't let them out, we'll have the lot this journey . . ."

— *From 'Blackbirding in the South Pacific,' Churchward, 1888.*

* * *

Melanesian workers on a Fiji cotton plantation.

Fiji's blackbirding era began in 1864, the year the first New Hebridean and Solomon island labourers arrived. Cotton plantations were springing up everywhere, and the Fijians just weren't interested in regular and sustained labour.

The white planters began importing labourers from other Pacific Island groups, and the trade in human cargoes, referred to on the waterfront as "black ivory", was underway.

Blackbirding verged on slavery. Sometimes it was outright kidnapping of unsuspecting people, stolen from their homes by the foulest means imaginable. More often, it was "recruiting" of people who didn't have the slightest idea what they were getting into.

By the time Fiji's cotton planters were desperately looking for help, the blackbirders and slavers had already received their training, supplying men for Queensland's plantations. They had some pretty novel techniques.

One was to send a gentle-looking man ashore, dressed in the black coat and hat of a missionary. He would tell the villagers that the Bishop had arrived, but was too unwell to visit them. Would they come out to the ship and see him?

As they stepped quietly below decks, they were seized and thrown into the hold, and their canoes were cast adrift.

Others were lured aboard with trinkets and then overpowered. A ship named the 'Challenge' decoyed six Torres Island men aboard in this manner, but when they began cutting a hole in the side of the ship, the captain ordered the hatches uncovered. The men scrambled up and jumped overboard, only to find the vessel was already seven miles from land.

Not all the labourers brought to Fiji were kidnapped, particularly as time passed and regulations governing the 'trade' were passed. But it is doubtful how many of the islanders understood that three fingers held in front of their nose — their 'contract' — indicated years service.

Some ship owners tried harder than others to look after their human cargo; after all, they were paid by the head, and bodies were worth nothing.

But other ships worked on different principles . . . ships like the 'Daphne', the 'Young Australian', and the 'Carl'.

When the master of the Carl was finally brought to trial in Australia on a charge of murder on the high seas, the ship's owner gave evidence in exchange for his freedom.

The owner's name was Dr James Patrick Murray. He told the court that the Carl had left Melbourne in June, 1871, for another labour cruise, and that it had begun its kidnapping expedition in the New Hebrides. His story:

"We went to several of the islands, and captured the natives generally by breaking or upsetting their canoes . . . we smashed the canoes by throwing pig-iron into them, and then seized the natives in the water . . . sometimes hitting them over the head with clubs or slung shot as they were at times very hard to get hold of.

"In this manner, 80 natives had been collected; they were kept in the hold at night and allowed to come on deck during the day. On the night of 12th September, there was a disturbance heard below . . . the men

appeared to be breaking down the bunks, and with the poles so obtained, they armed themselves and fiercely attacked the main hatchway.

"The attempts to pacify the men below having failed, the crew commenced to fire on them, and firing was kept up most of the night. I think everyone on board was more or less engaged in firing into the hold. This firing lasted for about 8 hours . . .

"At daylight, all appeared to be quiet, and it was considered advisable to save what remained; the hatches were thrown open, and those who were alive were invited to come up.

"They did so — about five came up . . .

"In the hold there was a great deal of blood with about 50 bodies, the dead were at once thrown overboard; the 16 badly wounded men were also thrown overboard . . . some tied by the legs and by the hands.

"After all this, the hold of the ship was thoroughly cleansed and whitewashed, and every trace of the late event being removed, we then proceeded on our voyage to Fiji . . .

"On our way, we met the Rosario, which overhauled us . . ."

HMS Rosario, in the islands to intercept blackbirders.

HMS Rosario was a British warship which had lately begun investigating the morbid tales of labour ship cruelty in the islands.

Ironically, when the Rosario fired a warning shot and then searched the Carl, there was nothing to indicate trouble.

"The second lieutenant had strict orders to make a most rigorous and careful investigation of the ship and her papers" wrote Rosario's captain, "and on his return, he reported to me that everything appeared to be correct, and as far as he could make out from the "passengers", that they were all on board of their own free will, and that between decks she was clean for a slaver, and freshly whitewashed . . ."

The slaver was allowed to go on her way.

Generally, the "recruited labourers" — men from the Solomons, New Hebrides, Santa Cruz, Ellice and Tokelau groups — had little recourse to their conditions. They didn't speak English, and if they tried to complain, they knew what was in store for them.

But back in their homelands, hostility against the blackbirding ships was building up. So when the first Bishop of Melanesia, Bishop Patterson, stepped ashore at Nukapu in the Santa Cruz group, he was murdered. His body was floated back to the mission ship with five knots tied in a palm leaf — symbols of the five islanders taken by kidnappers who struck Nukapu just before the Bishop landed.

In 1870, 180 Solomon Islanders were brought to the auction centre at the mouth of the Rewa River, the "slave market". One hundred were sold at prices from $20 to $30 per head, and 80 others were loaded aboard a small ship, the Peri, to be taken to other plantations. Near Naselai, the Solomon men turned on the crew, murdered all but one, and tried to sail the ship to the Solomons.

Instead, they drifted for five weeks until the Peri ran aground on the Great Barrier Reef of Queensland. During the journey, they killed each other for food until only 13 were left.

The survivors were shipped to Fiji aboard a navy cutter, and at Matuku they escaped — probably according to the navy's plan. They were allowed to settle there, victims of a labour system that by then was worrying not only Australia and Britain, but Cakobau's government as well.

By 1870, there were more than 2000 Pacific Island labourers in Fiji. They were paid 3 pounds per year and issued with a blanket and four *sulus*. Some of the pay was made payable to the "company store", where a clever storeman could ensure the men from the bush got little in return.

It has been said that the majority of Fiji's planters treated their labourers reasonably well. Just before Cession, Commodore Goodenough sent navy patrols to inspect plantations and found that most "treated their men kindly".

Nevertheless, it appears that about half of them died during their stay here. Sir William MacGregor, who became Chief Medical Officer in Fiji in 1875, listed a mortality rate of 540 out of every 1000 labourers, a staggering death rate for such a short period of time. It would be compared with 20 out of 1000 among the Indian indentured labourers who would begin to arrive in 1879.

Whenever blackbirding cruelty was discussed, planters said they were not responsible for what happened aboard ship. And on land, they cast a blind eye to fatigue, depression and illness which took its toll.

During the early years of the labour trade, the promise of a free passage home was easily forgotten by the recruiters. Then, when authorities began to insist on return passage, it was easiest to dump the bushmen on any remote island, far from their own.

Criticism of blackbirding was becoming an international incident, and Queensland was the first to do something about it. Its Polynesian Labour

Act in 1868 required recruiting ships to be licensed, to provide prescribed quantities of food and medicines along with reasonable accommodation aboard ship, and to offer security for the return of labourers after three years.

At first, a ship owner was required to produce a certificate signed by a consul, missionary or other known person, showing the labourers had voluntarily agreed to the contract and that they understood the conditions.

But when it was pointed out that there were no consuls in Melanesia, and that missionaries refused to sign the certificates, the law was changed. A Government officer was assigned to accompany each labour ship.

As Queensland cracked down, the slavers just shrugged their shoulders and carried their cargoes to Fiji instead, where there was no real government to carry out inspections.

But then, in 1872, the British introduced the Pacific Islanders' Protection Act — and sent 7 warships out to enforce it!

Island labourers, finally, began to see some improvements.

It is interesting to read the account of a crewman aboard the 'Bobtail Nag', as two New Hebridean men were returned to their homes . . .

"One of them had on a black Paget Coat, riding trousers and a black belltopper hat of the latest cut on his wooly head, with a pair of lemon coloured kid gloves on his hands, a red necktie, and a silver watch and chain . . . in his hand, he carried a Snider rifle, which he had taken the precaution to load before landing. Frequently, it happens that whilst he is in Queensland, the village he formerly lived in is burnt down and his tribe annihilated, and being ignorant of the historical events of his country during the past three years, he deems it advisable to be prepared . . .

"Our second return boy . . . displayed himself in a suit of light tweeds, deerstalker hat and patent leather boots. The gun he carried was a brightly-polished Enfield to which he had affixed a bayonet . . ."

The two might have been a bit unusual. Most labourers returned home with little more than they had when they left, usually to find their pigs and wives had been taken from them during their absence. Nor were they any wiser for their "training" abroad.

The new laws didn't exactly put them in heaven, but the warships and changing attitudes put an end to the bitterest of the blackbirding era.

During all this time, the Fijians had been able to quietly ignore the mess. They weren't involved with the labour scandal . . . at least, they weren't until Cakobau put the Lovoni people on the auction block!

The people of Lovoni were made to crawl on their hands and knees, bearing baskets of earth.

Then the whole tribe, every man, woman and child, was prodded and pushed into line and marched into the centre of Levuka.

A few days later, they were sold at auction as plantation labourers.

Their land was sold as well, and the proceeds from land and people provided the income to begin a new government.

It was 1871. It was Cakobau who sold them. And it was slavery.

* * *

Ratu Isikia Rogoyawa, the Roko Tui Wailevu, tells the story of the events that led up to that fateful day. He also talks of the current politics and land struggle which, because of it, is still going on.

Ratu Isikia, the Roko Tui Wailevu, at Lovoni.

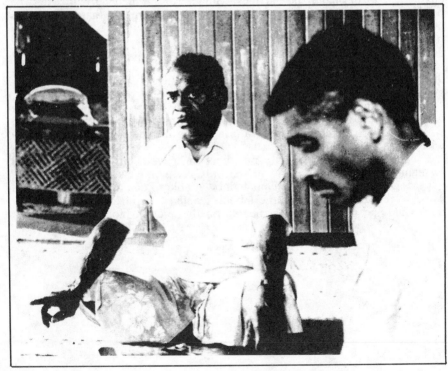

The story has been shortened, but it is entirely in his own words, translated from the Fijian following an interview with him at his home in Lovoni.

Ratu Isikia's story:

"The Lovoni people originated from Nakauvadra when Verata was being settled by various tribes from there. The Lovoni's leader, Rakavono, was a fighting and energetic man, but sometimes mischievous, and so he and his followers were told to leave Verata or be punished. They crossed over to Ovalau which was then unpopulated, becoming the first settlers and claiming sovereignty over the whole island. Their first village, a fortress, was built on a hill and named Nakorolevu . . .

Now in 1871, a battle was raging at Lovoni. This is how it started:

Lovoni had long been related to Bau. We have a house foundation here named for the Vunivalu. But, though the clans are closely related, yet they were constantly wary of the other.

When Levuka was settled by Europeans, our ancestors used to burn their houses because it was Lovoni land that the white people occupied. They burned it and burned it again.

The white population called a meeting and eventually sent a representative to the Vunivalu — I think it was David Whippy. The Vunivalu was angry, very angry.

And there were other troubles which had been going on at Lovoni for a long time. Ratu Cakobau was angered by the death of Ratu Ilaitia Varani, a great general in Cakobau's army, who had been killed at Lovoni, even though it was Bauan treachery which caused it.

Cakobau had long been angry; so had the Lovoni people. When some Lovoni women were fishing on Tutu Vakabola reef, Bauan men molested them. Another reason was the capture at Lovoni of Ratu Mara. His grandmother was the daughter of Tui Lovoni and he sought refuge inland after the Bau-Rewa war. When Ratu Mara was being sheltered here, his uncle Ratu Joeli Colata arrived and told him: "Let us go. There is no more anger in Bau". But when Ratu Mara went to Bau, he was hanged.

This was the cause for deep sorrow and anger.

All these things added up and eventually, war broke out. During this war, the people of Lovoni moved from the present site to the old one on the hill, Nakorolevu, and it was made stronger. Each section of the fort had its own tribe to guard it, and a great amount of engineering work by our ancestors went into it.

There were three main fences or ramparts. Smaller fences, all of stone, were built within the larger ones, so if a large fence was breached, there were smaller ones inside to reinforce it, guarded by more men. Trenches and moats ran right around all the main sections, surrounding Viro and Rukuruku.

If you came down from the top, the first defence which winds right around the fort is called Sonabukete, and this is the priest's quarters and temple. His words and commands were final.

Descending further, you cross three lines of defence before coming to the second large fence right round, which runs down to Viro. Smaller trenches are so intricate they are known only to the builders and occupants.

The old fortifications must have looked beautiful and awe inspiring, with the women and children's quarters right at the very top. The time will come when these old fortifications will be a tourist attraction . . . they would marvel at the intricate and clever workmanship of the old folk.

Well, Nakorolevu was assaulted by the Vunivalu's forces several times, but without success. One of Ratu Cakobau's sons, Ratu Naulivou, led one attack with 600 warriors, but most were slaughtered and the rest fled to Yavuadrau. Other Bauan forces attacked Lovoni, from Vugalei, and one led by the *Gone Sau* of Nakorotubu, Ra, but they met the same fate.

Lovoni was being supplied with arms by friends from Naceva, Yacata, Rewa, Cakaudrove and by the Tongan chief Ma'afu. The fighting dragged on, and Ratu Cakobau could not do anything further.

Ratu Cakobau was nearly caught in pincers between Ma'afu's fleet of war canoes anchored off Wakaya Island and an attack by the Lovoni people. He would have been killed on the Ovalau coast, but he was warned by the Tui Levuka, Ratu Samuela . . .

The Vunivalu called a meeting of the white settlers of Levuka, the Tui Levuka, and the two missionaries, one of whom Rev. Frederick Langham, was stationed in Bau.

During the meeting, Rev. Langham said he would go to the Lovoni people himself.

I wish to recall something at this stage. When the war was raging, the heathen priests were in a central deep trench from which all the Lovoni warriors received their orders.

But when the lone Rev. Langham came climbing up the hillside towards the fort, carrying the Bible in his hands, the heathen priests declared to the chiefs, "an army is approaching, a one-man army. Lay down our arms."

Mr Langham went over to them and there held a church service and read a sermon from St Mathew about the lost sheep. He ended the service by saying: "Let us all go down to Levuka. The Vunivalu and the Tui Levuka are preparing a feast of peace which we all must share together and end these hostilities."

They went down to Levuka, but they heeded the heathen priests' advice and kept their weapons on their shoulders.

On arrival, the Vunivalu greeted them: "Chiefs of Lovoni, rest your arms. The war is over. This magiti is a feast of peace for our enemity is ended."

Our ancestors stacked their muskets on the side of the qara-sara cliff and sat down to eat. As soon as they were seated, Ratu Cakobau gave a sign to the soldiers.

The Lovoni were immediately seized in a most pitiful and degrading manner. They were held in captivity at Levuka and after seven days, they were distributed like goods to various parts of Fiji. They were divided, fathers and mothers and children all sent to different parts of the country. If a woman and her children stayed together, it was just luck.

They worked, worked hard. One party that was sent to Taveuni was housed at Vuniduva, the name of their first defence moat at their old fortress of Korolevu. They took the name to Taveuni, to Lagiloa Tea Estate at Muaicake.

Only some escaped. While the Lovoni people were still at Levuka awaiting transport, some were told to go into the hills and gather wild yams, and they escaped into the bush and settled in hide-outs for two years on a piece of land called Nakavika. A few others were told by the bete (the heathen priest) that it was all a trick even before they arrived in Levuka, and they ran off.

The Vunivalu received three pounds cash per head for our ancestors. From this money, he was able to finance his government which was ruling before Fiji was ceded to Great Britain.

The Government always said the Lovoni people were captured in war, but this was not so. We were tricked. The Lovoni were too strong to be conquered.

Three years after that sale, the first Governor was named, and he said that what was done to our people was very wrong. He ordered the return of the people and they were settled in the villages of Visoto and Nacobo, on land belonging to a clan subervient to Bau, the Qali Vaka-Bau from Natokalau village.

Our ancestors were dependent on the land owned by these people because all the Lovoni lands, totalling 4000 acres, had been sold. Yes, sold to pay for Cakobau's government. Our ancestors were sitting on nothing!

In 1878 when a Lands Commission appointed in England came to inquire about the illegal selling of native land in Fiji, they had a look at Lovoni land already sold. That was about the time Sir John Thurston became Governor.

The Governor saw to it that Lovoni village was given back to the rightful owners, our ancestors. A tabua was presented in remembrance of this, and the date is July 6, 1878.

The tabua is still with our priests, and it signified the release of our people to resettle our land. But at the same time, Government ordered the Lovoni not to touch 2350 acres because it now belonged to a bank . . .

This is the land we have been striving to get back for so long. If our land had been sold for smoking pipes or muskets we might not have fought back, but the sale of Lovoni land made no sense to our forefathers.

We kept up with our struggle, on and on. We presented tabua to the Vunivalu, we took 34 tabua, a large pig and a huge pile of dalo to the Governor-General, and he told us that he would try and get the land back to us . . . the Government came, the police came, the District Commissioner came, and I chased them away in my hot temper. I told them: "It is better to come with bullets, rather than let anyone but Kai Lovoni till this land."

The land totalling 2350 acres contains our ancestral village site and the sites of our old temples. It is the traditional site for the installation of the Tui Lovoni, our ancestral burial grounds, and the sacred site where the aged were peacefully fed each day before their lives ended.

Where their bones lie is a sacred spot. I want Lovoni to be on top where it belonged and where it had been for years in the old days. O Lovoni ga i cake — rise up!

Ratu Isikia's story is not without contradictions. It seems strange that events which happened in the 1850s could have been the principal reason for a war in 1871, particularly since the Ratu at one point refers to it as the Religious War, *A i Valu ni Lotu*. And if the Tongan chief Ma'afu really aided the Lovoni in a "pincers" move against Cakobau, it was less than a month before he would pledge support for Cakobau's government.

Veteran historian R.A. Derrick had a few things to say about the Lovoni. He noted they refused to pay taxes levied on them by Cakobau, and that when a chief of Yarovudi came to the village to discuss the tax, the Lovoni hacked him to pieces.

They also destroyed the village of Natokalau in the first months of 1871, killing 10 people — supposedly after accepting a tabua promising Natokalau peace.

Derrick says the Lovoni people "surrendered" and were marched into Levuka "wasted and haggard" from lack of food during the long siege. They were sentenced to transportation on the plantations of European settlers, and their land confiscated and mortgaged.

In addition to three pounds per head, the planters paid a yearly hire fee, and Cakobau collected 1100 pounds from the sale of about 365 people, followed by 1500 pounds in 1872-73, and nearly 2000 pounds the following year — Cession year — for the "hire" of Lovoni labour.

Three of the Lovoni men, including the bete, suffered the strangest fate of all. They were sold to an American circus company, where they were exhibited in travelling sideshows as "Savages of the South Seas"!

Levuka in 1880: rebellion and growing-pains.

25 ROUGH AND RUM-SOAKED LEVUKA

Levuka in the early 1870's: a town filled with derelicts and debtors, runaway sailors and rogues. A town in which every second shed housed a grog shop, and ship's captains supposedly could find port just by following the line of floating rum bottles.

On a Saturday morning in March, 1872, Cakobau called the settlers of Levuka to the town square. Only about a tenth of the 600 whites living in the town showed up. The rest were probably fortunate, because they missed a good brow-beating.

"We Fijians understand revenge and the law of the club," the King said. "You white people said such things were cruel and savage. You brought us civilisation and you brought us law. I thought law and order was a good thing. When a native does wrong, there is no rest until he is punished, yet three natives have been killed lately and nothing has been done . . .

"Perhaps you think the laws are to protect one race only, but if the law punishes a native when he does wrong to you and does not punish a white man when he does wrong to us, it is all one-sided. Your sided.

"Now, I understand there are divisions among you and an appeal to force. If you resist the laws and force us to settle matters in our old way, there will be a war of races. I appeal to you to support law and order."

Cakobau's little lecture, should have hit home. Levuka was practically lawless. The greatest threat to settlers was not the Lovoni people — although in 1880 special constables were enrolled to guard the town from attack — it was from Levuka's own wild citizenry.

There was one particularly good source of information about wild and wooly Levuka during that period — the Fiji Times.

The newspaper began operation in 1869, and it played an important role in shaping public opinion during the pre-Cession turmoil. It also pointed a finger at some of the town's more notorious characters.

Some of the stories carried in those early issues include:

Sept 11, 1869 — "Our little town was thrown into no little excitement last Sunday evening by the intolerant behaviour of some of its unruly members, whose too frequent imbibings had rendered them perfect madmen and fit inmates for a lock-up . . . one individual appeared in this disgraceful scene with a knife somewhat under a foot in length which was ultimately taken from him before he could effect his evil designs . . ."

Oct. 2, 1869 — "A meeting was called on Monday morning at four o'clock to consider the advisability of arresting and putting under restraint a Captain Morgan and Mr Minton who threatened a breach of the peace in the shape of a duel with revolvers . . . During the preparation of weapons (for the intended duel), a lamentable accident occurred by which one of our most respectable settlers, F.W. Hoyle, was shot through the leg. Anxious to prevent a duel, he ran from the billiard room of the Criterion to the room where Mr Minton was examining a pistol.

"Mr Minton fired it towards the open door just as Mr Hoyle entered, and the ball went right through the leg. Great sympathy was felt for Mr Hoyle . . . Capt Morgan was so excited and violent as to threaten the lives of several persons and was strictly guarded until safely placed in irons on board the Young Australian."

January 11, 1870 — "Oh, for a lock up. A murderous assault was made on Monday by Stephen, alias Coko Smith, who struck a man named Reed with the butt end of a gun until his weapon was broken. How long are we to suffer him to keep the north end of the beach in a chronic state of drunken rowdyism?"

And on November 22, 1871, a Fiji Times editorial noted "one of the nuisances of Levuka is the constant report of firearms, which lasts almost without intermission day and night . . . only the other day we were somewhat startled to hear a charge of shot rattle on the roof . . ."

But perhaps the best commentary of the times was an advertisement in the paper, on October 8, 1870: "WANTED, at the Star Chamber, Levuka — informers, spys and scandalmongers. Apply early, as the situations are likely to be eagerly filled up."

The Fiji Times wasn't the only critical voice in the town. A barrister who reached Levuka in 1872, Robert Philp, obviously wasn't too impressed, either.

The white residents, he said, "spent a great part of the day and the night too, tippling in the public house bars, and of the row of houses that make Levuka, fully half are hotels or public houses. Swilling gin and brawling are the principal amusements." The houses were "shanties built as they would be built on some Australian goldfield, and furnished as if they were in England."

Food was "nothing but the dirtiest, greasiest work," and the town was a breeding centre for dysentery. There was "roguery and scheming at every hand" and government "was undertaken by a set of adventurers from Sydney and Melbourne who would most certainly be sent to the treadmill" in their home cities.

And yet, Philp wrote that, in contrast with the untidiness and filth of Levuka, the Fijians were clean and their villages tidy and cool.

The newspaper added to this, by comparing the creditable manner in which the natives governed themselves with the lack of control among the Europeans.

That was the whole problem — there wasn't any real government to enforce the laws or clean up the brawling settlement!

The Levuka Charter of 1870, signed by Cakobau, supposedly gave the Europeans the authority to set up police and municipal regulations, but the town's more lawless inhabitants refused to recognize any rules which might upset their 'freedom'. What's more, the dissidents were backed-up by a letter from the Governor of New South Wales, saying Fiji's by-laws were powerless.

There was no unity among the Levuka people. One group sent out circulars trying to establish a Republic; others favoured annexation by one of the Great Powers, and even Prussia was considered.

As Cakobau had pointed out, there were no laws — but a lot depended on who broke them. About 70 armed men tore the door off the gaol to rescue a white man charged with murdering a Fijian.

A sailor named Rees was persuaded to ignore a summons on the grounds that there was no government and so it was invalid. He was gaoled, and a group of anti-government men swore they would liberate him, by force if necessary. Levuka's new civil servants were armed as special constables and no further efforts to free him were made.

And when a debtor who fled Australia was arrested and carried out to a ship to be returned, his friends boarded the vessel and began firing pistols in the air, but this rescue attempt also failed.

There were other wild incidents in the little town, but none quite as bizarre as the story related by a Rev. Nettleton.

One of Levuka's white residents was sentenced to death for murder, before a "jury of his own countrymen". But there were problems in finding a hangman, and the event was postponed for a day. During this time, the rope was left dangling out in the rain, slowly becoming waterlogged.

At 6am the next morning, a deputized hangman finally did the deed, and the man was left suspended in the air.

But no sooner had the crowd moved away, then he "began to struggle, and, freeing one hand, seized the rope above his head and pulled himself up."

"Shoot me", he cried out. "I can't die this way". The Chief of Police cut the rope, and an hour later, the man was eating a hearty breakfast of beefsteak which had been prepared for the hangman.

He fled on a ship to California, after the Chief Justice decided he was legally dead . . . and after being "led past his coffin and grave in the sad procession to the scaffold."

Settlers began pouring into Fiji in the 1860s.

By 1870, it was a flood.

There were planters anxious to take advantage of the cotton boom, following the collapse of America's cotton trade in their Civil War.

Colonial newspapers overseas gave a glowing account of homestead life in Fiji, right at a time when Australia's colonies were in the midst of a depression. The Maori wars in New Zealand had dampened the spirits of settlers there. And as talk of Fiji's possible annexation to Britain or France grew, settlers decided the risk of homesteading in the islands would be worth it.

Besides, gold had been discovered in the Navua River, and the news quickly spread, exaggerated as usual.

Before long, every available ship was crowded with adventurers, planters, homesteaders and opportunity seekers. A lot of them were reasonable, honest men looking forward to a life on the soil.

A lot of them weren't. With the ships came the derelicts of the Australian gold fields, and hundreds of men hoping to make easy money — the commission agents and auctioneers, so many that "there was not enough legitimate business in all of Fiji to support even half of them".

There were no extradition treaties in Fiji, and convicts, absconding debtors and runaway sailors headed for the islands and sanctuary.

By 1870 there were 2000 Europeans in Fiji. During the year, 1000 more came. About a third of them were in Levuka. They lived in weather-board corrugated iron sheds, and the town, except for the consulates, mission stations and a few trading stores, looked like a squatter's camp.

Gin cost a shilling a bottle, and "gunbarrel rum", distilled in back-sheds from sugarcane, was even less. Everything else was expensive — boom-town prices.

The cost of land soared. On Levuka's Beach Street, a tiny piece of land which housed the Criterion Hotel sold for enough money to buy an entire island in other parts of Fiji.

And then, of course, there were the problems with money. Since there was no recognised government, there was no official money. Traders used coins minted in Bolivia and Samoa and bartered with practically anything else that appeared to have some value.

Business accounts were settled with "IOU's" and makeshift paper money — until Europe's cotton market collapsed and the price of Fiji's cotton fell from 4 shillings a pound to one. A number of the planters were ruined, and their promissory notes, based on the cotton crop as security, were worthless. Besides, there wasn't a court to enforce payment of debts, anyway.

Philp commented on the situation by saying "if you have hard cash to pay for fresh fish, you can get it . . . but if you have not the coin, you must do without, for the Fiji man knows as well as you the difference between a silver dollar and a paper one . . . he won't have your paper money at all."

When annexation seemed assured, men wanted by the Australian police disappeared a jump ahead of the gun, and Levuka began to get a house-cleaning. A visitor who accompanied Sir Arthur Gordon to Fiji in 1875 said the town "greatly exceeded our expectations. We had imagined it was still the haunt of uproarious planters and white men of the lowest type . . . instead of which we find a most orderly and respectable community . . ."

But before things got better, they got a lot worse.

When Cakobau talked of "divisions among you and an appeal to force," he was referring to gun-toting groups of settlers who were taking sides on the issue of government.

His government.

Early Levuka.

On a June morning in 1871, Levuka's residents woke up to the clammer of drums beating.

Some said it was a fight . . . others thought it was a wild *meke*. But it was neither of those.

As the curious followed the noise to the north end of town, they saw Cakobau standing in the shade of a dilo tree. He was wearing masi, and there were a few Fijian chiefs on one side of him, a few Europeans on the other.

Before a crowd nearly too amazed to respond, the settlers and merchants were briefly told that 'Cakobau Rex' had formed a government. The names of the ministers were announced, most of them Europeans, and the ceremony ended minutes after it began.

But Levuka's residents weren't quite ready to accept the surprise. Before long, the Cakobau government would be facing threats and guns of men who called themselves the Klu Klux Klan!

* * *

Seru Cakobau, 'Tui Viti'.

At first, the announcement was taken as a bit of a joke. The colonialists had seen Cakobau crowned as king before, and the earlier ceremony nearly resulted in open laughter except for the overpowering solemnity of Cakobau himself. They'd also witnessed other efforts at government, and with the exception of Ma'afu's well-organised system in the Lau Group, they'd watched these efforts fail.

Besides, Levuka's settlers knew what kind of government they wanted. It would be headed by Europeans and operate for the benefit of Europeans, and the Fijians would simply be spectators.

So when Ratu Savenaca Naulivou and Ratu Timoci Tavanavanua, two of the newly-named ministers, stepped forward and asked the planters to accept the new government, the reaction was initially fairly quiet.

But at a meeting that night, a number of Levuka's townsmen angrily voted to resist the government, and to protest the way in which it was set up "without the consent of the Europeans".

Cakobau countered the move the very next day, with a hastily-printed Government Gazette in which he apologised for not calling a public meeting, saying they were invariably rowdy, fruitless, and accomplished nothing.

The same Gazette had a message from the Premier, Charles Burt, promising that only matters of urgent necessity would be considered until a House of Representative was asssembled. Burt also reminded them that "thoughtful men must admit the necessity of responsible government in view of the daily reproach of the colonial newspapers upon our lawless state", and the refusal of the major powers to accept cession of he islands.

Most of the white population seemed willing to give government a chance to prove itself. They settled down to wait and see what would happen — particularly among Fiji's high chiefs when they heard about "their" king.

They didn't have to wait long. Ma'afu arrived in Levuka the following month. He was openly regarded as the man who should be king, and his ambitions to the title were only too well known.

Ma'afu's prospering Lau Confederation — Na Tovata ko Lau — was a model of island government. And so it came as a total surprise when he acknowledged Cakobau as King of Fiji, took an oath of allegiance, and gave up any claims to territory outside the Lau Group.

The man who would be king settled for a salary of 800 pounds a year, a title of Lieutenant-Governor of Lau, and clear ownership of three islands: Moala, Matuku and Totoya.

Ma'afu had defected. Slowly, the other chiefs followed his example, including those who swore they would never submit to the Bauan.

Tui Cakau was the last, and he came to Levuka, "his eyes swollen with gin", bringing with him the allegiance and wealth of the white planters of his powerful district.

Before the year was out, Cakobau had the signatures of all the major chiefs, pledging support for his government.

If they had been fully aware of what they were supporting, they might not have bothered. The structure of the new government — a king, ministry, House of Representatives and a Privy Council — was cleverly designed so that it left little authority to the chiefs.

In fact, the Fijians, who outnumbered Europeans 100 to one, soon found out they had no votes at all!

The first session of the House of Representatives met on August 1, 1871, and it gave government its "constitutional existence". But before the two-week session were over, the Fijians had grown tired of the technical discussions of Parliament which they neither understood nor cared about — and disappeared.

After that, native representation was confined to the Privy Council, which had no veto power over the House, and its only power was to "suggest" amendments.

The white settlers exclusively controlled the House of Assembly, and the ministers didn't seem particularly concerned to stand up for the obviously neglected rights of the Fijians.

That first Legislative Assembly did, however, manage to achieve some worthwhile results. It established a postal service, currency, bank regulations, and a land commission to deal with the growing number of disputes over property claims. Land had been sold (sometimes to different purchasers at the same time) by chiefs who had no title to it; boundaries were inaccurate, and many of the deeds were proven to be incomprehensible to the natives who signed them.

The landing of arms or ammunition on any part of Viti Levu was prohibited. Foreign ships were to be licensed, and there were strict controls over the sale of arms and liquor.

Blackbirding abuses were to end, not only among the stolen natives of Polynesian islands, but among Fijians forced into "involuntary servitude" by their chiefs.

It was a reasonable start for a government — even though the more lawless grumbled about restrictions on booze and weapons.

But then, things began to break down.

The British Consul, Mr March, had refused to recognise the new government right from the very beginning. The "King", he said, was only a chief of Bau. March told people to refuse to pay taxes, advised ship owners to ignore harbour dues, and denied the authority of courts over any British subject.

People were also becoming alarmed at the complete disregard for the Legislative Assembly. Day after day, bills and laws were being passed "by order of the King-in-Council", without even a pretence of support by the representatives.

The ministers were also becoming very unpopular. Some, like Charles Burt, the Premier, became arrogant and big-headed with their appointments, power-hungry little men who forgot they were ex-auctioneers and shopkeepers. Others gave the best jobs to their friends, and high-salaried civic appointments were still being given to new arrivals months after the formation of government, in return for political favours.

The civil list was out of all proportion for such a small country, but Parliament authorised it without any hesitation.

Cakobau's government was plunging into hopeless debt. During the first financial year, nearly half of the budget went into the "Privy Purse" . . .

Cakobau and his household, and five Cabinet ministers.

Government had begun with 11,000 pounds — the proceeds from the sale of the Lovoni people. To keep it running, Cakobau needed much, much more.

George Austin Woods, a retired British naval officer and the man most responsible for prodding Cakobau into setting up a government, left for Sydney early in 1872 on a dual mission. He was to raise money through the sale of Crown lands, and raise complaints against March for his activities against government.

He wasn't particularly successful in either.

While he was gone, discontent in Levuka turned into open rebellion.

All the malcontents, and by this time there were a lot of them, met at "Keyse's Place", the home of the most outspoken of their lot. It was a former hotel, built on piles over the water near Nasova, and it was a fitting fortress for a mob.

They formed a secret society pledged to overthrowing the government — and they named it the Klu Klux Klan!

The name came from the United States, where Klan members at this time were showing what they thought of freed negro slaves in the South by terrorising them. In midnight raids, the South's white-sheeted KKK horsemen set fire to negro settlements, captured and whipped freed slaves, sometimes murdered them.

The Klan in Fiji was not quite as aggressive. But its members swore to carry arms, to rally at the signal of three canon shots, and to do all in their power to "depose the present Government".

They sent a deputation to Cakobau, demanding that Burt (the Premier) be sacked, and that a New Assembly be elected to replace one which was "contrary to the welfare of the country".

The King ignored them.

As Levuka waited for the explosion, a Levuka planter named Smith wandered into town. He was wanted for the murder of a Fijian and a warrant was out for his arrest. He openly defied it by placidly sitting on the railing of the Criterion Hotel.

The Klan went into action, circling and parading around the Criterion with rifles and fixed bayonets, warning that no one had authority to touch Smith.

The British Consul stayed out of sight and refused to do anything about the situation, which wasn't surprising, since he was a known ringleader of the Klan.

But Smith was turned over to the authorities after 120 Fijian Police, led by two European inspectors, quietly move in and disarmed the mob without a shot being fired.

Government won that round, and when Burt resigned a few days later, practically everybody was relieved. Things were better still when a well-respected cotton planter from Taveuni, John Bates Thurston, joined the Government.

Planters in Rewa and Lomaloma took no part in the anti-government demonstrations, and they warned the rebels that any shooting could lead to a situation as nasty as New Zealand's Maori War, a bitter battle between black and white.

They weren't the only ones who were worried. Some of Levuka's residents had formed a Mutual Defence Corps to support a government.

And then a Neutral Party was formed, which swore it would join the party attacked in any clash.

By this time, the Klan was known as the British Subject's Mutual Protection Society and Volunteer Corps.

Levuka had just about all the societies a town that size could handle, but political conditions weren't getting any better.

Those who were neither for or against the government were waiting for the arrival of a British warship which, they hoped, would clarify Cakobau's position.

It arrived — HMS Cossack — and it reached Levuka just as two Klan members were imprisoned on charges of assault. The Klan was waiting for a fight, and now it had an audience. With the signal of three cannon shots, the Klansmen assembled, armed to the teeth.

HMS Cossack's commander. Capt. Douglas, let Thurston know the situation: if government controlled the mob, it was truly in power, but if the mob released the prisoners, he would assume that Fiji's government was a farce.

Thurston was Acting Premier in the absence of Woods, who was still in Australia, and he didn't waste a second. He gathered together the police and civil servants and armed about 200 of them. One group surrounded the gaol; the other occupied Parliament House.

The Neutral Party, as promised, stood on the sidelines, waiting to see who would fire first.

Thurston was fairly direct. The Constabulary, he said, was to "load with ball cartridges, to arrest any malcontent carrying arms, to shoot those who resisted arrest, and to shoot any person attempting to break gaol."

Cannons were loaded with grape shot. Thurston's army moved out into view.

Faced with this inspiring obstacle, the Klan moved back to Keyses, and as the Taveuni planter made plans to storm the place, he received a message from Captain Douglas ordering him to maintain the situation as it stood.

Douglas sent for the Klan's leader, a Mr Beatson, and made it known that in any attack on Cakobau's government, the British would have to be reckoned with.

England, indirectly, had just given a firm nod of assurance to Fiji's King!

A fortified village in Vanua Levu, from a painting by J Glen Wilson aboard HMS Herald.

27   TROUBLE IN THE HILLS, TROUBLE AT HOME

Spiers and Mackintosh went out duck shooting.

They were shot instead, the first of the Ba planters to be murdered by the 'Kai Colos' — the mountain men.

An expedition went up in the hills to get revenge but, except for skirmishing with the wrong people and burning the wrong village, it accomplished nothing.

The Kai Colo decided they were free to do what they liked. That was unfortunate for the Burns family, whose cotton plantation was in the foothills below them.

It was also unfortunate for the Cakobau Government, because the Ba Campaign would pit not only settlers against mountain people . . . but settlers against the Government's own troops!

Spiers and Mackintosh were murdered in 1871. They made the mistake of handing their weapons to some Vatusila men to carry while they forded a fast-flowing stream. Their bodies were carried to a village in the Yalatina area, cut up and eaten.

When the word got out, settlers from all parts of the group assembled at Varoko on the north coast to get revenge. But when they moved into the bush, the Vatusila simply went into hiding, and it was impossible to find them in the thick, rugged country. Rather than go back without some action, the settlers burned Cubu, whose people were totally ignorant of the deaths, and went home.

* * *

Ba River valley was good land for farming, and there were already a lot of settlers and cotton planters by the river.

After the death of the two planters, they armed their New Hebridean and Solomon Island labourers and placed a 24-hour watch on their homes. For more than a year, the Kai Colo kept out of the valley.

But then Government moved in. The Armed Constabulary came to Ba, not so much to put a check on the mountaineers as to awe the whites. A Government minister named Clarkson told them they had no right to defend themselves against the hill people or to arm their labourers.

This, Clarkson said, was the work of the King's troops alone.

He warned the labourers to put away their guns, saying that if any of them shot a Kai Colo, he "would certainly be hung" . . . and then Clarkson and his party began the trip back to Levuka.

The planters were seething with anger. If they went about un-armed, they felt sure they would be attacked again. And they were right. Clarkson had barely returned to Levuka before news of a Ba massacre reached the town.

Early on a February morning in 1873, an exposed and unprotected plantation at Vunisamaloa was raided. When neighbours went to visit the Burns family the next day, they found the planter, his wife and two young children, 15 New Hebridean workers and a Solomon Islands woman all dead.

Ba's settlers vowed vengeance on the Kai Colos. But they despised Government just as much, because it was Government that had disarmed their workers, then left them without any protection.

They began to gather at Rarawai, men from up and down the coast, from Nadi and Nadroga, Ba and Rewa. Members of the still-notorious British Subject's Mutual Protection Society arrived on the steamer 'Pride of Viti', and with them came two radicals, White and DeCourcey Ireland, who convinced the settlers they must handle matters themselves.

The Government troops came a day later, led by Major Fitzgerald — only to find about 150 armed men at Rarawai telling them to go back!

The plantation workers had joined the settlers,and Major Fitzgerald was wise enough to see that the welcoming party was going to be a little wild. He turned the troops around, marched back down the river bank, and re-embarked for Levuka.

That bordered on indignity for Cakobau's forces, and soon after, they were ordered to return to Ba, this time under command of Captain Harding. At Sugunu, the home of the Tui Ba, the Government troops began fortifying the village.

The "enemy" moved into a native church, 50 paces away.

Two forces looked across their gun barrels at each other: Ba's settlers and their island workers, all well-armed, and "a handful" of Cakobau's men, woefully outnumbered.

If shooting had broken out, it is almost certain that Government would have lost.

But once again, a warship intervened. The rebels were warned that HMS Dido was on its way. When it arrived, Capt. Chapman listened to the grievances of both groups, won the planters over to the side of "law and order" — and arrested White and DeCourcey Ireland as ringleaders of the revolt. They were later deported to Sydney.

Both settlers and troops got down to the business at hand: the taming of the Kai Colo.

A Ba diary, written in 1873 by a now-unknown author, tells some of the story of the campaign:

" . . . *corn planted next to beans. Jack brothers returned from the mountains, reported 50 killed and wounded on the mountaineers' side, and 7 killed on the Government side . . . Government forces burned town of Karawa . . . planted kumala tops from Rarawai . . . the troops had a sharp fight with the Kai Colo, three of our natives were killed and eaten . . . Philip Jack and Gresham shot by Kai Colo, the latter died within an hour, the former the same night. Harding severely wounded . . . Rokogera, Tui Papalagi, was killed, his body cut into pieces by government native rooms and cooked and eaten with several others who assisted in the murder of Spiers and MacIntosh . . ."*

But by far the best record of events was written by Sgt. Wright, one of the King's troops. Some of the incidents he reported even had an element of humour to them.

When one of the Fijian soldiers was flogged for a breach of rules, the rest of the native soldiers deserted. Six 'very lonely' Europeans were left in a totally unguarded camp, and the officer who ordered the flogging spent the night in the bush searching for them. They returned, after being promised no charges would be laid against them.

Then, after days of treking through nearly impassable country, the troops managed to push the mountaineers into caves at Korowaiwai and Koroine.

Smoke and dynamite failed to get them out, and native "auxiliaries" were placed at the cave openings during the night as guards. At daybreak, the troops rushed to the caves — and found them empty.

Wright says the friendly Fijian auxiliaries "allowed the enemy to pass through their ranks unharmed, they simply paying toll by throwing to the allies any valuables they possessed in the way of whales teeth, pigs teeth, and likus . . ."

At first, the villages were easily taken. The mountain people simply fled into the thicket when the troops advanced. At Nakiki, a soro was offered, but was rejected: the Roko Tui Ba, who had joined forces with Government, was eager to get revenge on long-time enemies; Fitzgerald (who was back again), was eager to avenge the death of Burns.

By this time, a second force under Major Thurston (the brother of J.B. Thurston, the Chief Secretary) began a drive from Sabeto to Nubutautau. A number of forts and villages were taken, including Magodro, Bulu and Nawaicavu.

The hill people sent word they would make their "last stand" at Nacule. If they were defeated, they would surrender.

It was a strange force that prepared for the attack. Native auxiliaries who had joined Government troops and the European volunteers were *Kai Colo* themselves. They included the Naqaqa people, painted in red and black, lusting for the deaths of their old enemies.

Wright says "a force of men numbering some hundreds, following one another in single file, looked very picturesque, winding round the pathways in serpentine fashion, whilst up on the rocky heights, numbers of the enemy could be seen swarming on every point . . ."

Picturesque it might have been, but within hours, Captain Harding and 20 Fijian regulars were wounded, and a third of the volunteers dead. Nacule was taken, but it was the most expensive battle of the campaign.

True to form, the Naqaqa allies "carried on sticks bundles of what looked like yams, but which proved to be limbs of the enemy . . ."

The Kai Colo began to surrender.

Major Thurston reported to Government that they "are coming in daily in small groups and throwing themselves on the mercy of the Government . . . 46 men and 110 women and children arrived at daylight."

Other letters sent to Woods, the Minister for Military Affairs, reported "the mountain chief Ratu Dradra has surrendered with all the people from Bulu, Nasau, Nanukunuku, Savanunu, Nasautabu, numbering 232; 128 from Cubu, 126 from Magodro . . ." Only Nubutautau was left, a town so powerful it was considered nearly impregnable.

Despite its ominous appearance — the approaches to the village were lined with barbed lemon branches and skulls — it fell to Thurston in a surprise attack. It was a surprise because the Nubutautau never really believed the troops would try it.

The siege of Nubutautau ended the campaign. Less than 200 trained Fijian troops, with a little help from their friends the auxiliaries (who usually waited until an attack was over and then came in for the plunder) had defeated the hill people.

About a thousand men, women and children — the people of Magodro, Qaliyalatina and Naloto — were transported to Levuka as prisoners of war.

A few were hung. Most were hired out to planters as soon as the fee was paid to the Government, and their servitude lasted until Cession released them.

The Ba Campaign was a Government victory, but back in Levuka, things weren't any rosier.

Cakobau's Government was broke. Nobody paid taxes, and the few village people who did were the ones who could least afford it.

Just about everybody was talking about reforms or annexation.

England was "considering" annexation again, and when the Fiji Times said the British Government would probably annex the islands if both the chiefs and people wanted it, a Fiji Reform League took up the suggestions. Its purpose was to abolish the "bungling, inoperative and expensive" government for a better one — or secure annexation.

The Europeans were in the best position to do something about the situation, and at Nadroga, Nadi, Ba, Savusavu, Suva, Rewa and Tailevu, they called mass meetings of protest.

They passed motions of no-confidence, called for the ministers to resign, and demanded cession.

The third (and last) Legislative Assembly opened in May, 1873, just weeks after the end of the Ba Campaign, and only half the members showed up. Financial affairs were so messed up that it took a week before the Government's debt was disclosed — already more than $200,000.

There was chaos everywhere and Cakobau did the only thing possible. He dissolved the Assembly. But not before the ministers had negotiated a loan and a permanent revenue for themselves.

The ministers resigned, Cakobau refused their resignation, and then they governed without a Parliament. They said it would be dangerous to elect new members while Fijians were deprived of their right to vote and while whites declared they would prevent them coming to the poll.

Levuka's citizens, led by a deputation from a group called the White Residents Political Association, paraded to Nasova to beg Cakobau to dismiss the ministry.

Somewhere between four and six hundred of them came around the point . . . to face two loaded cannons and an army of 750 trained Fijian and Tongan troops guarding the King.

They were refused admittance, and as they stood facing each other, someone in the crowd fired a revolver. The soldiers charged, and the mob fled along the beach to town.

The guns of HMS Dido were trained on the Government offices, but the soldiers behaved with restraint. The 'Battle of Bull Run', as it was afterwards known, ended with no more bloodshed than a few bruised heads.

By now, however, there was absolutely no doubt in anybody's mind that the Kingdom's days were numbered.

David Wilkihson (centre) helped interpret the Deed of Cession to the chiefs.

28   CESSION!

The Fiji offer of cession to Britain was like a lightbulb.

It was on again, then off again, then on again . . .

In March, 1874, the high chiefs seemed in agreement: It was on again.

"We offer to her Majesty the government of the islands, but not the soil of the Fijian people," they said.

Exactly six months later, they were told that Britain was willing to accept the offer — but that conditions attached to it would prevent "good government" of the country.

Cakobau replied: "The Queen is right, conditions are not chief-like. If I give a chief a canoe, and he knows that I expect something from him, I do not say, 'I give you this canoe on condition of your sailing it on certain days . . . but I give him the canoe right out and trust to his generosity and good faith to make me the return he knows I expect. If I were to attach conditions, he would say 'I do not care to be bothered with your canoe, keep it yourself.' Why should we have anxiety about the future . . .?

"If matters remain as they are, Fiji will become like a piece of driftwood on the sea, and be picked up the first passerby. The whites who have come to Fiji are a bad lot. They are mere stalkers on the beach . . .

"Of one thing I am assured, that if we do not cede Fiji, the white stalkers on the beach, the cormorants, will open their maws and swallow us . . ."

* * *

But it wasn't just the stalkers on the beach that worried Cakobau. Ma'afu, too, was ready to swallow Fiji.

German merchants Boehm, Hedemann and others had urged Ma'afu to refuse annexation and return to Lau with the "Tovata" chiefs. Hedemann himself had ordered "several thousand stand of arms" to be held at Samoa in readiness for Ma'afu's order.

The country was in ruin. Fijians had no voice in government and no vote. A poll tax of 20 shillings for men and four for women went to a government in which the expenditure was almost entirely for the settlers. When they couldn't pay the tax, entire villages were sentenced to work as plantation labourers for months on end.

Village life was being destroyed to pay for a bureaucracy that offered them nothing in return.

When Swanston, the Secretary for Native Affairs, went to Vanua Levu to bring chiefs to the Bau Council, Ratu Kuila told him of the Administration's failures: ". . . the only act that is done in accordance with the law is the levy of taxes. The people are crying out in despair at the *lala* of the Chief; their time, their property, and their women are turned to his own account; the wealth of the Province is turned into the lap of strangers, and there is a constant horde of Tongans eating at the heart of the country ."

It wasn't all one-sided. The planter's world was collapsing, too. Cotton wasn't worth picking, the plantations had become worthless practically overnight, and with so much doubt about the political future, business was at a standstill.

Government was bankrupt.

England was debating the cession issue, but seemed antagonistic. Fiji's high chiefs couldn't decide, either.

Chaos.

Maybe a lot of the whites who came to Fiji were bad, but John Bates Thurston wasn't one of them. A Taveuni cotton planter, Thurston had spent years fighting for Fijian rights. "Justice to the Fijian nation", he wrote in the Fiji Gazette, "is of more consequences than cotton growing".

His chief concern about annexation was that it would give control of the country to the planters, and he didn't want to see the Fijian population turned into serfs. He was also behind a move to stop Fijians from being forced to work on plantations.

That made him extremely unpopular with the rest of the planter's community.

"I don't think" he wrote to a friend, "that I have a white friend in the country".

Thurston advised the Government ministers and chiefs to tear up the existing constitution in favour of a simpler, half-elected, half-nominated Legislature, or offer the Kingdom to Great Britain.

He and Swanston had spent hours drawing up conditions of cession, but at the same time, they were still hoping the Government would recover. They influenced the chiefs against it.

In August, Commodore Goodenough, the senior British naval offiver in Australia, and E.L. Layard, who had just been appointed to succeed March as Consul, were commissioned to make a full inquiry into Fiji's state of affairs.

They were told to look at four possibilities; recognizing the existing government (which Britain's warships had already done), giving the Consul powers of a magistrate, setting up a British protectorate . . . or annexing Fiji to the Crown.

The letter of appointment tactfully reminded them that the last of these shouldn't really be considered. "The British Government", it said, "is far from desiring any increase in British territory." Annexation "could in no case be adopted unless it proved to be the only means of escape from evils for which England might justly be held to be responsible."

Commodore Goodenough reached Fiji in November and immediately began a tour throughout the group — he went from island to island, plantation to mission station, school to bush village to "get the people's views" on government.

Even before Layard arrived, he was consulting Cakobau for an answer to his questions.

It must have come as something of a shock when Cakobau replied "I shall keep Fiji!"

The light went out again.

But the real decision would be made among the high chiefs who were already meeting in Bau. The Commodore and the Consul went to talk to them. They assured the chiefs that annexation would not endanger native rights on their positions as chiefs. Cakobau seemed to reconsider. If he could retain his chiefly power, there was something to be said for annexation. He didn't want to be trampled by Ma'afu, and England could save him from that.

During the meeting at Bau, Cakobau made the decision to cede — provided he kept his title of Tui Viti, and provided that he and certain other chiefs were given salaries for life.

His approval also hinged on establishment of a Great Council of Chiefs and laws restricting the transfer of land without the consent of Government and the tribal landowners.

That was March 3.

On March 4, he changed his mind again.

Ma'afu had come to the meeting supporting annexation. The chiefs hated the Tongan so much that, whatever he wanted, they didn't want any part of. They demanded that the offer of cession be withdrawn. Cakobau agreed, despite the fact that Rev Langham reported a conversation between the two great leaders, with Cakobay saying ". . . if you and I are of one mind, we need not ask a second chief in Fiji . . ."

Ma'afu wasn't in very good standing at the moment. What revenue he had collected for the Kingdom, he had kept, and the high chiefs were so angered by his insubordination that they talked of kicking all the Tongans out of the country once and for all.

Thurston went back to the drawing board with his plans for a revamped government, but in less than three weeks, the chiefs met again and decided to cede!

It was the first time the chiefs in council agreed to the idea, even though they pledged "government, but not the soil".

At the same time, missionaries and planters alike began to talk of the possibility (some said the certainty) of war, a land struggle which would be as bitter and devastating as the Maori Wars.

Goodenough and Layard made their report to Britain.

"We can see", they said, "no prospect for these islands should Her Majesty's Government decline to support the offer of cession, but ruin to the English partners and confusion to the native government."

The commissioners promptly declared the Government bankrupt and ordered British subjects to withdraw from any military service.

It was useless for Thurston and Cakobau to attempt to hold Government together any longer.

On March 21 they boarded HMS Pearl, anchored in Levuka Harbour. Thurston read a letter signed by the King, saying "It is our mind to give

John Bates Thurston.

October 10, 1874: the Royal Standard is raised.

the government of our Kingdom to the Lady Queen of Great Britain . . ."

In England, things also looked favourable for Fiji's annexation. Goodenough and Layard had been sent out under a government that warned Britain didn't need new colonies anywhere, saying colonies were overcostly jewels of the crown.

But by the time their report reached England, a new government was in power. Gladstone had been replaced by Disraeli, and the new Prime Minister favoured Imperialism and empire-building!

A British House of Commons debate in August decided Fiji's future. It agreed to Cakobau's requests, including title, allowances, and land-sale restrictions. The debts incurred by Cakobau's Government were also to be considered.

Sir Hercules Robinson, the Governor of New South Wales, was to be the final "investigator". If he gave the word, Britain was prepared to act.

Within two months, Sir Hercules had collected signatures of most of the high chiefs. And on September 28, the Council of Chiefs gave Fiji "unreservedly to the Queen of Britain, that she may rule as justly and affectionately, and that we may live in peace and prosperity."

This time, the chiefs had added a key word. Unreservedly.

The following day, Cakobau and four ruling chiefs also signed: "Ratu Epeli Nailatikau, Ratu Savenaca Naulivou, Ratu Isikeli Taba and Vakawaletabua, the Tui Bua.

Then Robinson, with Cakobau and Thurston, went on an island-hopping tour to get the other necessary signatures. Ma'afu and Tui Cakau signed, the latter "holding the pen while his name was written".

Ritova and Katonivere, fighting as usual, even stopped their war and agreed to go to Levuka together to witness the formal ceremony of cession on October 10.

October 10 was a rainy day. It rained so hard that the 10am ceremony was postponed until the afternoon.

It was short, so short that the Fiji Times complained it was "altogether void of ceremony".

That wasn't quite true. About 200 sailors from the two warships formed a guard of honour around Government Buildings at Nasova as Sir Hercules, Commodore Goodenough, Layard and others walked from the beach to the Council Room.

The King and his ministers received them. There were two copies of the Deed of Cession on the table, and the interpreter, David Wilkinson, read translations of them and the chief's resolution from September 30.

Ma'afu, Tui Cakau and other high chiefs watched in silence.

Just before they left the Council Room, Thurston produced a letter.

"The King", he read, "desires to give Her Majesty the only thing he possesses that may interest her . . . his old favourite war club" known as the blood-bather. This, Cakobau said, was the only law known in Fiji.

Now, British rule would replace it.

The men walked outside. As they watched, Cakobau's flag was lowered, and the British Royal Standard was raised.

The warships fired a 21-gun salute.

Fiji was a British colony.

Forty thousand Fijians died of measles and dysentery.

29   ONE IN FOUR FALL IN FIJI'S BLACK DEATH

It came like the plague, like Europe's Black Death.

The new colony was only three months old when the sickness struck, and then one out of every four Fijians died.

Whole families died. Whole villages died.

The dead were buried where they fell until after a while, there was no one left to dig the graves. People fled the villages — but there was nowhere to flee to.

Those who were left behind gave up any hope of life and meekly waited for the end to come.

Gardens were full of food, but the sick didn't have the strength to dig it, to carry or to cook it. The healthy wouldn't come near them to help.

Famine and dysentery took up where sickness left off. Forty thousand people died . . . of measles.

* * *

Just after Cession, Ratu Cakobau kept a promise he had made to Sir Hercules. He and two of his sons, Ratu Timoci and Ratu Josefa, went to Sydney to be the guests of the Governor.

They had a good time. They were wined and dined, they met a lot of people and a lot of people came to see and meet them. While in Sydney, Ratu Cakobau came down with the measles. On the way back to Fiji, the two young chiefs did, too.

But there was nothing to worry about, the Governor's own doctor and the ship's doctor saw to that. By the time HMS Dido reached Levuka, all three were feeling better.

When the Administrator, E.L. Layard, came out to the ship, he was told by the ship's doctor that the Fijians on board had all had the measles, and that the young chiefs had "another disease less to their credit" as well.

But Fiji had no quarantine regulations. Measles weren't considered terribly dangerous, and besides, it wouldn't look very good to lock the former King and his sons up in quarantine while crowds gathered on the beach to welcome them home.

In another 10 minutes, Cakobau, passengers, and the Fijian crew of a Government boat which had already come aboard to greet their chief, were on their way to shore.

He was still feeling weak, but during the next 10 days, Cakobau entertained visitors at Draiba (his home near Levuka) and then at Bau.

Some of the highest chiefs were among them.

Then the visitors returned to their homes, carrying with them a deadly seed of infection.

Soon after, the Commissioner for the Interior, Mr Carew, arranged a meeting of the chiefs of Viti Levu's hill tribes. They were to meet the Administrator and other officials and learn just what Cession meant.

Between 800 and 1000 of the hill people made their way to the meeting ground at Navuso on the Rewa River. The HMS Dido, some of them certainly carrying the germ, and several chieftains of Levuka who were already sick with measles, mixed freely among them.

It's possible the Kai Colo might have escaped the infection even then, but five of the leading chiefs were taken back to Levuka to be shown the working structure of a colony.

By the time they returned to the hills, all five were sick.

It wasn't just the Dido doing the dirty work. The steamer Wentworth left Sydney for Fiji in the middle of January and measles claimed two of its passengers before it arrived.

The Fiji Times on January 27 said it hoped the disease would not reach Fiji "as among natives it would spread rapidly".

The paper was barely published before it hit. It had been simmering for weeks, building up in intensity like a tropical storm.

Almost simultaneously, in village after village, people grew sick and died.

Young and old alike fell victim, and families were buried under their houses which were then pulled down, leaving nothing but patches of bright *sarasara* leaves to mark their graves.

At over-crowded Bau, there was a continuous ferrying of canoes bearing the dead to mainland graveyards, and with them went many of the best chiefs and teachers. The cries of the mourners and the death drums lasted day and night.

Among the first victims was Cakobau's brother, Ratu Savenaca Naulivou, one of the ablest and most respected chiefs of the time. He had been the Kingdom's first Minister for Native Affairs, and one of the first to sign the Deed of Cession.

Another who had signed the Deed was the Macuata chief Ritova. He died, too. In fact, by the end of April, five of the men who had signed their names to Cession a few months earlier were dead.

At first, the deaths occurred at Ovalau, Bau and Rewa. But the gathering of people for Cakobau's return and the meeting of the Kai Colo had been disastrous.

Measles spread to every part of the islands. Nearly all of the hill people who had come to Navuso died.

In late February, the Administration adopted New South Wales' quarantine laws, but it was too late. Way too late.

Thurston wrote: "People talk of isolation. They might as well talk of setting a barricade against the east wind."

He was right: those who fled their towns and abandoned the sick couldn't keep ahead of the epidemic.

When the fever began to burn, people hurried to the water to cool off. And that was fatal. The only way to beat it was to let the fever burn itself out. A sudden chill brought congestion and death.

The planters, the settlers, the Administration and naturally the missionaries went into action. They saved hundreds, not because they had so much medicine, but because they knew the basic rules.

Warnings were printed in the newspaper in Fijian: " . . .it is forbidden for those infected to bathe or sit in a cool breezy place . . . if a patient goes outside to cool off, he dies."

A Savusavu planter reported "the whites have done all they could, and in most cases get them over the measles, but a malignant type of dysentery follows and the result is death.

"They likewise seem quite indifferent about one another and neglect the sick, sitting and looking at them dying . . ."

With care, people did get better. At a Wesleyan mission station, Rev Waterhouse nursed all but one of his students back to health, and at Levuka, the Constabulary's commander saved all but 10 of the 143 men in the command.

But for the Fijians living beyond reach of help, there was no knowledge of the disease or of its remedies.

Two things made matters even worse: weather and rumours.

Warm days might have helped, but instead, February and March were stormy and wet, with day after day of chilling rain. When the weak tried to reach the gardens, they were drenched and pneumonia followed.

Rumours, some started by those who had been opposed to British rule, claimed that the disease had been introduced purposely by the whites.

The whites wanted the land, they wanted the Fijians dead, they had taken Cakobau to Australia to be infected, they used their medicines to spread the disease . . . and so it went.

The Fijians began to ignore advice, and they refused the medicines. Some carried to hospital escaped and the first opportunity and instantly headed for the streams or the sea.

It is ironic that among those who were willing to listen to the Europeans were the imported labourers from the Solomons and New Hebrides. Most of them survived.

Dysentery and starvation followed in the wake of the measles. Unburied bodies and lack of sanitation caused the dysentery. Parents lay too sick to move while their children starved. As the sick became weaker and "more offensive", they were left to starve.

The reports began coming in.

Rev Waterhouse, at Navuloa, said: "The people have been seized with fear . . . whole families have been taken ill and have been left without help. I knelt down to pray in the muddy lane rather than enter one hut out of which came the fumes of disease that almost felled me to the ground . . Viwa is, I hear, half-emptied . . ."

On Ovalau, a town of 150 inhabitants had "scarcely a house in which there was not one dead or dying . . . the pathways are empty . . . not a soul is to be seen."

At Lomaloma, Ma'afu had been so sick he had given up, but had somehow been nursed back to health. A number of Tongans on the island hadn't been so fortunate.

At Levuka, Tui Levuka was dead and bodies were flung into common graves. When even that became difficult, they were buried a few inches under the soil.

The Tui Nadroga was dead. So were nearly all of the village leaders in that area.

In late March, it began to subside and the death count began. The newspaper mentioned that Levuka's streets "are no longer traversed by natives carrying coffins . . ." But one third of Ovalau's people were gone, 450 out of 1500.

Taveuni's population had dropped from 20,000 to 4000.

At Koro, 688 had died out of 2543; Ba, 2214 out of 7295.

The losses averaged out at about 28 per cent, some places faring worse, some better. By the time the sickness reached Totoya and Matuku, the weather was warmer and there were fewer deaths. But Moala had been hit by the cold rain, and Keteira village lost 26 people in 48 hours.

Sir Arthur Gordon, the man who would be Fiji's first Governor, was just on his way. He learned of the disaster even before he arrived, and despatched a warship with a medical team and assistance. When he reached Levuka in June, the epidemic had all but died out. His final estimate of the number of deaths, based on a village-by-village census: "Certainly over 40,000 died, and probably many, many more."

The effects of the sickness on the population had been so devastating that, in at least one district, widows and unmarried men were ordered to marry. But it would take nearly a century for the Fijians to reach their former numbers.

Village midwives reported that, the first year after the epidemic, there were no births. The year after, all those who were born, died.

The people had lost their mana.

With the end of the onslaught, there were bitter attacks on the Administration. The newspaper on February 17 said "the first advantage derived from annexation is the introduction of the measles, and for this we are indebted to the Dido, which came and discharged her diseased passengers utterly regardless of any consequences that might arise."

Dr Goodman, the doctor aboard HMS Dido, was blamed by the Colonial Office for not having warned the authorities of the danger.

It seemed that *somebody* should have realised the danger. As late as 1860, measles had been introduced into the New Hebrides and New Caledonian islands, and about a quarter of the population had perished.

Commodore Goodenough put the blame with local officials, "who by long experience in the South Seas should have been aware of the fatal effect of the first introduction of measles among a population previously unvisited by the disease."

But it didn't do much good to blame anyone, now.

There was another repercussion to attend to. The hill people had lost nearly all of their leaders immediately after the Navuso meeting.

It wasn't surprising that they should believe this was witchcraft, an effort to poison them and take their land.

Hill villages which had just turned Christian thought their punishment was heaven-sent for forsaking their own gods.

They returned to heathenism and soon were in open rebellion.

Captain Knollys with Fiji Armed Constabulary.

30   THE LITTLE WAR ENDS WAR IN VITI LEVU

Capt Knollys stood bare legged, a rifle slung over his checked shirt, a force of 80 men lined up in front of him.

Some of the troops wore a white scarlet sulu, but most wore a long black *liku* made of water weed. Streamers of *masi* floated from their arms and head, and almost all had their faces painted a coal black — including one with horizontal stripes acrss his face, another with large white circles around his eyes.

They were a wild looking bunch.

They were the government's troops, just the same.

* * *

The troops were on their way to the "disturbed district" — an area that included the upper half of the Sigatoka Valley and hundreds of square miles of hill country on either side.

It was "disturbed" because the hill people were certain the measles epidemic which had just subsided was some sort of terrible sorcery in- flicted on them by the new colonial government.

Villages which had already turned Christian threw away any signs of the *lotu*, including clothing, and joined those that hadn't. They defied the government and went back to their old ways of warfare and cannibalism.

At first, a commissioner and a few of the Armed Native Constabulary were sent out to investigate the problems . . .

Walter Carew, Commissioner Colo, set up camp at Nasaucoko, about 35 miles up the Sigatoka River valley. He had quite an understanding feeling for the Fijians, mentioning that "the only thing I am afraid of is that some of our party may want to kill stragglers or messengers. Olive (the police superintendent) thinks we should arrest these . . . on the contrary, I should like to induce some of the old chiefs to come to me and talk things over." Capt. Olive, he added, "is of the same opinion as his men, that we have come here with the primary view of making war . . ."

The police superintendent might have been a little headstrong, but he didn't lack courage. When the constabulary faced armed mountaineers at Vatumoli, the captain ordered his men to stay where they were and went to the top of the hill where two rebel chiefs, Batikarakara and Na Gusudradra, waited. He approached them by pulling a fern leaf and sticking it in the muzzle of his loaded rifle — which he handed to Gusudradra.

In the rebel village, he was shown to a *bure* "at the door of which stood a man leaning on the handle of a very large battle axe. The most they could do, however, was to kill me, so I put on a bright face and entered the house, and on finding no one inside, began to think I was in for it . . ."

But the parley was peaceful enough. As he walked out of the village, a number of men dashed toward him with up-raised spears, only to drop pieces of sugar cane and bananas at his feet.

"We parted, one chief begging me to accept some sugar cane with tears in his eyes," Oliver wrote. "Were it not for one or two of the principal parties, I believe all this would be settled in a short time."

The one or two principal parties were Na Bisiki of Drio Drio and Mudu of Naqalimare, both strong leaders who were stirring up hostility towards the new government.

Carew had come to talk matters over, not to make war, but all that changed after April 12.

On that day, the Kai Colo attacked Christian villages in the provinces of Nadi and Nadroga and burned eight others along the banks of the Sigatoka River. The time for negotiations was over.

Esala Seru, the Buli Vatukarasa, appealed to government for help. "Our district is ruined", he wrote. "Those at Batiri are clubbed, all the towns until you reach Korotogo are burnt. A great number of men are clubbed." As an afterthought, he added "I beg of you some paper that I may continue writing to you . . ."

The 'tevoro' as the hill people were being called, attacked a number of villages before reaching the gates of one guarded by the Roko Tui Nadroga, Ratu Luke Nakulanikoro. They beat bamboo drums and asked to be admitted, saying they only wanted water.

Instead, the Roko and his men pushed them back across the river, killed eleven, and set fire to a half-dozen rebel villages.

"But the worst is this," he wrote in a message to Carew: "while the men of Batiri were absent fighting, the women and children had collected in a house ready to flee, and those that attacked Batiri came round at the back and killed 20 women and children. Only two women were left alive, taken prisoner. They threaten Sigatoka today . . ."

Sir Arthur Gordon had been governor for less than a year when the "Little War" broke out. But he knew it was a delicate situation. If he called in British regulars, it would result in a war between whites and natives. He also refused a suggestion that 500 Indian *sepoys* be brought over.

He decided that the Armed Native Constabulary and Fijian volunteers would have to settle it themselves, led by a few trained officers. In addition, he asked the Rokos of each province to pick 30 volunteers for service.

Double that number — 2000 men — actually turned up.

The Governor devised a plan: Capt. Louis Knollys, 32nd Lt. Infantry, would take a force in from the Ba River to Nadrau (which was pro-government) and descend the Sigatoka River to Bemana.

Mr A J L Gordon, the Governor's private secretary, would push up from Navalili with the Roko Tui Nadroga's forces. The Armed Native Constabulary at Nasaucoko, now under Mr Le Hunte, would assist whichever group needed it. And Carew would use his influence to try to get Ro Qereqeretabua and the Wainimala people to help in preventing the Kai Colo from escaping to the east.

The Governor himself came out to Nasaucoko to set the plans in action.

From the camp, he described the "plains of the Nasaucoko Valley below us, Magodro rising up like a great dome due west of us, eastward Naqaqa and some other devil strongholds and, far to the northeast, the mountains of Nubutautau".

He gave his officers a somewhat terse message: "I know you are fully aware of my abhorence of emptying the country by destruction of the towns . . . I give you fair warning you will have to give me a very strict account of every village burning."

Gordon was the first to move. He was in charge of about 1200 untrained auxiliaries who were eager to get started, and after continued delays by Knollys, he couldn't hold them back any longer.

On June 8, with the Nadroga and Namosi men, the auxiliaries took Koroivatuma and then Bukutia, a "natural fortress on the summit of precipitous crags and honey-combed with caves".

The enemy fled to Qalimare and Matanavatu, the latter a rock fortress so inaccessible that attacked seemed out of the question. But a few days later, the Governor got a message from Gordon: "Yesterday," he said, "the rock fortress of Matanavatu was taken by Ratu Luke and a small number of men from various tribes. The attack was unpremeditated on our side ."

He went on to explain that Ratu Luke and a few men were out looking for food when they decided to sneak a look at the interior of the fortress.

Much to their surprise, the inhabitants fled. That, anyway, was Gordon's account to the Governor. By the time he made a report to the Colonial Secretary, the story had been enlarged to this: "I next gave orders to attack Matanavatu, and the whole company moved up opposite to it. That evening, we attacked and took the town . . ."

At Matanavatu, 38 were killed and 11 taken prisoner. Bisiki and Mudu, both apparently in the fortress at the start of the 'attack', had escaped.

The only problem was, where was Knollys?

There was no one on the other side to stop the runaways, and Gordon complained to the Governor that "My people are becoming discontented; my force would dwindle to something very inefficient if kept waiting very long. By long, I mean a *week* . . ."

But by the end of June, Gordon's drive through the lower reaches of the Sigatoka was finished. Mudu had been captured by the Naqoqo of Nadi. The rebel villages south of Bemana were taken.

The rest was up to Knollys. And his job was getting easier all the time. The Wainimala people had talked a number of the rebel villages above Bemana to *soro*, including even Na Bisiki's.

Other villages in the north had 'soro'ed, too. The Kai Colo were so harried that they no longer even bothered to *bole*. And more Snider breech-loading rifles, accurate and quick to reload, had just arrived from New Zealand for the government troops.

One of the most stalwart of the pro-government leaders was the Roko Tui Ba, Ratu Vuniani Vuki, who had been with the government forces ever since the disturbance began. He was continuously praised for his efforts, and was later awarded a ceremonial sword of gallantry — after he had crawled on hands and knees through a burning powder house to rescue Nasaucoko's already-hot kegs of gun powder.

On Monday, June 26th, Knollys, 200 of Vuki's men, and the Armed Native Constabulary left Nadrau. At the first skirmish, one of the chiefs complained that the Kai Colo didn't fight fair. They "run backwards and forwards so they are difficult to hit".

Most of the *tevoro* villages were abandoned before Knollys reached them. The hill people had taken to the caves, and it seemed like an impossible task to get them out.

The caves were deep. Many had multiple entrances so small that an attacker would have to crawl through the opening on his belly. Larger entrances were guarded by earthworks and stone walls, and inside, there were springs of fresh-water and storehouses of food. One of them was described as "an immense room of a great height. Lighted bamboos used as torches failed to show the roof of the cavern."

They were taken, nevertheless. Slowly, sometimes by a talking process, sometimes by a fierce attack through the narrow entrances, the hill people were routed.

The forces marched past Nagatagata to Nadua. About 90 people were taken prisoner there. At Lobo ni Koro, it was harder, and it took days to collect 133 prisoners.

At Nacawanisa, it was harder, still. The people wouldn't come out, so the constabulary went in, four of them dying in the attempt.

The Kai Colo made their last stand at Nanuwai, and by the end of July, they were persuaded to lay down their arms.

During this time, one of the chief military strategists was the chief medical officer, a gun-toting, scalpel-bearing surgeon named Dr Mac-Gregor.

When he wasn't firing at the enemy, he was fixing them up.

During one such operation, he described the difficulties of "holding a forceps between the teeth and tying up blood vessels which are pumping streams of blood into one's face" — while 300 spectators imagined he was drinking his patient's blood.

(The patient lived, the crowd was astonished . . . "truly, he opens his eyes . . . he speaks . . .")

Another time, the officers surprised a rebel camp preparing to eat a cooked human leg. The doctor wrote in his journal: "a small leg with soft muscles and delicately rounded calf, a nicely-turned ankle and the skin smooth and soft . . . a gastronomic delight." Either the doctor had a sense of humour, or he'd been in the bush a little too long.

He was also outspoken in his demands for fair treatment of the captives.

"Speaking on behalf of the cannibals" he said, "I cannot believe that the great majority of the mountaineers ever resigned their independence, and with reference to past acts of cannibalism, it would be necessary to begin with the Vunivalu."

He recommended that all arms be taken, but that the people "be left in their native glens, under their respective chiefs" and said he "considered the preservation of tribal relations to be a necessity".

He had at least one listener. The Governor answered his request by saying "the strongest advocate for clemency is myself".

A sketch by Arthur Gordon of Nasaucoko.

Sir Arthur Gordon was at the trials, both at Sigatoka after Gordon's campaign ended, and at the mountain camp at Vatula when Knollys' prisoners were brought in.

Of the 850 people tried at Sigatoka, most were 'paroled' to other districts on an honour-system. One man pleaded that he could not be guilty, since he did not club a man, but only shot him in the head.

About 15 were held to be directly responsible for the Batiri deaths or for leading the rebellion. They were shot by firing squad or hung. Mudu was among them.

So was Na Bisiki. During the out-door trial, he suddenly made a dash for freedom and nearly made it to the edge of a thickly-wooded ravine. A throwing club felled him, and then a bullet shattered his knees. As he lay helpless on the ground, he was shot again.

It was the end of one of Fiji's most impressive warriors.

It was also the end of war on Viti Levu.

On the 28th of October, 1876, the Governor issued a proclamation pardoning all of the mountain tribes, including those still at large. They were free to return to their districts, to rebuild their towns and cultivate their lands. The only stipulation was that fortified places were not to be inhabited again.

A year later, Sir Arthur Gordon revisited these districts. At Fort Carnarvon, the name of the former camp at Nasaucoko, about a thousand mountaineers assembled to hear him address them, including several hundred school children.

He walked to Korolevu, where, according to an entry in his journal, "I was received in a fashion which I have never seen elsewhere. The people were arranged in rows on each side of the rara. As I came into it all the folks inclined their heads to the left shoulder, and as I passed them, sank down into a slanting position to the left, like a row of ninepins . . ."

"Every one of the people here was last year a prisoner. Later I strolled up and down by myself alone, but in perfect security."

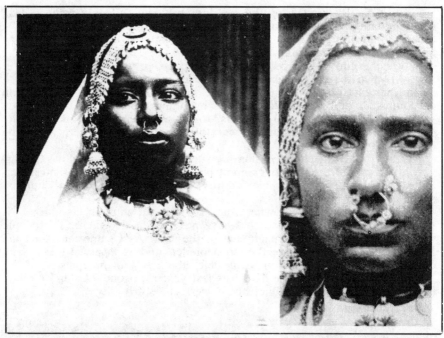

Many of the women who came under the indentured system were tricked, yet life in Fiji was usually no harder than it had been in India.

31   LEONIDAS BRINGS INDIA'S LABOURERS

The Leonidas arrived in Levuka late in the afternoon on May 14, 1879.

It didn't come into the harbour, but instead sailed up and down outside the entrance.

At first light the next morning, a pilot boat and a number of other boats went out to greet the arrivals from Calcutta.

But the Surgeon-General aboard called out a warning to keep away.

Cholera, smallpox and dysentery were aboard. Seventeen were already dead.

The ship anchored at Waitovu passage, as far from the shore as it could get without hitting the outer reef. Four boats with police guards were stationed around it.

The guards were told to shoot anyone who attempted to reach shore.

For the 463 immigrants aboard — the first of India's indentured labourers to reach Fiji — it was a very poor beginning.

* * *

They had come at the request of Fiji's government, or more exactly, at the request of its governor, Sir Arthur Gordon.

And they were to answer two of his most pressing problems; a dwindling supply of labour, and a means of preserving his 'native policy'.

As the colony's first governor, Sir Arthur has immediately taken steps to safeguard the Fijians. He made it unlawful for Fijian land to be sold. He made certain that Fijian customs and traditions remained intact, and that the authority of chiefs was maintained. And he set up a taxation system that required Fijians to work their own plantations rather than the settler's plantations, providing both government and themselves with a source of revenue.

In this, he was probably following the Colonial Secretary's advice. "The fact is," Thurston said, "that no Fijians will go from home to be worked from morning to night, upon paltry pay, indifferent fare, and anything but mild treatment, if they can avoid doing so . . . The native villager is a member of a commune, and to move out of that commune is opposed to his natural instincts and habits . . ."

The Great Council of Chiefs agreed. Long-term employment of Fijians, the Council stated, broke up families and interfered with planting.

Besides, the measles epidemic had carried off a big portion of the population, and this wasn't the time to be pulling men away from the villages. They were needed at home.

In Gordon's eyes, Fijian affairs would remain paramount. There would be no alienation of the land or the people.

The only problem was, the Colonial Office had made it very clear to the governor that the colony was going to have to support itself. Soon.

Large-scale plantations seemed to be the obvious answer. But plantations required cheap land and labour — and the governor had already placed restrictions on both!

Sir Arthur had previously served in Mauritius and Trinidad. In both places, he had seen both the colony and its immigrants prosper as a result of indentured Indian labour.

The day after his arrival in Fiji, he addressed a meeting of Levuka planters and asked: "Shall we attempt, not to supplant but to supplement Polynesian labour by that of Indian coolies? I think we shall do well to do so. I have nothing to urge against Polynesian labour, but I think we must admit that the supply is decreasing and the cost is increasing . . . The supply of labour to be obtained from India is practically boundless."

And, he added, "at wages so low as to be well known".

The governor was certain that Indians would be a benefit to Fiji.

Nobody else was.

The planters and the press all attacked his plans. Planters said they couldn't afford the initial expense of bringing labourers from so far, particularly when they'd just been deprived of Fijian labour.

The press said: "the interests of the country are better served by the immigration of Polynesians than the introduction of a class whose lives, traditions, habits and thoughts are so widely opposed to those of the people amongst whom they would have to reside . . ."

Gordon's policy, they said, was slavery for the Fijians and ruin for the Europeans.

It was an interesting situation. The governor was fighting tooth and nail to preserve Fijian social structures — at the sacrifice of Indian ones.

The 'coolie', as Gordon referred to all Indians in his government despatches, would take the pressure off the Fijians and bring industry to the colony.

That the Indian's family and religious background would begin to crumble the day the "coolie" first stepped aboard ship, was never mentioned.

The temporary loss of freedom which five years of servitude would bring was offset by advantages to the migrants . . . they would be able to remain in Fiji after their indenture finished, if they wished.

Sir Arthur won his case.

The recruiters went to work in Calcutta before the governor had even finished his proposal to the Colonial Sugar Refining Company.

CSR began operations in Fiji in 1880 — a year after the Leonidas had arrived!

If the indentured system was unpopular in Fiji, it was resented just as much in India.

There were religious objections. Hindus were not allowed to travel on foreign lands or cross the *kala pani*, the black waters. If they did, they lost caste.

Aboard ship and certainly on the plantations later, there would be mixing of castes, even to the point of eating food prepared perhaps by an "untouchable".

No sooner had the recruiters begun their task, than rumours moved ahead of them. Indians who went to Fiji would be hung upside down to drain the oil from their heads, some said.

Others suggested even worse: they could be forced to turn Christian.

In Calcutta and, later, Madras, the *arkatis*, the recruiters, soon discovered that it took a trick or two if they were to get any takers. They set up camp in fairs and festivals, any place where crowds of uneducated villagers, particularly those lost or separated from their friends or family, could be lured to the depots to sign.

To the least-educated, Fiji became "a district near Calcutta". The pay of a shilling (12 annas) a day was reasonable by current India standards, and it was always for "light and easy work". There was no mention of compulsory labour, or the penal laws which waited for the person too weak or ill to do his task.

Those who became lost in crowds were given a home for the night and "friendly advice". Women were shamed into signing the indenture agreement, sometimes were even kidnapped. They meekly submitted to their fate.

Not everybody was tricked, of course. The *arkatis* had silver tongues, but the migrants weren't all simpletons. Many had their own reasons for giving up family and religion, among them literate men of high caste. Others were running from the police.

Or from the land. Much of India was harsh, a land of "ever-recurring famine in the country and never-ending plague in the city".

Bihar, the 'land of sorrow', was one of those places where recruiting was good. It was devoid of industry. There was too little land and too many people. Uttar Pradesh, one of its provinces, supplied more than half of all Fiji's migrants.

They came to escape poverty and to find the promised security.

There were few families. In fact, there were relatively few women, despite the extra inducements paid to recruiters for indentured families.

Those who agreed to go to Fiji were taken to sub-depots run by the recruiters. They were well-fed, care being taken to have their food cooked by high-caste people, and they were kept isolated until the last possible moment. Even on their rail trip to Calcutta, the recruiters sent them in groups in hired private coaches, fearing that villagers from home would see them and persuade them to return.

In the Calcutta depot, they were given a medical check, and the Registering Officer interviewed them to make sure they were going of their own free will.

The indentured had already been prepared for this. "Say yes to anything the Sahib asks," they were told. Few thought to do otherwise.

From Calcutta, the ship which would take them to Fiji was towed down the Hughli River to sea. Even here, some jumped over the side, especially Hindus in despair at losing their caste.

The *kala pani* was fearful, but in fact the journey to Fiji was not nearly as dreadful as the horror voyages faced by those in earlier labour ships.

Slavers plying Africa, Pacific island and Chinese ports sometimes did well to land *any* of their human cargo alive.

The India ships were better. By standards of the time, they weren't even over-crowded. There was a Surgeon-General and hospital on each ship, and a set amount of "living space" for each passenger.

Deaths at sea averaged about one per cent, which was not considered bad for a voyage which usually lasted 70 or 80 days. For most, their worst recollection of the journey was sea-sickness.

For most, that is. Probably not those of the Leonidas.

After the disastrous measles epidemic, government was taking no chances. When it was learned that the Leonidas carried cholera and small-pox, the Chief Medical Officer, Dr MacGregor, ordered a platform built on the reef, with a floating trolley to and from the ship. Even the smallest letter or note from the vessel was fumigated in carbolic acid.

The Leonidas was sent away after dropping its passengers on Yanuca Lailai, an island near Levuka which was hastily prepared as a safe quarantine station.

There, the new arrivals waited for another 90 days. Fifteen more died before they were declared disease-free and were brought ashore.

Those on the Leonidas had a hard time . . . but not quite as bad as those who would arrive five years later, on the Syria.

The Syria left Calcutta on March 13 with 180 aboard. It had a smooth trip with good weather right up until the last, when stormy seas clouded out their first view of their new land.

If they'd had an experienced lookout in the shrouds who was familiar with the coast, they would have realised it was the wrong land.

An hour after sunset on a May evening, the lookout spotted breakers. Moments later, the Syria hit the point of Naselai Reef on the southeast tip of Viti Levu, four miles from shore.

Towering seas crashed down on the small wooden ship. All but one of the lifeboats was smashed.

Seven men, including the mate and three lascars, pushed the last lifeboat across the shoals and made for Levuka, 30 miles away.

The Penguin steamed toward the wreck as soon as it got the news. So did the Clyde from Suva. But when the Penguin neared, it was seen to be "utterly impossible for the steamer to approach, and certain death for the boats crew to launch into angry white foam. The mast was gone, only a bare hull remained . . . and about 20 or 30 passengers came to the weather side and seemed to gaze at the steamer, but no sign to attract attention was noticed."

Fortunately, between the Syria and shore, and in comparatively calm water, Fijian canoes and a boat were waiting to pick up anyone who made it through the raging surf.

The Penguin made a run to Nukulau for more help, and when it again approached the Syria, "not a soul was to be seen aboard the wreck".

The final death toll was 56 — 31 men, 15 women, 10 children.

But the rest were rescued. The Rev Langham in his boat from Bau, Dr MacGregor, aided by the Native Constabulary and with boats rowed by prisoners, and other small boats went into the surf and plucked out "the bodies of the drowned . . . and the struggling forms of the feebly living."

Between May, 1879, and November 1916, when the last labour ship arrived, there would be 87 journeys from India with workers bound for 'girmit' — five years servitude — in Fiji.

Sixty thousand people.

Deprived of caste, their traditional leaders and elders, and for some even the basics of their religion, they were to become very vulnerable.

The author of *Fiji's Indian Migrants*, K.L. Gillion, describes the five years which would follow this way:

"To a man with a wife and family, who had belonged to a middle or high caste in India, his new life was a miserable one, at best that of a well-treated animal — fed, looked-after if sick, driven to work, and given a stable to live in . . . Conditions in the factories and on the plantations in India were as bad, if not worse . . . but it was not without reason that the Indians called their life on the plantations in Fiji *narak*.

Hell.

Indentured workers, Wainadoi rubber plantation.

32 GIRMIT, THE TIME OF SORROW

In the labour depots of Calcutta, those waiting to go to Fiji spent their time eating and singing.

When they arrived in Fiji, they found much less to sing about.

The five years of indenture — girmit — was above all else dehumanising. The labour lines were 'kasbighar', a brothel.

The 'coolie', as he was commonly called, was given a room ten feet by seven, without windows, floors or ventilation. If he was single, he shared it with two others, along with all their food, belongings and, if they owned any, chickens or goats.

He cooked, entertained, slept and mated there. There was no privacy. The walls did not even reach the ceiling.

The line was not built for hygiene and even the cleanest among them found it difficult to avoid illness. Yaws, tuberculosis, hookworm and VD began to take the life from them.

Plantations were visited regularly by inspectors, but then the inspectors were for the most part ex-overseers who could be induced to overlook certain things, particularly over a cold beer on the overseer's verandah.

The death rates were high. Despair claimed those that sickness left, and suicides claimed still more.

They were given a daily task to do. A task was legally defined as the amount of work an able-bodied man could do in six hours steady work.

As defined by the plantations, it was how much you could make a coolie do without a rebellion, or the authorities causing trouble.

Those who failed to meet the task were beaten, or fined, or imprisoned. Those who complained were given harder tasks still.

Women were worked almost as hard as men. The pretty ones had an advantage, since there were five men to every two women, and both overseers and sirdars would reduce the task for a woman who didn't object to a turn in the bushes. The situation led to moral chaos among women, murder among the men.

Some girls became wives at the age of 11, mothers at 12. A child with a child at her breast. At 30, she was old.

Certainly, not all overseers or sirdars were bad. But good ones were hard to find and some were just plain rotten. Sirdars may have been the worst of the two, because many thrived off the misfortune of their own kind. They were in a perfect position to extort money or demand women.

It was not surprising that the cane knife and the hoe took the place of law, and that sirdars and overseers were frequently the victims.

The following personal interviews with Fiji's indentured labourers tells their story better than any text could do.

They were collected by Dr Ahmed Ali of the University of the South Pacific School of Social Sciences, in association with students and staff at USP.

The interviews used here are condensed and represent only a portion of a manuscript which Dr Ali expects to be published under the title 'GIRMIT'.

* * *

PANCHAM: "I had no intention of coming to Fiji or going away to any other islands. It was the month of *cheat*, the month of extreme heat, and the time to harvest *channa*. I was a farmer, all the channa in the village had been harvested except mine which became over-ripe and began falling off of its own accord.

A Brahman's son came to me and suggested we ought to go abroad and seek some other type of work.

I was then 16 or 17 years old. In the village we only knew our own home or that of our close blood relations, we were totally ignorant of the outside.

I answered "I have no intention of going abroad for the purpose of work, I have work here at home. Yet if you suggest that we should go abroad for the purpose of education, then I am willing." He answered: "Let us go for education."

An old woman lived in our house and I knew where she kept her money buried in a large earthenware pot. From it I took a handful which proved to be 50 rupees. This I thought was plenty.

We left Gwalior and went to Bhind, to Etawah, to Agra, then took a train to Kasi. In that place there were recruiters who were sharp-eyed persons able to detect individuals who were running away from somewhere.

A Muslim came to us and wanted to know our destination. I replied we were on our way to Kasi for education. The *arkati* then told me I was no longer of the educationable age, our time for education was gone.

The arkati asked us to accompany him. He called a closed carriage and took us to his depot, It was a large house. I saw some women cooking there. There were men, too. He left after giving us food and a place to sleep.

The next day, we were told we should have to go to a white man's office. 'The arkati told us that the sahib would ask 'Where did you come from? What did the man say to bring you here? Did he coerce you into coming?'

We went to the sahib. We had already been coached to give the right answers. He noted it all and called the arkati in and asked him to take us. The arkati told us that the train to go to Calcutta would arrive at midnight and we should be ready.

About 30 of us were put in one carriage, men and women, and it was locked to stop outsiders from getting in.

I began thinking of home. I could have returned, but I lacked the knowledge and wisdom to do so.

At the depot, our clothes were taken away from us and we were given new clothes. A fat Bengali doctor examined each of us.

We were not told how far places like Fiji were from Calcutta. I did not ask. What had happened had happened and I must go on.

Aboard ship, I ate only roti. When dhall, curry and rice were cooked, sea water was used and I could not eat such food.

There was no caste or religion on the ship. We were one.

After about a month the ship came to Fiji. Big punts came to take us to Nukulau. I felt terribly cold, which I could not bear. I don't remember how long we stayed at Nukulau. The sirdar there treated us very well. When I first saw Fijians, I thought they were *rachas*, cannibals.

I was taken to Navua, where we were required to weed the grass in the cane field and I had a task of 20 chains. Sirdars seeing sturdy workers finish early would say 20 chains was too easy and order a 25-chain task. We could do nothing about this. If we agreed to work slowly so as not to get larger tasks, then we got into trouble and were given a beating by the overseer.

Once I loaded a cane truck, thinking the more I loaded it, the better paid I would be in the end. I thought I would receive a monetary reward. Then I was told that if I were to do this again, I would be sent to gaol for six months. I was told overloading would wreck the engine of the truck.

When I got home and had cooked and eaten, it was 4am . . . at 5 I was to go to work for another day. I pretended I was sick.

The overseer suspected that I was trying to get away from work. He got off the horse, he grabbed my hand and he tried to kick me. Each time he tried, I moved. He was a fat man and we went in circles, he tried to kick me and my moving out of range. In the end, the overseer got tired of his unsuccessful efforts to kick me and gave me a letter to take to the doctor.

I took the letter to the doctor. He looked at me and read the letter. He had a stick near him and came down the steps to hit me, so I ran away and he ran after me. I decided to go to the doctor who lived with the 'free' (Indians who had completed their five years indenture). He gave me a letter to take back to the hospital, saying that if the doctor there were to beat me, he would see to the rest.

The sirdars were never on our side. Sirdars who were unmarried and the unmarried overseers got up to mischief with women. He would advise the woman it would be in her interest to go and see the overseer. He would also warn her that if she did not go, then the overseer in any case would take her by force and then everybody would know about it and she would have no self-respect left.

The Australian overseers who used to come knew how to herd cattle or to drive animals and this is how they behaved towards human beings as well.

It was just as well that indenture lasted only 5 years. Had it been for 6 years, I would have preferred to be dead, even by my own hands. During the 5 years, I counted each day to find out how many were left."

MAHADEO: "There was a South Indian with us. He used to do a lot of singing and dancing but he was not able to work and he used to get a terrible beating from the overseer. So he took off into the bush and hanged himself.

The sirdars used to wake up at 2am. At 3, we had to line up and go to our task. The 'free' were very good to us, they used to give us milk, yoghurt and food, in return we used to help these people a little.

ABDUL AZIZ: "I went to Naitasiri to serve my girmit. For a month I spent my time crying. Work was hard, but there were only two alternatives: work or a thrashing. My wife was weeding grass but she missed a patch. The sirdar kicked her. I would have killed the man for doing such a thing, but we were in a hopeless and helpless state. We became fed up with one sirdar and chopped off his hand."

GOVIND SINGH: "On Saturdays after we got paid we would meet the sirdar and would greet him and he would reciprocate. Then we had to slip a shilling quietly into his pocket. If we did not then on Monday he made certain that we got work that did not allow us to earn a day's wage. Just imagine, 300 people on that particular estate and almost all of them paid the sirdar a shilling.

Some of the Europeans were bad, but it was the sirdars who spoiled them. There was a chap called Badri who apparently could not work, both the sirdar and the overseer took him and pushed him into the swamp to drown him. But we managed to rescue him. After that, he was not given very heavy work.

There was a case where the sirdar took a man's wife and sold her for ten pounds, there was a court case over the whole thing. The sirdars became rich and were able to buy good land. They lent money and claimed it when the man could not pay, so they could take over his land and evict him."

LOTAN: "When we first saw Fijians we were scared. We were worried that we might become like them once we saw their hair. When we first came to Fiji all the Fijians wore banana leaves as skirts. They used to keep their money in their mouth and take it out to give to the shopkeeper.

There were many hangings and killings over women. Sometimes a woman had liaisons with two or three men and this was a source of conflict. I was strong then, and nobody bothered my wife.

Hindus and Muslims were all friends, they lived like brothers on the same estate. Those who knew how to say their *namaj* used to say it in the field when the time came. Indenture was harsh, but Hindus and Muslims retained their religion, without it they would not have survived or retained their identity. It was their religion which enabled them to survive."

MAHABIR: "In the estate where I worked the European overseer was very good. He looked after us well and helped those who had wife and children.

There was no conflict with Fijians, if you gave them something they reciprocated. Some Indians used to run away from work and go to the village. They were given shelter there and food."

LAKHPAT: "I came from Kanpur, Madhya Pradesh, but when I was 15, my father sent me to United Provinces to get married. I met a Brahmin who said that he would be able to take me back to my village, so I joined him. In Patna, the Brahmin took me to a big house and asked me to wait until he returned. But he did not come back.

I was told I was in a recruiting depot from where people were sent to work.

The inspector looked at my hand and said I must be the son of a Brahmin. He asked me to stand aside. I began to cry. He then said that they were not recruiting Brahmins, but I replied that in any case I had already lost my caste by eating with everybody and that if I returned home, I would be thrown out. He put me back in the line.

When we arrived in Fiji, we were all herded into a punt like pigs and taken to Nukulau. We were given rice that was full of worms. We were kept and fed like animals.

In the evenings after people had washed, men who could not read or write would come with a slate, asking to be taught. We were keen because we wanted to learn to read our religious books like the *Ramayana*.

Those of us who were single were told by the overseer to take a wife from our own ship so that the two indentures expired at the same time. When we were given that advice, this Muslim friend of mine and I ran off into the bush, hoping that while we were away the three women would find somebody else. We were right, by the time we returned from the bush, they had found somebody else.

I was eventually made the sirdar in charge of women. I did not want this, the women had a tendency to hit the sirdars."

BUHAWAN: "There was a physically weak man working with me. One day we found him hanging from a tree. Apparently he did not like Fiji."

PHALAD: "There was a white man who told an Indian woman that he wanted her. She asked him to wait until the next day. This woman with two other women devised a plan. When he came back, two of the women remained at a distance, and she asked him to take off his trousers. When he lifted his shirt to take it off, all three women jumped on him and beat him and threw him into a drain. There were no consequences for the women."

HUSSEIN: "At the end of a week I received only 3 pennies in wages. When I enquired about this paltry sum I was told that that was all that remained of my share after the overseer, sirdar and water-carrier had been paid.

That evening, my ship-mates and I got hold of the sirdar and gave him a thrashing. But someone reported to the overseer what was happening, and the European loaded a gun and came down. The woman of the lines, whom I called mother or sister and who treated me well, took up their hoes. The European retreated and moving backwards, landed in a sewer pit.

The women then threw the *tatti* (excrement) on him."

JAGAN: "In the depot we ate, sang and enjoyed ourselves. On board the ship, the food was satisfactory. I had no thoughts of home, my girmit was pleasant.

Each man was for himself, each kept his sorrow to himself.

There were many who committed suicide, their girmit was full of anguish."

GAFUR: "I came after being told I could continue my work as a teacher. When I arrived, I was told to cut cane. My days passed with hardship, only God knows how terrible the sirdars were.

There were times when our work became so tough that we thought death would be easier, but there was the divine injunction against suicide. It was religion that saved us from taking our own life."

Brewer & Joske's sugar mill, in the heart of what is now Suva.

33   A SWAMP BECOMES THE CAPITAL

"Suva at present consists of three or four houses, a small disused church, a large disused sugar mill, and this disused and deserted hotel . . ."

That was one description of the area which had just been chosen to be the Colony's new capital.

It wasn't any less kind than others, including an 1880 Fiji Times article which questioned the suitability of a site "almost one-eighth of which is represented by fetid and pestiferous mangrove swamps".

The town plan, according to the newspaper, resembled "a spider's web after a strong gale". Its narrow lanes and alleys "by courtesy called streets", wound tortuously through a "rookery specially designed to retain the malarious swamp airs".

Suva's citizens, it concluded, were unlikely to escape pestilence or epidemic diseases.

The few people who had tried to grow sugarcane in the area had failed. There was too much rain and too little soil over the soapstone. Brewer and

Joske's mill closed down in 1875, and with it went the hopes of those planters who had the misfortune to settle there.

The Governor's own niece claimed Suva could be a capital, perhaps — a capital for paupers!

As for Levuka's merchants, they just went on with their business, unconcerned. If government wanted to shift its offices to a swamp, then let it. But the commercial centre of Fiji, the heart of the colony would always be Levuka.

They were wrong, of course.

* * *

Levuka was already tickling the sides of the cliffs, hard up against the mountain side with nowhere to go.

A capital would have to be big enough to be the ultimate Fiji city, with a good harbour as well.

Nadi was considered. So was Galoa in Kadavu, which had been a stopover for the San Francisco-Sydney mail steamers even before they ventured into Levuka.

Rather than rely on local knowledge, the British did their usual thing and sent over an expert to pick the spot, and Colonel Smythe picked Suva.

He described its beautiful harbour and surrounding hillsides as a perfect location, one of the prettiest localities in all Fiji.

Somehow, the good Colonel had managed to visit the site on a sunny day.

But the real clincher came when two very smart Melbourne merchants made a little gift to government. They owned a large tract of Suva land which was, after the collapse of both the Polynesia Company and sugar efforts, next to worthless.

They offered half of it to government free — every second lot — plus a site for government offices . . . providing Suva became the capital.

Samuel Renwick and William Thomson knew that if their offer was accepted, the remaining half of their land would skyrocket in value.

The offer was accepted. By 1877, the Home Office and the Queen had given approval for the move. The swamp was to be transformed, and Colonel Pratt of the Royal Engineers was given the primary responsibility for it.

The colonel let his artistry run away with him. Streets which looked fine on paper didn't seem to follow the natural formations of the land. In the years to come, the planning would be termed a disaster. In fact, the work was hardly underway before the attack began. But no one seemed to suggest any alternatives.

Victoria Parade and Thomson Streets began to take shape, along with the wharf. Indian labourers who had arrived a few months earlier on the Leonidas, and numbers of New Hebridean and Solomon islanders still under indenture were used to clear the land.

In October, 1880, a small crowd gathered under an ivi tree in what would eventually be the centre of town to witness the first public sale of Suva land.

It didn't go very well. Only six or seven lots were sold. Levuka still seemed a better investment.

But two years later, the town was beginning to lose its backblock appearance. Victoria Parade was still described as having "barely room for a handcart, a danger to life and limb", and pedestrians still "floundered through the mud, unable to tell whether they were on the street or off it."

The difference was that government had arrived . . .

Just before midnight on August 30, 1882, the Governor, the Colonial Secretary, and numerous other department heads boarded the Ocean Queen in Levuka for the trip to their new capital.

The paper termed it a "heartless desertion", saying "such a serious defection in the manner of dignity and social consequences may probably have the effect of making Levuka rather dull for some time to come . . ."

The switch was complete.

At first, there were some fairly novel ties with the rest of the colony.

The famous pigeon post was in operation for years between Suva and Levuka, keeping both centres informed of significant events . . . including shipping and race results. One example of the message carried in a tube clipped to the bird's leg: "no appearance of either Melbourne or Sydney steamers. Lord of the Isles arrived on Sunday. In the Sheffield Maiden Handicap, Turner was first . . ."

Remarkably enough, the birds usually got through. One misguided pigeon landed aboard ship near Kadavu, but was despatched again after a rest, and it reached Levuka with its message intact, along with one from the ship's captain.

By the turn of the century, Suva had a weekly overland mail service to the new sugar area — Lautoka. A Fijian runner carrying up to 30lbs of mail in a leather bag would sprint to a point where another runner was waiting to receive it.

Runners ran day and night. The 'post' travelled along at an average 80 miles a day.

Suva's principal recreation was the meeting hall. There was the race-track at Muanikau, or a stroll along the 'Parade' (which ended in a bush track long before it reached the present day Albert Park), but nothing compared with a good, fiery meeting for socializing. One of the most frequent topics of conversation was annexation with New Zealand.

The annexation question never got anywhere, even though New Zealand's Premier said in 1900 that "the colony would be favourably inclined to consider any proposal of federation with Fiji".

Probably there was enough to do by the 1900s to keep people busy, and the annexation issue was allowed to die quietly. Suva was booming. So were its 'suburbs'.

Nausori, by 1902, could be reached by a pontoon ferry which crossed the quarter-mile of river in about 10 minutes, using a cable and winding gear. "Mr Abrahams in his buggy, Mr Gemmel-Smith and sons with horses and mules, and an Indian wayfarer with his packhorse" were the first ones to brave the device.

The trans-Pacific cable, linking America with Australia and New Zealand, reached Fiji the same year.

But that wasn't as exciting as the arrival of the first motor car three years later. Town dignitaries and Fijian royalty went out to the park to be photographed alongside the machine. It belonged to a visitor, but Henry Marks, one of Suva's leading merchants, was so impressed he bought his own, following it up a little later with a De Dion 'char-a-banc' (bus) which could carry 28 passengers between Suva and Rewa "enabling tourists to view the beautiful country in between". The tourism industry had begun.

One visitor commented that "motors are now in great vogue among the natives, who pay quite large sums . . . to charter them for a run from the post office to the cricket ground . . ."

Cumming Street, reclaimed from swamp in the 1900s and once named All Nations' Street, served as market site and the home of numerous curry houses, yaqona saloons and brothels.

Just above it, settlers opted for the best positions on the hill, the most exclusive area in town, Toorak.

There was no longer any question of the winner in the race for status between Suva and Levuka. One after the other, hotels and business houses began shifting to the mainland.

Renwick and Thomson's gambit had paid off. And as far as Colonel Smythe's decision went, he didn't have to put up with the rain . . .

Suva, about 1890.

"There Satan reigns, the sovereign owner," wrote a Catholic bishop in 1893. He was referring to a Wesleyan village.

A Wesleyan minister about the same time accused priests of exhibiting pictures of Methodist missionaries falling head-first into hell, where the devil waited for them — "pitchfork, horns, tail and all".

Fiji's holy war was raging. It was to last for years, a bitter clash between Catholics and Wesleyans. When they weren't fighting each other, they took on government as well.

About the turn of the century, that old time religion got pretty lively. It included the rebirth of a pagan cult promising immortality; a bible-burning incident which sparked protests as far away as Australia and Britain . . . and the tale of an excommunicated priest with a fortune to spend. And how he spent it.

* * *

Bishop's Court in Suva in 1894. Fr. Rougier is top row, centre.

Hostility between the two church groups began almost as soon as there were two teams on the praying field. The Wesleyans had arrived first, and they jealously regarded Fiji as 'their' mission ground.

But both Wesleyans and Roman Catholics resented government, which took away some of the absolute power they had enjoyed before Cession.

The result was a triangle of suspicion.

It was only natural that competition for converts among the missions, along with rival church training and even differing life-styles, would cause some conflicts. But the biggest problem was more basic than that.

The Wesleyans were British, most of them recruited from Australia. The Catholics were French — members of the newly-formed Marist Society which had been sent to convert the Western Pacific.

Even forgetting past political unhappiness, there were recent disturbances to remind them of their mutual distrust. One of them was that French warships had just kicked the British out of Tahiti, missionaries included.

The stage was set for battle.

Sir Arthur Gordon was one of the earlier antagonists. He attacked the Wesleyans for collecting church money in the villages under the threat that those who didn't pay would be taken to court.

Rev. Langham, the Wesleyan District Chairman, struck back by claiming Fijians were "overworked, driven like slaves, harassed and oppressed" because of government's taxation of villages.

When government decided to recognise Fijian marriages prior to 1877 as valid "if they had complied with Fijian custom," the Wesleyans raised hell because the contracts included "some understood to be temporary and a number of polygamous ones."

There were land squabbles, and the missionaries weren't exempt. The French priests, in particular, seemed to have difficulties accepting government rulings, and there were problems in Levuka, Solevu and Kadavu.

The Colonial Secretary advised a local government official in 1890 to "visit Solevu, see the resident Roman Catholic Priest, and explain to him that all the papers and all the signatures quoted by him relative to a donation of land are useless — the natives can neither give, lend, nor lease any land and . . . any attempt to procure the use of land outside of the Crown only creates trouble . . ."

Gordon had been accused of being anti-church. Now it was Thurston's turn. When a new Roman Catholic church opened in Levuka, the priests hoisted the papal flag above the British flag. Thurston politely informed them that the Union Jack must be on top.

The Bishop called the Governor "a Wesleyan proselytizer", along with a few other names.

Thurston warned both missions against recruiting in villages already converted, saying splits in loyalties would be harmful to the village way of life.

But the competition for converts *did* effect villages.

A journal held in the Catholic archives, written by an unknown author, discloses that Catholics in a Taveuni village were ordered by their Roko to help build a Wesleyan church. When a priest told them to ignore the order, half the village was in revolt.

Soon after, the Roko was entertaining a number of Wesleyan teachers, and the priest intervened and told Catholics not to assist in the customary preparation of food for the visitors.

The journal reads: "These things have not tended to increase mutual forebearance and good feeling between the Roko and the priest. Now, the Roko has refused land for the priest to plant, and says they (priest and nuns) can return to their own homes . . ."

For more than a decade, the Colonial Secretary's office was flooded with similar complaints — or with indignant reports of one mission buying allegiance away from the other *Veiqaravi Vakaviti*.

But it wasn't until the last few years of the 19th century that the real mud-slinging began!

The Wesleyans introduced a course in 'Popery'; the Marists taught the dangers of Protestantism.

When the Marist sent hygiene sisters into the villages, the Wesleyans hurriedly organised their wives to go into the same areas, to do the same job.

Those attending Wesleyan district meetings were told about the "persistent machinations of Papal agents in Fiji" and warned of priests entering villages to "revive old quarrels and foment discontent."

In an 1892 article in The Missionary Review, Wesleyan author Josua Chapman wrote: "We passed by the priests' new house in Solevu which has been erected of concrete. We would like to mention the work of the girls in connection with this house, but forbear . . ."

The Catholics claimed libel and sued for 2,000 pounds damages. Chapman won, but the Suva trial lasted a fortnight, and he was reprimanded by the Wesleyans for "placing our mission in fearful danger".

The Fiji Times quoted a priest as saying "Whenever there is an outbreak among the natives, they are sure to be led by a native Wesleyan teacher . .

Wesleyan missionaries think more of getting (coconut) oil and cotton from the natives than anything else . . ."

And so it went. When the Catholics printed that Fiji's Wesleyans were "spoiled cannibals with a little knowledge of hymn singing and much religious hysteria", the Wesleyans responded by saying Fijians had been converted from heathenism "without the aid, and before the advent, of meddling and unscrupulous priests".

The only difference was, the 'war' was spreading, Cardinal Moran, the Archbishop of Sydney, publicly stated that Wesleyan preachers had made their fortunes in Fiji — which of course was at least partly true. The Reverends Binner, Moore and Joseph Waterhouse had all profitted from land dealings, and there was a popular saying going around that the missionaries "came to do good and did well".

The Marists, on the other hand, were attacked for "monumentalism" — building churches far more grand than they needed to be, at the expense of the people.

There were reports of school children bruised and cut from hauling coral rock used in building the Rewa mission station, and at Tunuloa on Vanua Levu, the government sent officials to enquire into the neglect of food gardens during the construction of a Catholic edifice.

Much of the rivalry stemmed from differing life-styles.

Catholics, according to Basil Thomson, tried to make the lives of Fijians as joyous as possible.

The Wesleyans were puritanical. They prohibited smoking, drinking, and even tried to put a ban on the Fijian's most treasured and sacred ritual, the *yaqona* ceremony. Worrall in 1896 said chiefs were "dedicated to lust and avarice". Langham said mekes were often 'shamelessly indecent'.

One of the possible results of this squabbling was that villagers didn't know what or who to believe. Some gave up trying altogether . . . and the Tuka cult was reborn!

The Tukas had made their appearance before, but in 1892, a Fijian *bete* named Navosavakadua told followers in Colo East that the serpent god, Degei, would rid the country of Government and missionaries.

He raised an army of soldiers (with women attendants) to guard the cult, and promised them immortality. Neither the army nor immortality saved him from gaol, and the movement died out.

But if the Tuka cult created a little stir, the great bible-burning incident of 1903 created a much bigger one.

Namosi was a Wesleyan village in 1903, or at least it was until someone forgot to advise its chief of the annual Wesleyan district conference. Hurt by what he considered an insult, he decided to become a Roman Catholic.

So did 800 people in Namosi, whom he ordered to follow him.

To prove their new faith, they were told to give up their Wesleyan bibles and hymnals, and these were taken to Naililili, the Roman Catholic mission station on the Rewa.

Some, if not all, were burned.

For the next month, there were cries of outrage. The Wesleyans charged that the "public burning of 238 Wesleyan bibles had been a studied insult and outrage to the entire community."

Every issue of the Fiji Times had letters to the editor. Australia, New Zealand and British newspapers carried the stories, as well.

One witness, the wife of magistrate Samson Dobui, said that Fijian girls carried out the burning at the direction of two European sisters.

Another, a Mr Burns, wrote the Fiji Times: "Our grief at Rewa Mission on learning of the bible burning was great . . . almost as great as our amusement at the Rev Fr. Rougier's denial of the incident."

He went on to describe the two cases of hymn books and bibles, "most with their covers off and some bearing the stamp of Langham's recent 1901 translation," which were burned in the lime kiln at Naililili.

Father Rougier, the priest in charge at Naililili, said the whole incident was "twisted". The public is being led to believe, he said, "that a cartload of Wesleyan bibles were publicly cremated at Naililili . . . heralded by trumpet and drums and the Naililili Band, and the exulting shouts of applauding onlookers . . ."

He said that two Catholic sisters, aided by a few pupils, burned "one biscuit tin full of torn and useless Catholic books and church materials, and one kerosene case filled with soiled and useless Wesleyan testaments ."

It was not a public event, and he pointed out that it was church policy that sacred books of any nature which were not of any use were to be burned "to prevent them being put to viler uses."

The Wesleyans said they should have been returned, because they were useful to *them*. The papers had a field day; there were calls for public protests, letters to the Governor, and eventually a Mission Board Commission of Enquiry.

At the end of it all, people realised it had been blown out of all proportion. It was soon forgotten. In fact, it seemed to be the pressure valve that both sides had needed.

The holy war was over.

Surprisingly, Fiji benefitted from it all. The competition between missions resulted in a race to provide better schools and medical services, to do more for the people than the opposition.

So when, in 1899, Wesleyans heard about the "serious danger of the Roman Catholics getting our children into their schools on the plea of teaching them English" — they did something about it. They put more emphasis on teaching young Fijians English.

And when the Wesleyans seemed to be making inroads with the Indians, Bishop Vidal sent two Catholic missionaries to India in 1895 to learn Hindustani. The Marists opened their first Indian school two years later.

The missionaries were pioneers of rural development, in medicine, schools, and personal freedom . . . on BOTH sides.

And the priest with a fortune to spend? It was the man from Naililili . . . Father Petrico Emmanuel Rougier.

But the story of the fortune actually begins with another Frenchman, an aristocrat named M. Cecil, who drifted into Fiji in a whaleboat, nearly dead from exposure. It was 1904.

He had escaped from the penal settlement at New Caledonia where he had been sent 20 years earlier, a prisoner-resident forbidden to leave the colony.

In Fiji, he was sent to a fellow-countryman who could help. Father Rougier.

They became close friends immediately. When M. Cecil fell in love with a Fijian girl named Katarina Biaukula, the priest married them, despite a protest from the Bishop.

And when Cecil asked the priest to inquire about his estate in France, the aristocrat found he had inherited a small fortune . . . which he didn't want. All Cecil wanted was to be left in peace and quiet with Katarina, and he asked Fr Roguier to do what he liked with the money, as long as he and Katarina were provided for.

The next few years involved some complicated legal and business arrangements — loans, disputes, an over-spending lawyer and a little-publicised auction — but the result of it all was that the priest became owner of Fanning and Washington islands. Later, he bought Christmas Island. The three atolls would become money makers in the copra boom which followed.

Father Rougier was a Marist and had taken a vow of poverty. It was not the first time the priest had raised the Bishop's eyebrows, and this time he had gone too far.

Bishop Vidal told him to give up his money — or his mission.

Fr Roguier left Naililili, never to return. At first, he went to France, and on Cecil's request, took Katarina with him. She returned to Rewa to look after her husband, but Rougier stopped at Tahiti and set up a company to manage his copra plantations.

'Abbe', his long red beard a trademark, became one of the area's most colourful characters. He was known as the 'King of Christmas Island' and he bought a three-masted schooner, Marechal Foch, to visit his kingdom.

He was never defrocked, although he was deprived of his mission. He had broken the vow of poverty, but he had been one of Fiji's most energetic and effective priests. Prior to his departure, he had organised a district health service, written a Fijian-English dictionary and a book on traditional Fijian herbal medicine.

And he never forgot his promise to Cecil. Long after Cecil died. Fr Rougier was still looking after Katarina.

In his last letter to her, he wrote: ". . . don't spend the money (which he was sending to her) unwisely . . . listen to what the priest says to you . . ."

"I am dying," he told her. "Pray for me."

Father Rougier: told to give up his money or his mission.

35 HOPE BEGAN WHERE THE 'COOLIE LINE' ENDED

A small settlement of Indians completely isolated and independent, far in the interior of the island, had an air of quiet peace and happiness about the village which touched us very deeply, after what we had seen for so long in the coolie lines . . .

"Nature has wonderful healing powers, the powers of recuperation very soon began to have their effect . . . a new life of hopefulness began to spring up in the Indian settlements far away from anywhere . . ." — Rev. C.F. Andrews, 1916.

* * *

For most of Fiji's Indian indentured labourers, the time of 'girmit' was a very unhappy experience.

The only good thing about it was that it ended. Five years was not forever, and when it was over, they were given a certificate of residence.

The girmits had become *khula*. Free and untied.

They were also a long way from home.

The Muslim 'Tazia'. This one was at Tavua, 1905.

Fiji wasn't home, and very few of the indentured ever intended it to be. The catch was that their servitude was over, but they still had another five years to go to be eligible for a paid ticket back to India.

Very few wanted to pay their own fares back. Even fewer wanted to sign on for a second five-year agreement, despite incentives offered by government and the CSR.

So, without making a conscious effort to stay in Fiji, they began to look for ways of staying alive. The first indentured Indians, those who had come on the Leonidas, were free by 1884. They weren't convinced Fiji was paradise, but as they moved away from the coolie lines, they could at least see the potential.

For anyone who wanted to work, there was work. And because the caste system had broken down, those of low caste might achieve prosperity, something which wouldn't happen in India.

Besides, some had married across caste boundaries, and it would have been difficult to go home. There were fears of what they'd find when they got there. Stories grew of those who returned only to be humiliated as a *tapuha*, one from the islands.

They stayed. Small shops in the most remote and isolated corners appeared. So did market gardens, and in the towns, laundries and tailor shops.

By 1887, half the hawkers licences in Suva had been issued to Indians with boats, who were beginning a regular trade on the Rewa and along the coasts as far as Navua and Ba.

By 1898, a government official travelling through Naitasiri commented: "I was struck by signs of industry of the free Indian settlers. In fact, it is not possible to travel up the river without noticing on either bank evidence of the push and perserverence of the free Indian, with his stores, farms and plantations . . ."

There was a loose pattern of settlement. In India, it was governed by caste and religion, but not here. The free Indians settled wherever they could find land . . . which wasn't always easy.

Permission to lease land had to come from the *mataqali*, and before long, the land-owning groups realised the value of this. Cost of permission rose to include unofficial gifts and presents.

If the buyer didn't have enough money, and he usually didn't, he got stung again by unscrupulous money lenders charging huge rates of interest.

But despite the difficulties — government for several years limited the amount of land an Indian could lease for five acres — the *khula* moved onto the soil.

Thirty years after the first indentures finished, 16,000 acres were leased to Indians. Lautoka's sugar mill was receiving nearly 50,000 tons of cane a year from independent Indian growers, and Indian cattlemen were raising 10,000 head of cattle.

For most, life was improving. There were a few exceptions. One wrote: "I have cane land, bullocks and a house. Yet every night I am awake, listening to see if someone is trying to burn my cane or steal my animals. In the indentured lines, we slept well, we did not worry . . ."

But in fact, even on the plantations, things were getting better.

An inspector of immigrants in Ba said in 1918: "There has been a movement among planters of late to try and settle (their better workers) on their estates by giving them back blocks of rice land and assistance to build houses . . . no rent is charged, but it is stipulated that tenants shall work on the plantation when required at full wages."

At first, CSR refused to hire 'free' Indians, but as much of the labour force disappeared, taking advantage of an offer of land in Navua to grow cane for the Fiji Sugar Company, the CSR changed its mind.

Within a short time, 180 free farmers were settled on CSR land, growing cane for the largest sugar mill in the southern hemisphere.

Government still looked on the *kai Idia* strictly as a labour force, but since sugar was the lifeline of the colony, it began building housing tracts in urban areas to keep the free in Fiji.

By the turn of the century, there were nearly as many free Indians as there were indentured.

During the early years, the free had done what they could to ease the life of those in the coolie lines. But as the numbers of non-identured grew, a strange thing happened. Class-consciousness began to creep in, and the free decided they didn't like girmits. They didn't even want to be treated in the same hospital ward with them.

About the same time, 20 indentured labourers were transferred to a plantation owned by three Indian planters, who apparently treated them with the same disdain as their Australian overseer predecessors.

Relations were getting a little strained. Fijians felt contempt for servile labourers. Europeans still felt "coolies" should keep their proper place, which was in the cane field.

Free Indians with aspirations were resented . . . especially the newcomers who were neither girmit nor khula!

Indian migrants, especially Gujeratis and Punjabis, began coming to Fiji about 1900, paying their own fares.

In 1901, there were about one hundred. In 1907, there were a thousand. The government tried to convince them to become indentured for a refund of passage money.

They didn't, of course.

Instead, they leased land and took jobs as clerks and shop keepers. They brought something which had been lacking: leadership.

The Gujerati and Punjabi migrants set up a chain for others to follow. Those who arrived penniless were given a place to sleep and loaned a few bales of cloth and a few cartons of tinned food to begin a shop.

From the meagre profits, a little of the debt was paid back, a little more cloth purchased. In time, the new arrival was able to do the same for the next link in the chain.

One thing was obvious. Fiji wasn't a replica of India. The Indian community of 1900 was a single community. What customs it preserved were shared as one. It was free of politics. Hindus and Muslims ate together, and why not? They had shared the same de-humanising experiences together.

Occasional conflicts, such as when a Muslim slaughtered a cow in sight of a Hindu, were soon forgotten.

The newcomers who were arriving would try to revive the old India ways, but it wouldn't work.

So when there was a wedding, everyone came. It might even be a Hindi-Muslim marriage . . .

They watched as a Hindu priest tied the end of the bride's sari to the end of the groom's sash. Circling an altar a number of times, the two finally were seated — with the bride changing sides to sit at the 'weaker' side. A sacred thread called a *tali* was tied around her neck.

If they were northern Indians, they circled the altar seven times, and the bride and groom disappeared under a sheet while the part in her hair was dyed red.

Civil marriage followed, since government didn't recognise traditional Indian marriages until 1918.

In other public ceremonies, neighbours gathered to watch a calf named for a Hindu child being decked with flowers and led to a temple for perpetual protection. Or a Hindu youth during a ritual "re-birth" which supposedly separated him from lower castes at puberty. The ceremony had little more than prestige significance.

Sacred readings were popular. Under a shady tree or in the back room of some small shop, the Hindus held a *katha*, the Muslims a *kitab*. Both sects listened in to the other.

In the privacy of their homes, personal rituals continued to be observed, despite years of lapse in the lines. Hindus, who worship literally countless gods and goddesses, might honour Surya, the sun, or remember Mariam-ma, the goddess of smallpox.

This was a time to ask for favours — for children, good crops, better health.

But the biggest festivals were the best evidence of community sharing. In some cases, even Fijians took part.

The Muslims celebrated Moharram (or Tazia) by creating a paper and bamboo mausoleum dedicated to two Muslim martyrs, and parading the giant creation through the streets. It was ceremonially dropped into a river or pond.

During the full moon in March, Hindus gathered by the hundreds around the Holi festival bonfire. They sang epic songs called *chautal* which might retell a legend of Krishna's love tryst with a herdswoman, or relate current events in India. Red dye was tossed over everyone in sight.

The Ramlila festival was one of the most popular. By 1902, every market town had its own Ramlila festival and it lasted for days. On the final day, a mock battle portrayed the triumph of Rama and Hanuman over the demon king Ravan, and a straw effigy of Ravan was burned.

Fijians in at least one instance were given the part of Ravana's soldiers in battle, which was fun, even if it wasn't very complimentary.

Fijians and Indians didn't intermingle much — it was even frowned on by government — but slowly, each become more aware of the other's customs.

At Vunioki, an Indian farmer watched as Fijians came to show reverence to a grave on land he had leased. He felt there was a 'vu' on the land, and he decided to worship the grave as well.

After a few years, he stopped. But when his bullock died, he lost money, and his crop went bad; he said he resumed his ceremony with the Fijians at the grave site.

The Indian's community spirit was reviving. Away from the lines, there was a rebirth of personality and family.

Rev C.F. Andrews, an Anglican "freedom fighter" who would help end the indenture system, made a study of Fiji's Indians in the labour lines and out of them. "On their own land," he wrote, "the Indians recovered a healthier and cleaner moral life . . . the impression of servitude and moral degredation was lost."

But he could find nothing good to be said about the state of Indian education.

"The policy of the Government of Fiji with regard to Indian education has been, up till quite recently, one of almost neglect . . ."

He noted that there was the strongest opposition from the sugar companies to Indians being educated at all, since "it was said that such education would tend to take the Indian coolie away from the soil and thus make him spoiled for labour purposes."

As late as 1909, an Education Commission heard a report that education for Indians "should not be considered one moment by the government, for to educate an Indian is to create inducement for crime".

And the manager of the Vancouver-Fiji Sugar Company (the sugar companies were listened to by government) argued that "we most emphatically do not require an Indian community of highly educated labourers . . ."

Indians were here to work. That included children of 10 until 1892, children of 12 until 1908. There were no provisions made for educating the "coolie" children.

Late in the 1890s, a woman named Hannah Dudley came along, and set up the first mission school for Indian children. Classes were taught in Urdu and English on Miss Dudley's small verandah in Suva. The same year, other missions followed.

There had been numerous attempts by the Indian community to start their own schools, but they usually failed because of lack of money or suitable teachers.

"It is indeed pathetic," Andrews stated, "to see the attempt made by the Indians to supply the education needs which ought to be supplied by government." He listed a school being held in a Nadi stable, a few boys being taught the *Quran* in Ba, a school-house in Ba empty for want of a teacher, and numerous others.

In Suva, rates were actually being collected from Indian ratepayers for public schools which their children were forbidden to attend.

The Arya Samajis were the first to ease the situation. They set up centres in Suva, Labasa and Lautoka during the first years of the 1900s. They taught self-respect for Indians "demoralised by girmit" and advocated women's education and an end to the caste-system, child-marriages, and other social evils.

They began the first schools organisd by Indians which were to be successful.

In the years to come, there would be changes in the "single community" that made up the Indian settlements. There would be protests, politics, and splits. Men like D.M. Manilal and Totaram Sandhya would bring an end to the indentured system altogether.

But the 'free' were free. Andrews put his finger on it when he wrote in his report on the indentured: "For countless generations in India, the villager has lived close to the soil and he has gained certain moral qualities thereby. He has lost these, for the moment, by the un-natural life in the coolie lines. But he has not lost them altogether. They are far too deep-seated for that . . .

"And when they are recovered, we could hardly imagine any country in the world which could give them more scope than Fiji . . ."

Ratu Apolosi Nawai.

36   APOLOSI'S MANA WAS LOST IN EXILE

He was a self-styled saviour of the Fijians, a prophet who claimed supernatural powers, a heretic who said he had found the "mana" lost at Vuda by Lutunasobasoba.

He was a cultist and Degei worshipper; an anti-everybody-but-Fijian militant who promised an end to taxation and the return of all land to the Fijians.

He was the founder of the "Viti Kabani" — an all-Fijian co-operative which he hoped would one day monopolize all commerce until the only store in Suva would be the company's; all others would be closed.

He was Ratu Apolosi R. Nawai, and he was to spend most of his life in exile and in prison.

* * *

Ratu Apolosi came from Narewa Village, Nadi, a commoner who later would claim not only to be a chief, but *the* chief of all Fiji.

He was educated at Navuloa and Davuilevu, possibly the religious background which gave him the ideas for his own "messianic arrival".

By 1915, there were very few people in Fiji who hadn't heard of him. Or the company.

The Fiji Company was going to unite the Fijians through commerce. Thousands of shareholders would control growing and selling of all native produce. They would boycott European planters and convince the villagers to sell only to the company. It would be a "taukei" takeover.

Their timing was right. The Government just before World War II had relaxed its ruling on the sale of Fijian land, and there was a rush of overseas land speculation, much to the unhappiness of a number of Fijians.

Apolosi found an immediate following.

He or his agents methodically went from village to village, province to province, collecting share subscriptions. Specially-appointed *ovisas* (officers) with red arm bands threatened enemies of the company with fines and imprisonment if they sold to anyone else.

In their initial enthusiasm, villagers even gave their produce free.

It was the beginning of a huge nationalistic movement, and it was having monumental effects on Fiji — fast.

The Fiji Times in March, 1915, noted: "The Viti Company's influence seems to have made the Fijians consider that their time is a very valuable asset . . . it is nothing unusual for natives to demand 5 shillings for a day's work . . ."

A missionary on the Bau Circuit commented: "During a trip inland in July, I noticed a great change in the character of the natives. They are consumed with the desire to make money, especially by supporting the Viti Company. On every little stream in that magnificent interior the Fijians are growing bananas."

The Reverend didn't know it then, but the Viti Company would have complete control of the lucrative banana export industry almost before the year was out.

Apolosi held the company's first general meeting at Draubuta Village, Tailevu, in January 1915.

Four thousand people came.

Among them were Government-appointed native officers (*bulis*) who Apolosi had ordered to attend. When the Secretary of Native Affairs, Mr Allardyce, heard of it, he told the *bulis* they couldn't go, and reminded them the only orders they need listen to were his.

They went anyway, and 10 of them got the sack.

The Government tried to counter the meeting by sending out notices to the *Rokos* that the company didn't have Government support. But the notices were ignored. Apolosi followed them up with his own letters saying "Government cannot stop the business or the company".

For Apolosi, the meeting was a colossal success. The people were told that, soon, there would be no more Europeans, taxes, Indian shops, or Government restrictions. A resolution was passed abolishing "cleaning of towns and similar Government work."

The Fijians were jubilant. Government wasn't. Neither were the planters, merchants, churches, or high Fijian chiefs.

Planters and merchants resented this new and formidable competition. The churches were upset because large numbers of Fijians who had made regular contributions to the mission were suddenly putting all their money into the company, instead.

The Council of Chiefs met in 1914 and decided Apolosi was insulting them by usurping their power.

And the Government was watching Apolosi like a hawk. District commissioners were told to report any action of Apolosi's which might be considered dangerous to the peace and good order of the colony. The reports began rolling in: threats to growers who were anti-company, along with Apolosi's continued directives to ignore Government.

In each instance, the Governor sought legal advise and was told not to take action. The time wasn't ripe and, considering his large following, a false step would be disastrous.

Then, a few Suva businessman decided to fight fire with fire. Viti Company wasn't legally registered. So they stole the name and incorporated a company with a similar objective: to buy and sell native produce with a fair return to the natives and a "reasonable profit" to shareholders.

There was confusion. Villagers had purchased shares, but in whose company? Apolosi continued on as if the legally, registered company in Suva was his own, despite the company's frequent announcements that he had nothing to do with it.

The showdown came in March, 1915.

Seven Europeans who were directors of Viti Company Ltd scheduled a meeting in Suva's Town Hall. Apolosi immediately announced his meeting would follow.

The first meeting was no sooner underway, than angry Fijians shouted the Europeans down, forcing it to be cancelled.

Then Apolosi arrived, decked out in a silk suit, stepping out of a shiny black car.

A Fiji Times report said the hall was packed, every space crammed with Fijians who had been arriving for days. There was "a fair sprinkling of whites and the police force was well represented".

Apolosi mounted the stage.

"I have no class" he admitted. "I am a *kaisi* (commoner). For a long time I have been blind, I did not see until a few years ago . . . that the *taukeis* were not getting a fair deal and that a company of this kind would be a way to uplift them.

"Who called the meeting and assembled thousands of people at Draubuta?" he asked. "I sent men as agents to all parts of the group on hired cutters . . . what have I got out of it? There are seven European directors here . . . but no taukeis. Why? Ask your directors . . ."

"Why did you break up today's meeting?" he went on. "I have taught you all these months to support the company, to support the taukei venture and today you break up a meeting called solely for your benefit. Why?"

At this point, a man rose from the crowd and said "because we did not like the laws laid down".

Apolosi: "If you do not like the laws laid down, whose do you want?"

The answer came from hundreds of mouths simultaneously: "Yours!" Within minutes. Apolosi had a unanimous show of support. The taukeis decided to withdraw their shares, unless the company's management was changed.

Apolosi had won. Viti Company's directors found it next to impossible to continue business, and they sold out — to Apolosi.

The victory was short-lived, because two months later, the Government decided the time had come to act. A warrant for Apolosi's arrest, for embezzlement of funds, was issued in May, 1915, while he was visiting the Yasawas. A police constable went over to get him.

The constable returned alone, the summons torn in half. The same thing happened to Inspector Scott-Young, who followed with several constables. They found Apolosi on Yaqeta in the Yasawas, "surrounded by some one hundred natives, their faces blackened and all armed with spears, knives and clubs."

As the police stepped ashore, they were told they were likely to be eaten. They turned around and went back to Lautoka.

The Inspector-General of the Armed Constabulary, Col McOwen, who by chance was visiting Lautoka, sailed that same day in the Government boat Ranadi for the Yasawas with a contingent of well-armed police.

On their way, they noticed three cutters anchored near the mouth of the Ba River and decided to investigate. Waiting until dark, they silently boarded the cutters and found Apolosi and his followers — all sound asleep.

There was no resistance. By the time the sleeping men woke, Apolosi and his brother-in-law, Kini Williami, were in irons. Forty-two were arrested.

Apolosi was gaoled for 18 months. *Ovisas* kept the company going.

A month after his release, he called the biggest meeting yet: the Bose ko Viti, the Council of Fiji.

It was December, 1916, and 5000 people journeyed up the Wainibuka River in a nearly-endless parade of boats.

Apolosi was treated not as a chief, but a king.

From a carved wooden throne surrounded by body guards, he told them that "any who have not yet joined the company may join by paying one pound. Enemies of the company may join by paying 200 pounds.

The Viti Company was to take over Fiji. It would mint its own money, run its own towns and schools, manage its own ships, industries and wharfs. It would have its own police and magistrates, along with its own tax system. It already had its own flag — a sun, moon and star — which Apolosi said would be the new flag of the Fijian race.

It was all too much for the Government.

He was arrested and, in 1917, exiled to Rotuma for seven years.

Viti Company collapsed, despite his efforts to keep it alive with directives mailed from the island.

According to all reports, the seven years were spent quietly. His wife was with him. There were few disturbances, although he stormed out of a church, never to return, after being reprimanded for sitting in the front row, the area reserved for "nobility."

But on his release from exile in December, 1924, it was a new man that emerged.

He had always been a hypnotic orator. This was now coupled with prophesies and mystic revelations and the announcement of a new church, *Na Lotu ni Gauna* — the Church of the Era.

He supposedly talked with the old gods of Fiji, with Degei and the twins Nacirikaumoli and Nakausabaria. His sacred powers, he said, came from the sacred box lost from Lutunasobasoba's canoe at Vuda, which he had retrieved.

He had the "mana", and his flock began to return. Just to clinch the matter, he would hold up a document which he said was the "Crown Grant" signed by Queen Victoria, giving him supreme power in Fiji.

The next five years were spent sermonising. It did not seem to matter to his congregation that the Governor, Sir Harry Luke, had accused him of "intrigue, sedition, lechery and debauchery on an heroic scale, ranging from drunken orgies to rape and incest". Or that his "abnormally developed sexual appetites" including harems, more than a dozen wives, and a daughter supposedly bearing his child.

What mattered to his devout followers were the tales of miracles he had performed, the prophesies which came true.

In one of these, he touched the earth near Nadi and said people from the four corners of the world would come here. He was standing where Nadi International Airport is now.

His sermons began to carry other predictions, too; predictions again harmful to Government.

He was sent back to Rotuma, this time for 10 years.

It was the end. He was no sooner released in March, 1940 (at the age of 62), then World War II broke out and he was hustled back to Rotuma as a security threat.

There were rumours that the Japanese would attempt to free him, so he was secretly shipped to New Zealand for the duration of the war.

Apolosi Nawai was exiled in Yacata Island, Cakaudrove, and finally Yanuca, where he died at the age of 68.

In one of his final sermons, he was said to have claimed to be The *Tui kei Vuravura*. The King of the World

Ratu Joseva Lalabalavu Vanaaliali Sukuna (left) and Ratu Josefa Cakobau in Vancouver, on their way to Europe.

37   THE LEGION HAD A RATU IN THE RANKS

"Those of us who were soldiers knew the severity of the fighting there . . .

". . . during the second grand attack in the Champagne, the First Battalion of the French Foreign Legion was before Fort Navarin.

"The French troops had made three attempts on this strong point, but three times had been repulsed. Finally, volunteers were called for a final attempt. The First Company of the First Battalion of the Foreign Legion volunteered and led the attack on September 26, 1915.

"A young chief of Fiji was a member of that company, and he was wounded as the attack reached the enemy's third line.

"The First Battalion returned — that is, 35 men out of 2,500 returned."

* * *

World War I broke out in 1914 and Fiji mobilized its defences, or at least what there were of them. The Fiji Constabulary was the strongest faction, but there were about a dozen rifle clubs with fanciful names (the Rewa Mounted Rifles, the Legion of Frontiersmen) whose members had sworn to "resist His Majesty's enemies."

The rifle clubs, along with members of the Medical Department, carried out tactical operations and manoeuvres on the Suva waterfront and at the wireless station at Vatuwaqa with as many as 150 men taking part.

There were difficulties in organising a proper Fiji Defence Force, because government at first restricted it to persons of European descent, and the Europeans weren't interested in home defence. They wanted action overseas.

Rather than stay home, 700 Europeans left for active service with the British, Australian and New Zealand forces.

Government countered the exodus with a decision to send its own force to the war, and on January 1, 1915, the 1st Fiji Contingent — 60 Europeans, although by now the Defence Force included a Fijian platoon — sailed for Europe aboard the RMS Makura.

All but six of them were assigned to the King's Royal Rifle Corps.

During the next three years, more volunteers from Fiji joined the Rifles until Fiji had a permanent bond with the Corps. But they suffered horrendous losses: the battlefields in France and in Belgium claimed 131 Fiji-Europeans.

It wasn't that Fijians weren't eager to serve. They were. The British War Office instructed the Fiji Government not to let them.

So there were less than a handful of Fijians in active service. One was Ratu Vuiyasawa, the son of Ratu Jone Madraiwiwi, who first joined a Maori division in New Zealand and served two years in France, then served until armistice with the Royal Field Artillery in Palestine. At war's end, three-fourths of his battalion were dead or wounded.

Another was Ratu Sukuna.

The young chief was studying at the University of Oxford when war was announced. He tried to join the British army, but was refused.

Determined to fight, he crossed over to France and in January, 1915, joined the First Battalion of the French Foreign Legion.

He was to prove just how adept the Fijians were at soldiering . . .

According to the records of the French Ministry of Defence, Ratu Sukuna, on May 9, 1915, "charged a very strongly entrenched German position with fixed bayonet, without being led by an officer, in spite of stubborn resistance by the enemy and in the face of machinegun fire".

On September 20, at Navarin, "with an admirable spirit of sacrifice, charged a position which had to be taken at any cost. In spite of heavy fire from the enemy trenches he was able to break through right to the German trenches."

And on September 25, he "launched an assault on the enemy trenches north of Souain with superb zeal and courage, taking many prisoners and seizing several machineguns."

The next day, on the 26th, the Legion once again attacked Fort Navarin.

The Fijian Legionaire was hit in three places and evacuated to a hospital behind the lines.

Ratu Sukuna sent a postcard to his friend, ex-Fiji governor Sir Everard imThurn, who was by this time back in London.

"Please do not mention my wounds to my people," he wrote. "The three are all superficial of which two are very slight, the third is by an explosive ball and will take longer to heal. I am very comfortable here (the hospital at Pre au clercs, Lyon) and the rest is an agreeable change after the strain of the last few days. It was a stirring time and the division was heavily engaged. Yours sincerely, J.L.V. Sukuna.

"P.S. — Would you send me a pipe and a razor strap?"

When Ratu Sukuna spoke of 'a stirring time,' it was with an understatement which was to become one of his trademarks.

Thirty five men out of 2500 returned from the First Battalion's assault on Navarin!

Released from the hospital in January, 1916, it is likely that he would have gone back to the front. He probably wanted to.

Instead, he was discharged by special ministerial decision in France "at the request of the Fijian authorities through the Colonial Office."

Ratu Sukuna reached Suva on March 30, 1916, aboard the RMS Niagara. A huge crowd was on the wharf to greet him. So were the defence forces, cadets, and two brass bands.

"Cheer after cheer rang through the air," the Fiji Times reported, "as Sukuna stepped down from the ship on to the wharf and attempted to make his way to the motor cars. But the natives would have none of this modesty.

"Shoulder-high they reared their gallant brother and with an enthusiasm that broke all records, carried their hero to the cars . . ."

France had awarded him the Medaille Militaire — a medal given solely for gallantry in the face of the enemy and one of the highest honours which France can give to a soldier.

There were problems with the medal, of course — 15 years after the French decision to award it, the high chief still couldn't wear it.

It wasn't until 1931, after a barrage of letters between the French Consul in Suva, Major C.B. Joske; the Governor and the Colonial Secretary that the British Secretary of State for the Colonies decided "this should be treated as a special case and that permission be given to Ratu Sukuna to wear the decoration."

The Governor pinned it on his chest, saying that Ratu Sukuna's military record was an example not only for the Fijians, but for the Colony.

It didn't do much good for Ratu Sukuna to set an example, when Fijians were still barred from serving overseas.

But in 1917, that changed. Henry Marks & Co in March offered the government 10,000 pounds to cover the cost of "raising, equipping and transporting to England or France, 100 Fijians for transport duty at Calais".

The Fiji Labour Detachment was born.

Less than two months later, Marks' Boys, as they were known, were on their way.

Ratu Sukuna, now a sergeant, was with them. So were 15 other paramount chiefs.

Their major function was to load and unload ships supplying the Allied troops. It wasn't particularly noble duty, yet it was recorded that, where-ever Fijians worked, they reduced the manpower needed by 30 percent.

Paramount chiefs and commoners worked together, at Calais, at Marseilles, and then in Italy. King George V inspected the Labour Corps while they were in France. They wore British Army uniforms for the occasion.

Soldiers or dockworkers, what was most important, and The Times (London) mentioned it in June, 1918, was that "Fiji . . . did a great deal more than those who knew the islands best thought possible. It had not occurred to anyone that the realities of the great issue could have burned so deeply into the hearts of these simple islanders . . . ."

Years later, these 'simple islanders' would prove to the world that they were capable of a far greater war effort than unloading ships.

But World War I hadn't really come close to Fiji.

Except for a rise in food prices caused by some restrictions and rationing, and a little hysteria over people with German names, the war wasn't being fought in the islands.

Or so people thought, until the stories of a German sea-raider in the Pacific began to reach their ears . . .

When a New York newspaper reported that the German raider "Seeadler" had been sunk in the Atlantic by the British, there was a sigh of relief from ship-owners around the world.

Seeadler was the scourge of the seaways, and it had been plaguing allied merchant ships for far too long.

On October 1, 1917, the Fiji Times picked up the story, along with a number of other Reuter telegrams about the war.

The only thing was, Seeadler wasn't lying on the ocean bottom in the Atlantic. She had been on a "sporting mission" in the Pacific — and her captain, along with five of the crew, was already in Suva Gaol, captured by six unarmed men of a "knee-pants army."

* * *

Officers and crew of the 'Seeadler' soon after the fake Norwegian ship ran the blockade.

Seeadler ran the British blockade of the North Sea in December, 1916.

She was disguised as a Norwegian ship, a disguise so carefully worked out that the British found nothing wrong even after they boarded her at sea.

She was under the command of Count Felix von Luckner, and the Count had obviously taken pride in his work. He was so thorough in his task of duplicating an existing Norwegian vessel that he took a job as a dock-worker in Norway until his "study" was complete.

Slowly, Seeadler began to take shape. In reality, she was an American cotton ship which had fallen prize to the Germans, but when von Luckner was finished, she was as Norwegian as any ship in Oslo.

The Norwegian-speaking crew, all hand-picked from the German navy, chewed Norwegian tobacco. The pictures of their sweethearts bore the stamp of Norwegian photographers on the back. Von Luckner even had "Knudsen," a typical Norwegian name, embroidered on his underwear!

Seeadler, or Sea Eagle as it meant in German, passed the blockade with flying colours. The inspecting British officers went on their way, without noticing the one thing that would have given this sailing ship away: two propellers just below the waterline, the shafts connected to two huge diesel engines deep down in her hold.

A few more days out to sea, and the "Norwegian" crew donned the uniforms of the German navy and unpacked her guns. The raider was in business.

Ship after ship was intercepted by this "friendly" vessel, only to sudden-ly face an alarming display of cannons as the German flag was run up.

Seeadler sank them all, Antonin, Buenos Aires, Charles Gonoud and many more. Passengers and crew were taken off first, and the "guests" were accommodated in the raider's special cabins.

For the captives, life wasn't unpleasant. After a ship carrying a full cargo of champagne was plundered, prizes of bubbly were given out to the first to spot allied vessels.

Seeadler worked her way around the horn, into the Pacific.

But eventually, the 64-man crew needed land. They had beriberi and scurvy brought on by the lack of fresh fruit and vegetables.

The Count selected Mopelia atoll, a dot in the ocean 225 miles west of Tahiti in the Society Islands, for their hideaway. The ship couldn't squeeze through the narrow passage in the reef, so they tied her offshore, and that would have been fine if it hadn't been for a freak tidal wave.

The wave tossed the raider onto the reef, snapping its masts and filling the hold with water.

Before another week was out, the Germans had saved what they could, built a tent-town on shore, and burned the wreck so it wouldn't be noticed. They were castaways.

At first, everything was fine. The men regained their health and lived well on coconut, fish, crab and wild rootcrops. The Count even held a ceremony and 'officially' named it a German colony.

But after a rest, von Luckner decided it was time to go raiding again. This time, their ship-of-war was an 18ft-long lifeboat, "not in any too good condition" which leaked 40 buckets a day in a calm sea. The tiny boat was christened Cecilie and loaded with fresh water, hardtack, machine guns, rifles, hand grenades . . . and an accordian. Five of the healthiest men were chosen to accompany the Count as crew.

Their plan was to find a ship at anchor, steal it, and return for the rest of the crew at Mopelia.

They sailed that "overloaded cockleshell", as von Luckner called it, to the Cook Islands 800 miles away. But there was no ship to steal.

What's more, the Cook Islanders were suspicious about these gentlemen. They knew about Germans, and they swarmed around the boat in a show of obvious hostility, finally bringing the British resident commissioner down to inspect the craft.

He was quietly told to play along with the game — or face the consequences. According to Lowell Thomas, who wrote the story of Count von Luckner (the Sea Devil) at the end of the war, the inspection went like this:

"The resident raised a tarpaulin, but dropped it quickly. He had seen rifles. He raised another. There were neat rows of hand grenades, as easy to pick up as apples . . .

"Well," I asked, "how do you find everything?"

"Quite all right — quite all right." He smiled a very acid smile, and turned to the crowd on the pier.

"Everything is in order," he called. "These gentlemen are Norwegian sportsmen, as they say."

Since there wasn't a ship in the Cooks, the mini-raider and its crew of six sailed on — to Fiji.

It was a bad journey. Before long, their lips were swollen, their teeth loose and they could hardly stand. But luck was still with them. At Katafaga, in the northern Lau group, they struggled ashore to find a house and garden filled with food — but no owner. In the absence of Mr T. Stockwell, a retired Lomaloma storekeeper, they rested, ate, and revived.

They even left their unseen host a letter which today hangs on the wall of the Ovalau Club in Levuka: "We are very sorry that we have not meet you here. Although we had a good time on your island. I and my mates sleep in your house. We had a good meal, and are now quite fit to proceed on our sporting trip. The wonderful stroll around your island we shall never forget . . . all things we took is paid for — turkey, 10 shillings, bananas, 2 shillings. Me and my men are thankful to you . . ."

They sailed on to Wakaya, and were pleased to see several ships in the bay. The Count and his crewmen were just making plans to seize the best of them, when a handsome three-masted schooner, shiny-new and with auxilliary engines, dropped anchor nearby.

It was provisioned, they soon discovered, with large stores of fruit and vegetables for six months cruising.

Under his breath, Felix von Luckner was already calling her by a new name.

Seeadler II.

To make things even easier, the captain agreed they could take passage on the ship when she left Wakaya, bound for Australia.

She wasn't going to ever reach Australia, of course. A few miles out to sea, the passengers would come out of their cabins in full navy dress, machineguns at the ready.

But then, yet another vessel slid into the bay — an ugly little cattleboat called Amra. And as the Germans watched, she lowered a boat with a half-dozen men in uniform which began heading straight for them.

Von Luckner recorded that the boat had "an officer and four soldiers . . . Indians who wore puttees and those funny little pants".

Except for the officer, they were unarmed.

"We could easily have shot them down, or thrown a hand grenade in their boat," the Count narrated, "then we could have captured the ship and sailed away . . ."

But there was something bothering the German aristocrat. He wasn't in uniform.

"Our uniforms were packed in our bundles, stowed below. We would have to take the ship in the guise, not of naval officers, but of civilians, and that not only went against the grain, but it went against the unwritten laws of the game."

To make war in civilian clothes, he told his men, would see them hung from the yardarm as "international bandits".

In the account by Lowell Thomas, the uniformed officer and his four men came alongside Cecilie (the Germans were on their way to the schooner) and inquired who they were.

The Count introduced himself as the commander of Seeadler.

There was a long pause from the disbelieving officer.

"We have," the Count continued, "hand grenades and firearms enough to send you and your knee-pants army here to Kingdom Come, and if we were in uniform, you would be our prisoners. However, be that as it may, you have caught us in civilian clothes . . ."

In von Luckner's account, his men cut open their bundles, displaying their weaponry while the arresting officer "stared aghast" and the "soldiers developed goose pimples, edging to the rail ready to tumble overboard"

The captain and crew of the schooner were also gaping.

Supposedly, the man who was known throughout Europe as The Sea Devil then ordered his men to throw their weapons over the side, and told the officer "we are at your service".

That is not the story the arresting party told.

Actually, they were members of the Fiji Constabulary, not the army; they had heard a rumour about Germans at Wakaya and had come to investigate.

Inspector Hills of the Fiji Constabulary told a court hearing (to decide on the disposal of the Cecilie) that: "On the 21st September, 1917, I, together with Inspector Howard and other members of the constabulary proceeded in the SS Amra to Wakaya Island . . ."

"On arriving, we sighted a motor launch in which there were six men talking very excitedly in German. I called upon them to surrender.

"The commander, who gave his name as Count von Luckner, said 'We surrender, we are done. I am in command. We are of the German Navy!'"

The launch, Inspector Hills reported, contained "one machinegun with a large quantity of ammunition, hand grenades, revolvers and ammunition".

It also had nearly 500 pounds worth of gold and Bank of England notes in a tin box, a German flag, and "German naval uniforms respective to the rank of the captives".

Whichever account of the capture or surrender is accepted, it is obvious the Count could have made things difficult if he'd chosen to. His men were against the decision to surrender. The men at Mopelia, relying on him for help, certainly would have been. Maybe he was, as he claimed, an officer and a gentleman . . . not a

The prisoners were taken to Levuka first, then Suva, where the Count reported "our arrival was the event of the year, the only warlike happening that had come along to break the monotony of life in the dreary South Seas".

He said that "a company of infantry lined both sides of the approach to the pier with bayonets fixed, and a huge crowd gathered at the pier to look us over."

Actually, war-time censorship prohibited a news release about the capture, and there was no mention of his arrival in Fiji, so it is unlikely he was met at the pier by more than a handful of Defence Corps members.

Long before Fiji's citizens learned of their aristocrat visitor, he and his crew had been sent on to New Zealand.

The story doesn't end there — von Luckner escaped after stealing both a boat and a New Zealand army officer's uniform, was recaptured, and was planning a second escape when the armistice was signed.

Back on Mopelia, the rest of Seeadler's crew lured a French ship through the passage, captured her, and reached Chile and safety.

But the effect of the Count's short stopover in Fiji had other repercussions.

For months, controversy had been raging in Levuka and Suva about Germans living in Fiji. The calls for internment of all Germans, naturalised or not, was ignored by the Government — until the sea raiders reached Wakaya.

After von Luckner's arrival was made public, war hysteria grew. A Fiji Times editorial stated that the Germans had made a moonlight raid on London, and suggested "now is the time for a moonlight raid on the enemies within our gates".

Most of the Germans in Fiji were naturalised British citizens, but it didn't seem to matter: letter after letter in the press demanded their arrest and internment.

In October, they were interned. Most were sent to camps in Australia, and their land was seized and sold at auction.

In Levuka, Karl Kraft, the timber merchant Reichart, the baker; Volk, a retired publican and half-a-dozen more were shipped out of the country.

One of them, Mr Kienzle, even had his name carved off the corner stone of Levuka's Masonic Hall, the stone he had helped lay.

In November, 1918, the war ended, and all of Fiji celebrated.

Townspeople in Suva "filled the streets, there was joy-making with little restraint, and cadets and Fijians paraded to Government House to sing the National Anthem. At Lautoka, the mill closed for the day and "the place was simply turned upside down with excitement, mill whistles blowing, cars hootings, flags flying and men shouting".

A court report of November 7, a few days before the actual signing of the armistice, noted that a Fijian was fined 10 shillings for being under the influence.

He said he knew no one celebrating the victory over Austria, and thought someone ought to start things going . . .

Count Felix and Countess Ingaborg von Luckner.

Overseers and Indian servants.

D.M. Manilal.

39 A STRIKE SPELT THE END TO INDIAN SERFDOM

The bridge at Samabula was guarded by a detachment of soldiers, armed as if they were still in the trenches of France.

The Inspector-General of the Constabulary and about 30 police were also there.

On the Rewa side, two to three hundred Indians gathered. They said they wanted to come to Suva.

They were told they couldn't.

It was Friday the 13th, an "unlucky" day . . .

It was also the worst day, the bloodiest day, and the last day of the 1920 strikes, a day which would change the Colony's outlook toward its Indian community.

* * *

Tension had been building for a long time, but for years it stayed submerged beneath threats of colonial overseers.

The Indians were without leaders or politics, considered even among themselves as mere workers in the fields. Voiceless.

They didn't begin coming of age until about 1910. That year, 200 Suva and Rewa Indians asked for political representation. A year later, they formed the British Indian Association, and the association's first task was to ask Mahatma Gandhi (who was leading the struggle for Indian rights in South Africa) to send a lawyer.

It was D.M. Manilal, or Manilal Doctor as he was originally known, who responded.

Manilal was a Gujerati lawyer from Mauritius and he had made a name for himself by speaking out in India against the indenture system.

He arrived in 1912, was met by hundreds of Indians at Suva's wharf, and immediately commanded a wide following. He wasn't particularly anti-government, at least not until 1916.

But that year, against all the expectations of the Indian community, Badri Maharaj, a pro-government, pro-indenture 'puppet' was named as the sole Indian member in the Legislative Council.

Manilal was told he was ineligible . . . because he came from Baroda and so was not a British subject. Petitions came from all over the Colony asking for him, but they weren't considered.

After that, the Gujerati lawyer's attacks on Indian life in Fiji, the indenture system, and government in general became more intense and bitter, and they began reaching India where Fiji was becoming a dirty word.

Burton's book, The Fiji of Today, had just been published in Hindi and Urdu, describing the hardships of the girmit's life. Totaram Sanadhya, author of My 21-years in Fiji, had returned to India and was campaigning for the end of indenture, too, along with veterans like Rev C.F. Andrews.

Gandhi agreed to use his non-violent resistance movement, so effective in South Africa, to picket labour ships leaving Calcutta or Bombay.

Manilal's letters to India helped sway opinions, and in March 1916, the Viceroy's government in India announced the indenture system would end "as soon as possible".

Fiji's Indians celebrated by burning effigies marked "coolie".

When the British Government in India stubbornly said the system would continue for five more years, Fiji's planters rejoiced — and all India went on a rampage.

Indian women marched on the Viceroy's office; Andrews and Ghandi held meetings which had more support than any other movement in India's history.

The economy of a few tiny sugar-producing islands wasn't worth the price of Britain's self-respect in India. On March 12, 1917, all labour recruiting was stopped "for the duration of the war (World War I) and two years after". It would never re-start.

And with the success of the national movement in India, the threads of Indian equality began to come to life here.

Manilal, the only Indian leader with any power between 1910 and 1920, held meetings in Suva, Navua and Rewa. The British Indian Association was replaced by the Indian Imperial Association, led by Manilal.

It was formed in a Flagstaff cottage in 1918 and within a year, it presented government with a list of requests which included the repeal of the Masters and Servants Ordinance, a minimum wage fixed by law, abolition of the 'hut tax', and various forms of assistance for Indian farmers.

The governor, Sir Cecil Rodwell, ignored the requests.

Hundreds of Indians thronged to Suva town hall in 1919 — the day after Christmas — to hear Manilal tell them they must demand their rights, and that government must realize they were something more than just a labour force.

Indenture officially ended on January 1, 1920.

The Indians were free. Now, they wanted their rights!

Exactly two weeks later, Indian workers in Suva's Public Works Department went on strike. By the end of January, the strike had spread throughout Suva, including council employees, and to the sugar mills in Rewa and Navua.

The Commissioner of Works said the strike was "nothing more or less than a strike against the high prices of Indian foodstuffs".

Which was probably true.

India's rice crop had failed; Australia, which got its rice from India, stopped sending sharps to Fiji; and the rice or sharps which was left doubled in price in a fortnight.

In the five years between 1915 and 1920, war, inflation and other things had sent the Indian's cost-of-living up by 85 per cent. But wages stayed the same.

The strike was orderly at first.

Strike leaders told the gatherings to respect law and order. They moved back and forth along the 12-mile road linking Suva with several thousand striking sugar workers at Nausori, Viria and Vunidawa.

But then on January 27, about a thousand Indians gathered at Naduruloulou on the Rewa to "rescue" three men in court on a charge of intimidation.

They went home when more than 30 special constables and the machine gun section of the Defence Force told them to disperse.

A few days later, a delegation of prominent Indians, headed by Mrs Manilal, went to see the governor. They asked for a minimum wage of 5 shillings a day and a commission to look at food prices.

Rodwell agreed to the commission, but told them they must return to work before a wage increase could be considered. The commission was appointed the next day, and the Chief Justice was to recommend any adjustments to insure the Indians a "reasonable livelihood".

The strikers stayed out; "consideration" of a pay rise wasn't enough.

Rumours of violence began to grow. Some planters evacuated their families to safer areas, notably the west where the Indians on the land seemed content to keep working. In Suva and the Rewa, many Europeans went about armed.

Two Indian leaders criticised the stationing of returned soldiers with machine guns at Rewa and objected to the seizure of sticks from Suva Indians while European volunteers carried guns. They said the move was "designed to increase the panic among the Indian population".

By Wednesday, February 5, the Defence Force had mounted a 24-hour-a-day guard on the pontoon ferry at Nausori to prevent Indians "in large numbers" from crossing.

The same day, the Commission on Wages and the Cost of Living held its first sitting, and the governor ordered all "loyal" Indians to return to work and wait for the results of the commission. They didn't.

The commission met daily and a number of Indians gave evidence which pointed out not only alarming increases in food costs, but obvious cases of profiteering. It wasn't totally sympathetic, and reports in the press noted that some of the witnesses were "wearing 35 shilling boots" and that others were "in the habit of eating a fowl a week," which appeared to be a high standard of living.

But the commission did recommend subsidising the cost of imported rice and a system of intensified planting for Indian foodstuffs, which government approved.

Early in February, the governor hurriedly pushed through "public safety" ordinances prohibiting "certain classes of persons (Indians) from entering certain areas at the discretion of the governor in council". There were also restrictions banning gatherings of more than five (Indians) on the street, or seven in private dwellings.

Still not satisfied, he called for help. Australia promised a cruiser, gunboat and 90 ratings; New Zealand agreed to send 60 soldiers, a Lewis gun section and 200 rifles.

"The inevitable result of a collision between several thousands of Indians," the governor said, "and a (local) force which they believed they could overpower, although in the end the armed force would probably have prevailed, would have been a resort to rifle and machine-gun fire involving serious bloodshed . . ."

Everything was still fairly orderly among the strikers, except that Indian women had organised gangs to intimidate strike-breakers and any men who had not yet joined their ranks.

The newspaper noted that parties of six to eight women "hunted in packs" and used "cruel, filthy and hideous methods" to taunt men into joining the strike. In a society in which the male ruled supreme, it was easier to strike than suffer humiliation.

Women were spurred on by Mrs Manilal, who also advised them to discourage their husbands from going back to work until 5 shillings a day was offered or food prices reduced. In the meantime, she said, the women should give up smoking, picture theatres, and jewellery to minimize expenses.

Sixty soldiers from New Zealand arrived on the 12th and were moved to checkpoints at Suva and Nausori. The governor sent a telegraph to London saying that the disturbance was now racial. Strikers, he said, had pushed economic grievances aside and turned the strike into political agitation.

Friday dawned with an air of apprehension. Soldiers and constabulary manned the checkpoints and the whole Rewa delta was tense.

Three hundred Indians moved resolutely to the bridge at Samabula. They were stopped from crossing to Suva by a Major Knox.

They said they wanted to buy food and that they were cut off from both Suva and Nausori by armed guards. Major Knox said a certain number could pass through and buy food for all, but this was rejected. Told to disperse, they remained where they were and said "go ahead and shoot".

The Inspector-General of the Constabulary, with 30 police, charged with batons. There was a helter-skelter dash for a few hundred yards, but the Indians regrouped on a hill where a reserve of sticks and stones had been hidden.

In the melee that followed, a number of constables and Indians were injured. Three Indians were hit by pistol fire. One of them died.

That was the end of it.

As abruptly as it had begun, the strike ended and the men began returning to work.

There seemed to be no immediate accomplishments — they were returning at the same wage, and the hostilities which had erupted on both sides left both government and the Indians feeling a little less secure.

By far the worst blow for the Indian community was that Manilal — the only leader they respected and trusted — was deported. Late in March, he and his wife and two other strike leaders were banned from living in Viti Levu, Ovalau, or Macuata Province, the principle areas of Indian settlement, for two years. It wasn't really deportation, but there was little Manilal could do but leave.

In reality, the strike *had* made improvements to the Indian's life-style. Within months of the strike, government officers were stationed in principle districts whose sole duty was to work with the Indians and their problems. Advisory committees were set up, duties on essential foods dropped, licence fees reduced and the hut tax repealed.

But for many, it was too late.

Some had been humiliated by hostilities which grew out of the strike; others doubted if there would be any real improvements in their economy. Most fell totally disillusioned. They had no trust in government, no one to turn to, and now they were leaderless again.

There was a rush to leave Fiji.

By August, 1920, nearly 12,000 people — 15 per cent of the Indian population — were registered for repatriation.

The exodus didn't materialize and many of those who had planned to leave, remained. But the strike had definitely changed some things . . . for Indians, Europeans and Fijians.

The era of absolute colonial rule and serfdom was drawing to an end.

The corner of Cumming Street and Waimanu Road after the inferno.

40   THE CUMMING STREET FIRE

Cumming Street on February 9, 1923, was a hodgepodge of ramshackle shops and kava saloons.

Back rooms in some of the refreshment parlours offered other entertainments as well.

It was the centre of activity for the "little man", the meeting place and social centre of the poor.

On February 10, Cumming Street was none of these.

Just before dark, in a combined grog shop and boarding house on the northern side of the street, a man named Mittu spilled a can of petrol.

Mittu bent over to investigate, a flaming lamp in his hand . . .

★ ★ ★

It was Saturday night. Cumming Street was alive with people, inside the shops and out.

In Mittu's shop, flames swept across the tinder-dry, fuel-soaked floor and climbed the stairs to the boarding house above. Then they began leap-frogging from wooden building to wooden building, fanned by a north-east breeze which sent them racing towards Renwick Road.

The fire bell rang about 7.00. By that time, anyone who ventured to look out over Cumming Street could see the spiralling smoke and red glow coming from its centre.

The street's residents, both temporary and permanent, swarmed out like bees from a hive. One witness said it was a "torrent of maddened people"; another, a shop owner named Mr McGowan, said people "rushed wildly out of eating houses and kava saloons and ran about shouting, adding to the general confusion".

McGowan added that a number of Indian shopkeepers outside the fire zone scrambled to get together everything they could from their stores and carted them right out of town. Some apparently remembered big fires which had swept through cities in India and were convinced the whole town would go . . .

. . . which wasn't altogether impossible. Flames were now spreading in two directions at once. They were stopped at Renwick Road by the two-storied building owned by Henry Marks, but in the other direction, the inferno swallowed shop after shop until it reached a gap near a building occupied by Kwong Tiy's and the Coronation Bakery.

Then the fire crossed the street, methodically eating everything on the Nubukalou Creek side except one shop. For some unexplained reason, Jack Kee's fragile and wood-filled furniture factory remained alone, an unscathed island surrounded by smouldering debris.

Finished with Cumming Street, the fire moved down to Renwick Road, razing all the structures in its path until it reached the bridge over the creek.

Bish and Co's plant, a large structure next to the bridge, was one of the buildings levelled. Only a steam boiler was left standing above the sheets of iron.

The fire brigade — seven Fijian constables under an inspector — were slow in arriving. When they did arrive, they had the wrong nozzle for the hose, and it was some time before a new nozzle was found.

When at last hoses were connected to six fire hydrants, there wasn't any water pressure. The best of them squirted water about 20 feet, which the newspaper the next day reported was hardly enough to wet the verandahs.

In fact, the press went on to say the fire brigade was a "bad joke". It was the volunteers and bucket brigades which saved the whole town from going up.

When flames had first broken out, a cry went through town that it was the timber yard, Marlow's, which was aflame but a bucket brigade was already on the job in the yard, dousing the timber with water and pushing the fire back.

"It was an anxious time," Alf Marlow recalls, "but we had a good gang. As soon as sparks reached the timber, they pounced. They saved the town, because if the yard had got going, much of Suva would have burned."

The crew of the steamer Kaitoke were among the best and most willing firefighters. Other volunteers fought a scorching battle to save the Municipal Market, which was near the Thomson and Cumming Street junction. The building's walls were scorched, but the market was saved.

Across the creek, another bucket brigade forced the flames back from Suva's most imposing store, Morris Hedstrom's. Under the guidance of Sir Maynard Hedstrom, store clerks and volunteers erected a hessian screen along the colonnade and kept it soaked with water. Only the windows were damaged.

As the fire crept towards Thomson Street, merchants dumped tons of clothing, groceries, hardware and everything else they could save onto the Nubukalou bridge. A frantic shuttle of men and women deposited merchandise and their belongings at other selected "safe" spots until they stood in heaps.

Unfortunately, almost as fast as helpers could move the goods to safety, others moved in and helped themselves.

The press commented that "we are safe in saying that on Saturday, half the goods salvaged were stolen. We saw children running off, each holding a tier of one or two dozen children's hats" and people "disappeared into corners and reappeared with as many as four new singlets or shirts on".

Looting was so widespread that the police were helpless. One witness recalls people scrambling away from the stockpiles wearing new but unmatched shoes . . . or new boots, both for the right foot.

Still, most of the people who came to help did just that. The result wasn't always for the best, but at least they tried. In the excitement, people saved all sorts of things, many comparatively worthless, while more valuable items were lost to the flames. In an upstairs room near Thomson Street, a group of Fijians "rescued" a piano by throwing it over the balcony to the road below.

Cumming Street, by Sunday morning, was nothing more than an expanse of flattened sheet metal. Forty-five shops, including nine tailor shops, 18 refreshment rooms and a number of retailers, had been destroyed.

The damage was estimated at an unimpressive 40,000 pounds which, considering inflation, was about the same as damages in the 1891 blaze.

But to the Indians and Chinese who were the primary tenants of the street, the damage was catastrophic.

Mittu, in whose shop the fire started, told a magisterial inquiry that he lost from 600 to 700 pounds in jewellery and gold sovereign. For days after the fire, he was raking and sifting through the ashes in search of his treasure hoard.

So were countless others. Also by custom, they had hidden their sovereigns and valuables in cracks and crannies of the ramshackle shops and sheds.

In the debris of No 26 on Sunday morning, an iron pot was found containing 50 sovereigns, along with a melted mass of silver which was all that was left of Indian jewellery.

A tin box in another shed yielded the ashes of 150-pound notes which had been hidden by their owner only the day before. One of the tenants explained that his father had lost a fortune when a bank in Calcutta folded — so he hid his money at home.

The Governor and the Colonial Secretary arrived on the scene while the fire was still raging, and made arrangements for housing the homeless. They announced that the bakery in Suva Gaol would provide bread to any who needed it, and they said a Government depot at Korovou would house any who needed shelter.

The Fiji Times reported the "pathetic sight of a procession of Indians, many of whom had lost their all, carrying bundles and boxes to a place of safety".

Just two years earlier, Government House had burned to the ground after being struck by lightning. Now, the centre of Suva was gone. The fire made one thing clear: it was time for a properly trained and equipped fire brigade, and the coals were hardly cool before the Municipal Council sent a telegram inquiring about fire-fighting equipment.

A Dennis fire engine arrived in May 1923, the Fire Station was completed a few weeks afterwards, and by September, there was a permanent and salaried Fire Brigade.

There might have been some other advantages, too. A number of residents called the fire a blessing in disguise . . .

Cumming Street in the early 20s might have had three double-storey buildings to impress the tourists, but it also had the seediest collection of "ill-flavoured kava saloons and brothels" for a few thousand miles. There were periodic outcries from Suva's sophisticates clammering for action against the "dens of inquity".

Sanitation was poor or non-existent, food shops were accused of selling "nefarious poisons disguised as food" and there was concern that some of the back room entertainments might come as a shock to visitors and villagers.

"Oh, you could find any sort of things you wanted on Cumming Street," reminisced one old timer."

After the fire, the kava saloons shifted to Marks Street, which soon took over the reputation of its predecessor. Suva Market moved into the ruins that was Cumming Street and remained there for 20 years.

Oddly enough, the Fiji Times in its midday edition on Saturday, February 10, noted that "Cumming Street is again developing smells".

"It would be a good thing," the paper stated, "if the Health Authority carried out a surprise visit to the street."

Eight hours later, the street was wiped out in the most surprising visit of all.

"Some of the advanced cases . . . were truly human beings alive in dead bodies.

"Many during the last months of their lives had absolutely not the smallest sound area of skin on their bodies — face, mouth, nose — all were ulcerated, and only with the greatest difficulty could they swallow a few drops of liquid . . .

The odour was almost unbearable, and even their fellow patients would refuse to approach them. Caring for them was the special task of the Sisters.

A visitor told a Sister, "I wouldn't do this for a million dollars."
The Sister quietly replied, "Neither would I."

— *From Sister M. Stella's book, Makogai Image of Hope*

Mother Mary Agnes (centre) ruled Makogai with 'kindly authority'.

The Fijians called leprosy 'vukavuka'. In pre-mission times they had a variety of cures for it. Lepers were smoked over a fire of *sinu gaga*, a poisonous bark, most often until they suffocated. Or they were sent into isolation. Or, as in Colo, simply clubbed to death.

As early as 1876, Dr MacGregor admitted to the governor that he had been "dreadfully mistaken when I said that leprosy was almost unknown here. It is very common indeed."

By 1900, government health inspectors estimated that there were more than 1000 lepers in Fiji, and there was a particularly bad outbreak of the disease among children in Macuata.

In Suva, arriving labourers from India were given a medical examination and any suspected of having leprosy were sent back.

But for lepers who could not be repatriated, there was a small settlement in Walu Bay where about a dozen advanced cases were quartered. They were allowed out in public, providing they didn't break ordinances prohibiting them from riding in public transport, using public baths or guest houses, or working in prohibited trades.

Suva's residents however, weren't so keen on the idea. There was an outcry about "lepers roaming Suva's streets."

So the lepers were moved to an isolated point on Beqa, Soliyaga Peninsula, despite objections from the nearest village and from the Colonial Secretary, who felt a leprosarium shouldn't be anywhere in view of anticipated tour ships.

Father Guinard of Namosi visited the Beqa colony and noted that it was "enough to say that it is run in a Fijian manner" and that "some of the lepers are shouting out and demanding opium to relieve their pain". The report was probably correct, because in 1902, the Indian patients there threatened to burn down the village if they weren't given opium.

Government was still looking for a permanent station, particularly after it introduced a new policy of compulsory segregation.

Rabi, Yanuca and Wakaya were considered. There was a public protest meeting in Levuka saying Wakaya was too close.

In 1908, government bought Makogai for a little under 10,000 pounds.

The next problem was staffing it. There were few enough people qualified to care for the patients, and fewer still willing to do it.

Almost 20 years earlier, Father Bertreux had volunteered the services of the Catholic mission "in the event of the government deciding to bring together the lepers of Fiji on to one of the islands . . ."

Governor im Thurn sought the Bishop's help, and Bishop Vidal upheld his predecessor's offer. But at the same time, the governor stipulated that Makogai was not to become a Catholic colony.

Makogai, the governor said, "needed the best trained leper nurses we can get hold of, and, as it happens, leper nursing . . . has been almost exclusively undertaken by Sisterhoods."

"Bishop Vidal," he added, "should be made to clearly understand that we are not asking for nuns — but nurses."

A request for a chapel on the island was denied, and it was to be several years before missionaries of any kind were allowed on the island.

The newspaper in Suva complained "the sooner government prepares the island of Makogai for the reception of lepers, the better . . . a most glaring case has been brought to our notice. An Indian woman living on Waimanu Road is in the last stages of the disease, yet cultivates a garden of vegetables for sale . . ."

It was 1911 before Makogai was ready. On November 29, the government ketch Ranadi towed two cutters with the first 40 patients from Beqa to Dalice Bay.

Some among that human cargo were barely recognizable as living beings. All were in various stages of decay and misery, outcasts which society regarded with disgust.

They were frightened: leprosy was still considered incurable, and most must have known they were going to 'the island' to die.

The appearance of the island, with its neat and trim buildings, might have softened some of those fears. Four Sisters — two Fijians and two French Sisters — went immediately about their tasks. The doctor was less effective, saying he was already suffering from social ostracism and that most of his friends had already told him not to call.

He was replaced by Dr Hall, an energetic and devoted man who set the pace for the leprosarium. It was important that the island be relatively self-sustaining (for the patients' mental as well as physical health) and soon after his arrival, there were herds of cattle, sheep and goats, a piggery, and plantations of kumala and rice.

It was reported that, under his guidance, the "good food, cleanliness and regular attention had marked effects".

Makogai filled rapidly.

As it grew, there were appeals from other parts of the Pacific, and the Legislative Council agreed to bring the new patients in, even though one colonial officer warned that Fiji would be regarded as an unsavoury place.

Seven Samoans were the first, and within three years, there were Cook Islanders, Tongans, Solomon Islanders, Niueans. Outside criticism claiming "Our neighbours make full use of our enterprise while we allow our own diseased people to mix freely with their healthy fellows" was countered by a statement from the Fiji medical department reporting that, by 1927, there were no known cases at large.

Makogai's villages were separated by race on the assumption that the patients would be happier in their own ethnic groups and would lead a more normal village life.

There were villages in each cove, and Sisters came daily to care for those too sick to reach the central nursing station.

Fishing was good. The island was pretty. Patients sold their fish or their dalo to the management, and then were given the food back to cook as part of a system to encourage self-help. But it wasn't any resort.

"During the short span of life left to (one patient), the odour could be detected a quarter mile away," a Sister noted. "In wards reserved for the sickest patients, the odour was almost unbearable."

A letter from the Bishop's office to the Chief Medical Officer in 1920 reported that "Sister Emilie is not yet very well, as she is still losing part of her meals. I expect it is the air they breath over the tub where they clean the leper's wounds that tells on the health of so many of the Makogai nuns . . ."

The Bishop went on to explain that two more Sisters were enroute and that "Dr Hall told me it was imperative that Sisters destined to go to Makogai should go straight there, and not at first the more congenial life of teaching in a school, which makes it difficult to willingly take to the very peculiar work of the leper settlement."

Patients got up at 6am and were told to retire at 8.30. Once a week and sometimes more, they went for injections of Chaulmoogra oil (a tree derivative which was later grown on the island) which supposedly slowed the wasting process down.

They kept their minds off their fate by working. Women with barely any fingers learned to embroider; men worked in carpentry shops and became proficient as boat builders and tradesmen.

For recreation, the Fijians went fishing and the Indians hunted goats which had been introduced to the island and gone wild. Soccer and cricket were questionable activities — limbs which had lost all sense of feeling were too easily injured. The two biggest drawing cards were films and visitors.

There was no intermarriage of patients. That turned out to be one of the hardest things to bear, a life with little promise of togetherness.

In 1916, Fijians at Makogai petitioned the government "to prosecute our wives sinning with other men . . . since we are absent."

The Secretary of Native Affairs said it was too much to expect wives to remain faithful, "since there was little chance of husbands ever leaving Makogai".

It might have been correct, but it wasn't very tactful.

Each year, several patients were discharged. Their disease had stopped being active for the required two years, and they were able to get the governor's signature of discharge. But others had a negative reaction for nearly two years, only to be 'positive' just as they were on the verge of freedom.

And freedom, even for the lucky ones, was met with mixed excitement and fear. What had happened to their wives and families? How would they be treated 'outside'? On the island, there was sympathy, help and understanding. Outside their little world, there wasn't.

Dr Hall and later, Dr Austin, who was Medical Superintendent for 24 years, were rightfully praised for the way Makogai was run. But there were a lot of people who made Makogai what it was, and one of the most important was Mother Mary Agnes, who is said to have exerted a "kindly tyranny" over the island.

Makogai's people were described in detail in Sister Mary Stella's book, from which much of this material is taken. There's Ernest, a 17-year-old Tongan schooling in New Zealand when he was told he was a leper. He died at Makogai when he was 40.

There was Fritz, who tapped out letters to his many friends on a typewriter, using a pencil stub held between the stumps of his fingers. And Ioane, a young man married for only a month when a leprous spot appeared on his cheek.

Makogai's people had an enthusiasm for life that was catching. New arrivals, filled with despair, were invariably met at the wharf by crowds of 'old-timers' who were singing and smiling. It did a lot to ease their fears.

The staff, too, learned resignation. The island was probably the hardest calling a Sister could have, yet they went about their task with tremendous energy. Hour after hour was spent each day in the dressing stations, covering the multiple skin lesions of the patients who were in reaction. Sometimes, it took more than an hour to dress one patient, all the time enduring the heat and nauseating smell peculiar to lepers.

It was almost inevitable that some of Makogai's staff would come down with the disease.

One was Fr. Nicouleau, who after 9 years of work at Makogai joined the ranks of the lepers and died five years later. He had been the replacement of Fr. Schneider, whose boat capsized three miles from the island's entrance in 1913, and who was never seen again.

Sister Filomena was another. After 14 years of service, she quietly took leave of the Sisters and moved her few belongings into the hospital and took her place among the patients. When she died 30 active and helpful years later, Mother Mary Agnes recorded in her journal: "the news was received in the community with a deathlike silence . . . we can only ask for the strength, as Sr Filomena had, to carry our cross joyfully."

As each new drug was tested, the patients' hopes revived. Perhaps this would be the one . . .

In October, 1948, it came. It was called sulphetrone, and within a week of starting treatment, a change took place. The sores dried up, the smell from the wards of the very sick was gone. All Makogai held a party.

As each patient watched the improvements in his fellow patients, the optimism became nearly electric. The Medical Superintendent in 1949 wrote that "the 43 patients somewhat tamely described as 'much improved' would, if I had expressed my feelings more freely, have been described as 'astoundingly improved'."

In the years to come, there would be other changes. The archaic laws isolating people on an island would be changed; lepers would no longer be prisoners, and leprosy would be just another infectious disease.

Financially, the island was coping quite well, due to the year-in, year-out assistance of the New Zealand Leper Trust Board.

During its 58 years of existence, Makogai cared for and treated 4500 patients. More than half were restored to full health.

It ceased operation in 1969, when the last 17 were moved to Twomey Hospital in Suva.

The island is deserted now — except for the 1500 who still rest on the hill.

Southern Cross in Albert Park.

42 THOSE DARING MEN IN THEIR FLYING MACHINES

The radio went out an hour after take-off, about the same time the plane entered a wall of great black storm clouds.

Lightning ripped across the skies, and the navigators were thrown about so badly that they gave up any attempt to find out where they were.

Unable to get above the weather, the pilot brought the plane down almost to the wave tops.

He was flying blind, trying to hold the aircraft on a compass course in spite of winds which were tossing him about like a leaf in a storm. He was beginning to lose all sense of direction.

Headwinds were pushing them back, costing them far too much fuel. If they didn't make some headway soon, they'd plunge into the sea hundreds of miles short of their destination.

The weather finally cleared, and a quick sextant reading showed that, miraculously, they were only slightly off course.

A few hours later, the four men aboard the Southern Cross could see the islands of Fiji.

* * *

Charles Kingsford-Smith and his crew were to become the first men to fly across the world's largest ocean. But there were other air pioneers who made their mark on Fiji — in big and little ways.

One was a Mr Fleming, who in 1922 built an aeroplane and tried to fly it on Laucala beach. He kept his maiden flight a secret, saying he was not offering a "bob-a-head show" to let people see him break his neck.

His neck remained intact, but the plane didn't: it buckled when the wheels caught in the soft sand and the machine nosed into the mud.

Captain Gordon Fenton was probably the first true Fiji aviator. He assembled his British-built Simmonds Spartan bi-plane in front of the Metropole Hotel (initially with the wings on backwards, until the mistake was discovered) and registered it as a commercial aircraft, VQ-FAA.

Between 1930 and 32, VQ-FAA made frequent hops to Levuka, Lautoka and Savusavu. Captain Fenton set up the first Fiji Airways only to be wiped out by the depression, and he later offered himself and his plane to government, at a salary of 300 pounds a year.

On his first flight as part of the new, government-subsidised Fiji Air Services, Captain Fenton covered the 112-miles between Lautoka and Suva in a breathtaking one hour 35 minutes. He followed it up the next day with the first scheduled flight to Labasa via Levuka, Makogai and Nabouwalu.

Then there was Alf Marlow's flying boat.

The flying boat was a Dornier Libelle, built in Germany in 1922. Alf used to spend "two and a half days on my bloody feet" getting between Suva and Lautoka, not counting a possible lift on the CSR cane train on the Sigatoka side and a launch trip between Navua and Suva. So when he was on leave in New Zealand and heard about two Dornier Libelle flying boats for sale, he bought them.

Probably he assumed it would be an end to his long cross-country treks. He was wrong.

They had belonged to a veteran World War I fighter pilot, Major Donald Harkness. Harkness had been killed when the flying boat plunged into Auckland harbour on its first New Zealand test flight.

It was learned later that the Major had crammed a large rock into the tail section of the aircraft because the flying boat had a tendency to be nose-heavy. The rock broke loose and rolled forward.

The wreckage of Major Harkness's craft and a second Dornier were shipped to Suva. But Alf's problems weren't over. The Dornier was more a flying fish than a flying boat, and its slow, low and uncertain leaps over the water were usually shorter than planned.

The log book for VQ-FAB, still in Alf Marlow's possession, reads like a pilot's nightmare:

"Feb. 27 (1931) — performance poor, take off bad . . . Feb. 28 — Forced landing owing to bad performance . . . March 3 — Forced landing after 5 minutes in air. Revs dropped suddenly to 1200 . . . March 6 — Engine failure, forced landing . . . March 18 — forced landing owing to failure of tail plane through corrosion. Machine laid up indefinitely . . ."

The Dornier remained in Suva back sheds until 1978, when it was shipped back to the parent company in Germany, the only one of its kind left in the world.

"But it was really beautiful," Alf recalled, "looking down over the land it used to take me days to walk over. It could do about 120 knots." Then, reflecting, he added "Sometimes."

Aeroplanes and the men who flew them were a novelty, and they drew a crowd wherever they went. None, however, stirred the spirits or imagination of the public more than the historic trans-Pacific flight of the Southern Cross.

Charles Kingsford-Smith, called 'Smithy' by all his friends and later by much of the world, was the perfect example of the dashing and daring airman. He was decorated during World War I for action in France with the Royal Flying Corps. His combat career ended when he was wounded during a dog fight with three German planes, so he went to Hollywood where they needed stunt pilots.

Smithy became one of their best. Then he flew commercially for companies in America, Britain, and back home in Australia.

He flew for Digger Airways until an insurance company decided the fledgling airline had had too many mishaps. Looking for new money-making schemes, he met Charles Ulm, and the two decided they could cut the current round-Australia flight record in half.

They did — and during the luncheon given to honour them, they announced a new plan. They would try to fly the Pacific, from the USA to Australia!

Within weeks, they were in California. They bought a large Fokker monoplane and outfitted it with three new engines, with much of the money donated by Australian well-wishers.

They signed on two Americans as crew — navigator Harry Lyon and radioman Jim Warner — even though the men were seafarers and not airmen.

With Ulm and himself in the open cockpit and Warner and Lyon in the closed cabin behind, Smithy practised flying blind until he was certain he could hold a steady course in thick cloud.

When the big day came, May 31, 1928, the Golden Gate bridge was covered in mist as the Southern Cross slowly lifted off from Oakland airfield and passed overhead.

Exhaust from the engines streamed into the cockpit which was open on the sides. So did the rain. Lyon and Warner were slightly better off in the closed cabin, but had nothing to hang onto when turbulence threw them around. When sextant readings were impossible, Lyon watched the drift of the ocean below, the most rudimentary navigation imaginable.

They reached Hawaii without incident, although dense cloud had obliterated the stars for hours. Smithy's practice in flying blind was paying off.

The welcoming speeches in Hawaii went unheard; the two co-pilots were nearly deaf from the unremitting engine noise.

At first light on June 3, the heavy plane lumbered along a beach at Kauai. It was carrying the maximum possible fuel load to cover the longest of the three sectors, and Smithy gave it full power.

Even so, after 20 minutes of flying, the Fokker had reached a mere 300 feet!

Within an hour, the radio was out of action and a storm was raging.

Smithy and Ulm flew in circles trying to gain height, but with the fuel weight, it was impossible. They got one break in the clouds, enough to see the Southern Cross constellation glittering above them, and then the weather worsened and they were lost again.

It was hours before they finally sighted Fiij, and with it came golden sunshine.

At 2:21pm on June 5, after covering 3,290 miles in 35 hours, the Southern Cross came in to land at Albert Park.

A row of large, shady trees which stretched through the middle of the park had been cut down in anticipation of Southern Cross's arrival, although in typical 'Fiji time', the airmen were already on their way before it was done. The Colonial Secretary (Seymour) and the Mayor (Henry Marks) both were certain the aircraft would never reach Fiji.

Most of Suva's residents were out watching for the plane, but the first to see it were those on the roof of the Grand Pacific Hotel. There were shouts of "there he is" and then the Southern Cross came in low over the Rewa Delta and swooped over the hotel.

It banked, flew out over the sea again, then made a bee-line for the park and the opening in the trees.

Smithy later said he was horrified when he saw that the park was only 400 yards long. He was dead tired, and the Fokker touched down halfway along the field, racing towards a group of uniformed men standing horror-stricken at the far end.

He waited until the last possible moment, then swung the plane around in a ground loop.

The crowd cheered. They raced forward in one wild rush, but the Defence Force and police got there first, forming a cordon around the plane.

As the aviators climbed out, the Governor, Sir Eyre Hutson, stepped through the cordon to congratulate them.

The Fiji Times reported that "all four men showed in their faces that they had come through a terrible experience. They were ashen grey and bunched up . . ."

Smithy himself said he never wanted to go through another night like it.

It is doubtful if the men fully appreciated the ball held in their honour that night, or fully realised the significance of the whales tooth which Ratu Jone Mataitini presented to them.

But it is recorded that, about 1am, Ulm and Smithy walked over to the plane in the bright moonlight.

As they approached, the police on duty stopped them. When they tried to convince the police that the plane was theirs, they were told the instructions were that no one was to go near it. The two men shrugged their shoulders and went to bed, probably considering the problems they would have in getting the aircraft aloft again.

Fully laden, Southern Cross would never get out of the park. Smithy and Ulm had looked at possible runways and chosen Naselai beach as the best.

With everything taken out to lighten it, and with only a few gallons of fuel in the tanks, the empty aircraft was flown to the sand beach. Lyon and Warner, along with drums of fuel, came around by sea on the government boats Pioneer and Adi Beti.

On Friday, June 7, just after 1pm, the Southern Cross made a perfect take-off to the north, swung again over the beach, and crossed over Suva. Huge crowds lined the waterfront along Victoria Parade as the plane swept low over the town, and the roar of the engines was drowned out by a burst of cheering.

Just over the Club Hotel, one of the airmen put his arm out of the portside and waved a handkerchief. Then the Southern Cross turned out over the seas and headed towards Brisbane.

Almost before Suva had disappeared on the horizon, there was trouble. Lyon reported that the main compass wasn't working. Then the visibility dropped, and the plane began bucking in the most violent storm they had encountered yet. It took the combined strength of the co-pilots to handle the dual controls.

The storm lasted for hours. Navigation was impossible. Smithy and Ulm battled on, by now simply concerned with survival rather than direction. At least they were heading towards the east, towards Australia.

When at last the Australian coastline came to view, they realised they were 100 miles too far south. They also realised victory was almost theirs.

As Smithy turned the 'old bus' north towards Brisbane, Harry Lyon reportedly looked at the ribbon of Australian beach stretching for miles on either side of them and said "Bully".

In 83 hours flying time, through two vicious storms, they'd crossed 7,565 miles of ocean. The greatest flight of all time had ended.

Smithy went on to pioneer more long distance flights than any man in the world. At the age of 35, he was knighted.

Three years later, he was dead. Perhaps not so strange, he and Ulm shared similar fates.

Charles Ulm was lost at sea in December, 1934, while trying to set a new speed record between California and Australia.

Less than a year later, Smithy and co-pilot Tommy Pethybridge made an attempt on the England-Australia speed record. Their Lockheed Altair developed engine trouble and crashed into the Bay of Bengal.

Neither were ever seen again.

Bill Borthwick ignored the experts and kept on panning . . .

43 OLD BILL OPENED A DOOR TO FORTUNE

"Old Bill sent a little tube through the mail, registered, about the size of my thumb here, and it was filled with gold.

"He sent in all the statistics, how much ore he thought there was to the ton, how much panning he'd done to get it, and it looked pretty good . . .

"We decided to go to see Bill and have a look for ourselves. We took a punt around the Ra coast, there wasn't any road yet, and when we got there, old Bill was sitting on a log with a rifle across his lap.

"What's the rifle for?", we asked, and Bill said it was in case someone tried to jump his claim. Well, we said, you better take us and show us where all this gold is, and Bill said 'just step aside,' and he got out a shovel and dug a little.

"Then he walked a couple hundred yards over to the water and panned it and when he came back, there was gold in the bottom." — Vincent Costello.

* * *

There had been reports of gold in Fiji for years. Baron de Este found it in the Nasivi River of the Tavua district in 1872. So did a New Zealand prospector named Fielding who began a systematic search of the Nasivi about 20 years later.

In July 1899, the Fiji Times reported a gold find "of a payable nature" in the upper reaches of the Rewa River, and noted that a few local residents had continued the search — until they'd run out of beer.

The newspaper went on to call it a treasure hunter's picnic, and the author complained "this is about the 99th expedition which it has fallen to this writer to record . . ."

A large ore body in Vanua Levu's Yanawai district was discovered in the late 1920's and the first bullion from Mt. Kasi was exported in 1932. But somehow, Vanua Levu's hills and valleys didn't seem to generate the excitement among prospectors that Viti Levu did.

From Rakiraki to Nubutautau, men 'just on the verge of something good' combed the creek beds and outcrops.

One of those men was Bill Borthwick.

Bill was an oldtimer of the goldfields. He was a veteran of the Australian and New Zealand digs, and in Fiji he couldn't help but notice the similarities between the volcanic slopes here and those of rich New Zealand goldfields.

He talked about it continuously to his best friend — Pat Costello — until Costello, too, was fired with the idea that the rugged mountains of Viti Levu hid a fortune.

Even at the age of 70, Borthwick never lost hope of striking it rich, and his genial Irish friend Pat backed him in his search. Costello was a man of means, with a cattle ranch in the foot hills of the Sigatoka Valley and a prosperous hotel, the Shamrock, in Lautoka.

So Bill and another oldtimer, Jack Sinclair, set off for the Koroboya Range. On a hillside above a small tributary of the Vunisina, they began digging into dirt that Bill thought looked promising.

When they took their samples down to the creek to crush and pan, the result was beyond their highest expectations. Sinclair, reportedly shaking with excitement, told Bill they'd struck it rich at last.

Bill replied: "Maybe."

If it was true, it was contrary to the reports of a team of New Zealand geologists who had already assured the Fiji Government that Fiji was not ever going to be a gold producer.

Not that a report from experts was likely to influence a die-hard prospector like Bill Borthwick, but, except for Pat Costello, it made it hard to find backers.

Bill summoned Pat to the site. Vincent Costello went along. They kept the strike a secret among the 'family' until Pat got the area (one square mile) surveyed and registered.

"Then," said Vincent, "Pat went out and told the world . . ."

It was November, 1932. Fiji's gold rush was on.

The great Australian and American gold rushes were more spectacular, because in Fiji most people remained at their work and were content to let the jobless head for the bush. But a lot of people were talking gold, and just about everybody with a few dollars to invest hired prospectors to peg a claim in the Tavua hills.

There were queues for prospector's rights, and pegs denoting claims went up everywhere. Costello's lease was surrounded on all sides. Before long, there were men digging up half of Viti Levu . . . many of them without the slightest knowledge of how to recognise what they were looking for.

The publican, meanwhile, had sent ore samples to a fellow Queenslander, E.G. Theodore, who had the knowledge of large-scale mining operations (and the capital) to set things in motion. Theodore was impressed. He bought an option in the area and sent a party of experienced miners to investigate.

John Fraser was one of them, and in his book Gold-Dish and Kava Bowl, he described some of his new neighbours:

There was Andy and his wife, who came over to the camp to weigh their weekly gleanings, and who accepted the regularly disappointing results with the stoic fate of true prospectors.

There was a camp of Madrasis who left in despair, probably because their exploration failed to reveal anything that looked like the gold they were used to seeing in Indian jewellery.

And finally, because the road from Suva around the north-east coast opened soon after the field was announced, there were sightseers trudging up to the trenches, cameras in hand.

Fraser records that, during the early days at Tavua, hundreds of people — villagers, shopkeepers and city dwellers — arrived at the diggings with specimens of rock collected from all over the islands. Most stared in disbelief when told their glittering sample was worthless.

Some of the better-educated gold hunters were certain that thermal activity had pushed the gold-bearing rock to the surface, and at Tavua, there was indeed a hot spring which Hindus called the Garum Pani.

Someone even discovered that a local fern, coral bracken, grew on mineralised zones and almost nowhere else, a botanical guide to possible riches.

But for everyone that panned out a bit of colour, ten times as many gave it up when their rations ran out.

Prospecting in Fiji was totally different than in Australia or New Zealand. The Tavua goldfield may have resembled other gold-producing areas, including the famous Comstock Lode in Nevada, but it had little in common. It upset the theories and well-tested rules of even the best prospectors, particularly those used to Australian fossicking.

When they didn't see evidence of tell-tale quartz reefs or find reefs of alluvial, 'float' gold in the creekbeds nearby, they went home. Fiji was newer than Australia; its gold was of a different type, which often showed up as strands of hair-thin wire.

Borthwick had not been fooled. Neither had Fraser, who "marvelled that these gold-bearing formations, in such an accessible position, should have remained so long undisturbed. For years past, families of Indians had lived in the area, cultivating the flat lands between the lode outcrops . . . and officials of the CSR regularly visited these Indian settlements, while all the time an observant passer-by could have seen specks of gold on dislodged boulders."

Geologists, however, weren't so sure. Tom Victor, one of the most reliable mining experts in Australia, advised against mining operations, saying the gold wouldn't go deeper than the surface.

For a long time, it seemed as if he was right.

On Costello's block, a venture which at first seemed very promising began to look doubtful. Wherever they dug, the wonderfully rich values on the surface didn't go down much deeper than three feet. The gold was lying in a thin horizontal line called a leader. It was fine for a small operator, but it wasn't likely to interest a big company.

Spirits began to fall, particularly at the end of the day during weighing-up time. Only Costello remained convinced that somewhere, like a handle on an umbrella, the gold went down.

For the next 18 months, prospecting continued, and when it finally seemed obvious that there was no huge lode of paying ore, an agreement was reached between Fraser and a few other miners to work it on a subsistence level.

With picks and handshovels, wheelbarrows and a tiny "pudding mill", Fraser and his cohorts won, in five months work, 250 ounces of free gold, a daily average of just over 2 ounces. Since they broke even at one ounce a day, they were paying for their beer, even if they weren't getting rich.

But then, late in 1934, an assayer on the site did a little arithmetic and decided that there were thousands of tons of ore worth more than two pounds per ton, not only on Costello's claim, but on adjacent leases.

More than two years after Borthwick's discovery, and after just about everyone in Fiji had ridiculed their prospects, three lease areas joined together to form the Tavua goldfields.

In October 1934, the Dolphin, Emperor and Loloma mines were born. The gold boom was renewed, this time with more vigour than ever. During 1935, an average of 50 prospector's rights were issued each month. Mining circles in Australia, New Zealand and England were interested in Fiji.

There were scores of companies and syndicates formed. In October 1935, 20 Fiji gold stocks were listed locally, and company promoters published fantastic stories of rich discoveries for almost every one of them. Shares soared skyward the minute they reached the market, even before any development or exploration had taken place.

The names of Loloma, Koroere, Aloha, Mt Kasi and Nasivi were on everybody's tongue.

Mining experts and company men arrived on every boat and property owners met them as they got off, offering options at exhorbitant prices.

Then the bubble burst. The boom of '35' was the bust of '36'.

Shares which had rocketed to 80 pounds were suddenly worth 5 pounds, and there was vicious talk of 'salting' the prospects. How else could samples assayed so high — such as those from Nasivi — come from areas which later proved to be so uniformly worthless?

Gold fever was replaced with a total and absolute pessimism.

Government stepped in and helped cool things even more. It let it be known that leases would be cancelled where little or no work had been done, then hinted that leases would be granted for only two years, hardly enough time to turn a good find into a paying proposition.

As it happened, some of the laws rumoured to be going into effect weren't even passed, but the new policies on mining were strict.

Potential miners "weren't able to get a penny for a good show — even if they did find one".

For Borthwick, Costello and a few others, it didn't matter. They'd made it.

Costello's block became the Dolphin mine, a man named Morton had the Emperor site, and Lawler held the Loloma.

Lawler. Lucky, lucky Lawler.

Bill Lawler had paid a visit on a man named Reimenschneider, one of the first to peg a lease as news of gold in the Tavua hills spread. Reimenschneider's 200-acre site adjoined Costello's, and he had brought in some Australian miners to look the land over. They found nothing, and they found it at a time when overseas experts were saying the Tavua area was unlikely to amount to much.

Bill Lawler was a country publican and he complained bitterly that "every hotel-keeper in the island except me seems to have got a leg in . . . stuck out there in the bush,. I never get any news until it's stale."

Reimenschneider told him if he wanted a lease area so bad, he could have his. In fact, he could have it right then and there for 20 pounds, enough to pay his out-of-pocket expenses.

Lawler grabbed it.

The lease area was to become the Loloma mine, from which the richest ore ever found in Fiji was to come. Lawler eventually cleared more than 80,000 pounds on his investment of 20!

Ten years after the Emperor, Dolphin and Loloma mines went into production, they had produced gold valued at well over 15 million dollars.

As for Bill Borthwick, he died comfortably in his house next to the Shamrock Hotel, where he and Pat Costello would invite friends in for a drink and tell them, "I told you so".

The First Battalion enroute to the Solomons.

44   DEATH IN VELVET GLOVES

The enemy convoy was first reported when it was about 60 miles north-west of Malolo.

All units were ordered to take up battle positions. By the time the convoy was nearing Beqa, the Fiji Defence Force was poised and ready.

Soon after dawn broke, an official report stated that Nadi airport was being bombed and shelled by the enemy. The news filtered through to the people in the streets, and almost immediately, a wholesale evacuation of the Indian section of the community began. Roads were blocked by hordes of people and vehicles, all loaded with everything that could possibly be carried, and then some.

Beneath the guava trees of Bilo, in specially-dug trenches on Suva Point, in Nausori and Vatuwaqa, the First Battalion (Regulars) and 2nd Battalion (Territorials), along with two New Zealand brigades, watched the horizon.

About 9am, two warships and a landing barge were sighted, and then news was received that two more destroyers were in the Rewa River and the enemy had landed near Bau . . .

As the impossibility of this sunk in, it became obvious that the attack was just another exercise. But the war had entered the Pacific the day the Japanese bombed Pearl Harbour. Nobody knew when Fiji would become the next target.

* * *

The war broke out in Europe in September of 1939. Government decided to train a small force in 1940 which could go overseas.

It began recruiting in earnest in 1941, and by 1942, what had been a home-guard effort of part-time territorials had swollen into a force of 6,500 trained men, including three regular battalions, two commando units, artillery sections, Labour Corps, and all the necessary supporting units.

It was a remarkable achievement, and it was primarily the result of the loyalty of the Fijians to their chiefs.

As each cry for recruits was sounded, there was a rush of Fijians to volunteer. If a district fell short of the required number, the 'buli' ensured that it suffered no shame by nominating 'volunteers'. They obeyed chiefly rule, and were sent off with a feast which filled them with pride.

Ratu Sukuna told the Fijians why they had to go to war: "We'll never be recognised," he said, "unless our blood is shed first."

They joined, along with more than a thousand Fiji Europeans. At first Indians offered their support, but when their demands for equal pay in the army with Europeans was refused, the Indian platoon was disbanded. That year 1941, the sole military effort of the Indian community represented two officers and 70 members of the Reserve Motor Transport Section, which had been guaranteed it would not have to serve outside of Fiji.

The Indian response to recruitment left them open to mistrust and criticism, and probably few of their antagonists thought about the reasons why, or about the obvious backlash of colonial oppression.

For the rest, training went on and on and on. New Zealand took over command of the Fiji Defence Force in late 1940, and for the next two years, Fiji's soldiers built defenses and practised manning them. When there weren't enough rifles to train with, they used bamboo sticks. There were long marches, sometimes 100 miles or more, and the Fijians, unused to wearing boots, came back with bare feet and their boots slung over their shoulders. Later, when their bushy hair was cut so they could wear helmets, the unhappiness was magnified: their long, traditional hair was part of their mana.

With the attack on Pearl Harbour, everything was intensified even more. As one Pacific island after another fell into Japanese hands, fear for Fiji grew. Reinforcements came from New Zealand, most of them officers, NCOs and specialists.

To the New Zealanders, it seemed as if the Fijians would never make good soldiers. Fresh recruits were so frightened of weapons they couldn't pull the trigger, and on the parade ground they were so hopeless that columns had to be kept in line with ropes.

But just when the officers began losing hope, the recruits would show remarkable abilities in some other field. Eventually, they proved they were crack sharpshooters and riflemen. Camps were established from Natabua to Nausori, sentries were stationed at key points, and there was an around-the-clock watch at gun batteries, including Suva and Momi where huge naval guns guarded the bays.

The only major problem was in preventing soldiers from breaking camp — particularly as make-shift grog shops went up around the campsites, offering a 'taralala' and specially-selected barmaids. Slipping camp was all the easier because, after Pearl Harbour, there were complete blackout restrictions. The cities were in total darkness.

Then, the situation in the Pacific began to change. By 1942, Fiji was no longer regarded as a likely war zone. The troops were tiring of the routine of army life. They wanted to go overseas. They wanted action. That same year, the Americans established bases in Fiji and the 37th Division took over New Zealand's role, commanding the Fiji forces.

The Americans were immediately impressed with the Fijian ability in jungle craft. In fact, they sent fresh groups of soldiers to train *under Fiji commandos* every six weeks. They changed the name of the Defence Force to Fiji Military Forces, a hopeful sign that they considered the army as something more than a home guard. But they still weren't convinced the Fijians would stand up to actual combat conditions.

It took the Governor of Fiji, Major-General Sir Philip Mitchell, and the commanders of the various units to convince the Americans to give them a try. At the beginning of December, 1942, 30 commandos — 22 of them Fijians — were secretly sent overseas. They weren't allowed to say goodbye . . . they weren't even told where they were going.

They were called the 'Special Party' and they were under the command of Captain David Williams. They landed at Koli Point on Guadalcanal and moved to Tenaru where the Americans were holding a beach-head.

In Fiji, they had been frightened of death. Here, death was all around them and bodies were still strewn everywhere. What's more, the Solomons jungle was thicker than anything they'd ever seen in Fiji, and it hid not only Japanese, but crocodiles and malaria-carrying mosquitoes.

In the Solomons, the Americans had the fire-power. But when the shelling was done, it was the Fiji special party they looked to — to go in, scout around, and see what was left. Patrol after patrol of commandos did just that. On one mission, four of them killed three Japanese on a sabotage mission, their packs filled with explosives and a map of the main airfield on Guadalcanal. The commandos sniffed out Japanese encampments, and when the mopping up operations were done, they began training Solomon islanders in jungle warfare, using captured Japanese weapons.

The Fiji commandos were "death with velvet gloves" according to one war correspondent, and he added they were "better qualified to drive the Nipponese from their South Pacific jungle defences than any troops in the field . . ." General Patch (US) was so pleased that he cabled to Fiji for more, and on the 23rd of April, 1943, the first Fiji commandos were united with the First Battalion and the 1st Commando Battalion, fresh from Suva, on Guadalcanal.

They were glad to see them. They were also disappointed when they heard of the farewell Fiji had given its troops, a farewell the first 30 men had been cheated out of.

The First Battalion and Commandos marched through Suva on April 13 and boarded the American military transport 'President Hayes' for the Solomons. Initially, the embarkation order had seemed like just another rumour. But when it was proved true, hospital cases climbed out of bed to rejoin the unit and men previously discharged were trying to enlist again.

There were parties all over Suva. From Nasese, 36 officers and 799 other ranks forced their way through the crowds with fixed bayonets as men and women alike broke through their lines to kiss them goodbye. It actually took another two days of waiting in wet, hot, sticky Suva Harbour before the convoy put to sea: four troopships and three escorting destroyers carrying the Fiji battalions and part of the 37th Division of the US Army.

Their landing at Kokobuna beach, Guadalcanal, filled them with horror. They were greeted by "booby traps, skeletons and the horrible stench of dead bodies". Kokobuna had been the last stand of the Japanese on Guadalcanal, and the barrage laid down by the Americans had turned the entire area into a wasteland of bomb craters and twisted stumps.

The Fijians, probably to calm their own nerves, frightened each other with skulls. Then they got down to serious war. They were told to dig foxholes, and they dug them the regulation depth. During their second night, there was an air raid and shells fell close to camp. The scrape of shovels could be heard until dawn as the new arrivals dug deeper.

During the first bomb raids, the Fiji troops piled into the trenches on top of each other, helterskelter, sometimes head-first. Some even dived into the wrong trench, probably realising their mistake an instant before they landed in the latrine.

But then they moved to a new campsite, Boromoli, on the island of Florida and it was a comparative holiday. For the next half-year, the First Battalion frolicked in the surf or went fishing. Their camp was so comfortable it was used as a rest haven for VIPs. The only discomfort was in knowing that, just 30 miles away, 5000 Japanese troops were still reported to be encamped on Santa Ysabel.

As the war and the Japanese moved further north, a smaller force was thought sufficient to hold Florida. The First Battalion prepared to move, this time to New Georgia and a small island in the war-torn area, Kolombangara. But there wasn't any action. The Americans already had cleaned it up, and most of the time was spent fixing up abandoned Japanese equipment, and trading war souvenirs. One of the Fiji men 'bought' a large Japanese truck from an American . . . for a watermelon!

The only brief period of excitement was when two prisoners were brought into camp. But they turned out to be Chinese who had been conscripted and brought to the Solomons as labourers. And when a Fijian cooked his taro too close to a 100-pound bomb. It exploded, but miraculously, no one was hurt.

The Japanese had escaped to Choiseul and Bougainville. The only enemy left were the mosquitoes, which continued to spread malaria. The battalion, once again, was cheated of the action, but the 1st Commandoes, who had preceded them to New Georgia, weren't. In late June, 1943, the 1st Commandos were assigned to the 43rd US Division to assist in capturing Munda Airfield.

The struggle for the airfield lasted until August, with the commandos scouting and patrolling into enemy territory, sometimes miles behind the front lines. They patrolled all day and helped defend the perimeter at night. Sleep was practically impossible: the Japanese would scream like dying men in the dark to make the Fijians jittery and trick them into firing. Then they lobbed handgrenades at the rifle flash.

On one patrol, the commandos were cut off from the Americans behind them. Led by Captain Tripp, they made a desperate bid to circle around again and in the attempt, two of their number were killed. It took them 12 hours to push their way back to camp — but the Japanese loss was estimated at 40 killed. Their action, and their report of a Japanese patrol which was later successfully ambushed, helped the Americans reach the coast and take a beach-head only three miles from Munda.

Up to this time, the commandos had led charmed lives. They were casualty free, even when Americans on the same patrols had lost their lives. Munda was to change all that.

The commandos were exhausted. Most suffered from malaria, and when they were taken for a rest at Rendova Island, the island suddenly came under heavy and constant bombardment. The wounded and sick were moved on.

On July 17, Captain David Williams, with 70 commandos, withstood an all-out attack by the Japanese, intent on a final effort to hold Munda. The captain later said he couldn't believe the effectiveness of the Fiji marksman. Thirty-four of the enemy lay dead along the perimeter. There were no Allied casualties.

Old friends, the 37th US Division, came over to assist the 43rd, and all three units made daily raids on enemy pill-boxes surrounding Munda, softening them up for August 5. That day, Munda was taken by the Allied Forces and more than 3000 Japanese fell.

Eleven of the 1st Commandos were killed. Twenty were wounded. At least half of the rest suffered from malaria.

Brigadier Dittmer, Commandant of the Fiji Brigade, said it was time they went home. The New Georgia campaign was over, and the 2nd Commando unit from Fiji was on its way to replace them.

Besides the 36 medals for gallanty won by the 1st Commandos, there were other honours. One of them was the message from General Beightler, Commander of the 37th US Division: " . . . the Fijians with their New Zealand officers have won the unqualified respect of all our troops for their skill and bravery . . ." The Commandos had proven themselves.

The First Battalion's turn was still to come.

When the Japanese surrounded Kameli Outpost in Bougainville, about 600 of Fiji's 1st Battalion were trapped inside.

They were cut off from the only known trail of withdrawal, 30 miles from safety, and with no hope of reinforcements.

The Japanese were mounting a massive attack and they reportedly had ten times the number of troops the Fijians had.

Kameli Outpost had been named after the first Fijian killed in Bougainville, and now it looked as if most of the 1st Battalion was about to be annihilated as well.

But the Japanese hadn't counted on one factor . . . a wire-thin missionary who'd spent 20 years in the Bougainville bush.

"There are 99 tracks on Bougainville known to the Japanese," Rev Usaia Sotutu told the Battalion Commander.

"I know the hundredth."

★ ★ ★

On patrol near Torokina, Bougainville.

The 1st Battalion landed at Torokina on Bougainville's Empress Augusta Bay at dawn, three days before Christmas. Torokina was a beach-head taken by the Americans, the only Allied-territory on an island which harboured 40,000 Japanese soldiers.

Four destroyers covered them as they waded ashore from their landing craft. They were barely on land before they were told that their commanding officer, Lieutenant-Colonel Taylor, was injured.

Colonel Taylor had flown to Torokina ahead of the battalion. During an intense air raid the previous night, an anti-personnel bomb had landed in his tent. Some of the Fijians cried as the officer, covered in bandages from head to foot, was carried on a stretcher to say farewell to them.

Major G.T. Upton was flown in from Munda in the Solomons to take command.

The first night on Bougainville, the battalion was welcomed with a heavy artillery barrage. It was to become a nightly occurrence: the boom of the big guns, the screech of shells overhead, and the bark of the American anti-aircraft guns just behind them.

On Christmas day, the first patrol went out. It was an all-Fijian platoon led by Lieut. Isireli Korovulavula, and it was the battalion's first true action against the enemy. When the patrol returned two days later, they had collected valuable information and taken three enemy lives. There was wild jubilation.

For the next two months, there were almost continuous night bombing raids on the camp, but at the same time, hundreds of Allied fighter planes and bombers were taking off from Torokina to bomb Rabaul, Truk, and other Japanese-held bases.

The Americans were kept busy holding the tiny perimeter around Torokina's vital airstrip. The Fiji battalion's job was to begin moving out beyond the perimeter, to survey Japanese defences on the other side of the island and find out just how strong the enemy really were.

On December 29, a patrol under Captain R. Freeman, with 200 men, set out on the unenviable mission of penetrating 40 miles behind Japanese lines. They reached the far coast, and during the next five days, patrols from Ibu killed 22 Japanese, with the loss of only one Fijian, Pvt. Kameli Rokotuiloma.

That was how the outpost at Ibu began. Seventeen hundred feet up, reached only by a narrow and steep track which crossed almost vertical gorges, Ibu was the mid-way point over the rugged Crown Prince range.

The Americans asked that the outpost be held as long as possible, despite its isolated location. But when Maj. Upton reached it, he said it would have to be abandoned unless there was an easier way to evacuate the sick and wounded . . . and so the men cut an airstrip out of the jungle with bayonets and trenching tools.

A Piper Cub from Torokina landed on 'Kameli' airstrip a few days later.

Ibu was cold, but it was out of the malaria zone, and the Fijians countered the cold by rolling up in silk parachutes or using torn ones as bright silk sulus. It might have been almost comfortable there — if the Japanese hadn't become so suddenly aware of their presence.

Three hundred Japanese soldiers came looking for them, but their advance party was discovered and ambushed, and the rest withdrew into the bush to regroup.

Several attempts were made to find them, and Lieut. Korovulavula, certain he pinpointed the enemy position during a ground patrol, set out in a light aircraft to direct an airstrike against them. On the way back to Ibu, the weather closed in and the plane was reported missing.

For several hours, the plane circled and searched for an opening in the clouds, and then the Cub crashed into the trees on a mountainside. Neither Isireli nor the pilot, Lieut. Charles Cross, were hurt, but the plane was 50 feet up in the trees. It was a shaky climb down to the ground.

Their compass was broken. The rain was coming down in torrents, but they found signs of what had once been a track and they began walking.

They walked for 10 days without food, and then Lieut. Isireli climbed a tree and saw an island. With horror, he realised it was Buka — the main camp of the Japanese.

They had been walking the wrong direction.

As they retraced their steps, they got weaker and weaker. When Cross could go no further, Isireli carried him. But eventually, even that was impossible and the pilot begged him to build a small shelter and go on alone. His final request was that the Fijian write to his mother.

Isireli, now able to move only pitifully small distances at a time, struggled on for another week. He was found by friendly Bougainvilleans, who hid him from the Japanese for another five days while he gained strength, and then took him to one of the Australian Coastwatchers, Captain Robinson.

No search was carried out for Charles Cross. It was too futile. Lieut. Korovulavula had been only half-conscious during the final week of his trek; he had no idea which direction he'd come.

It was the 28th of February, one day and one month since the plane had crashed, when Lieut. Isireli Korovulavula finally reached Torokina again. His efforts to try to save Charles Cross earned him the Military Cross, and the commendation from Brigadier-General Dunckel, the commander of Cross's unit, read: "Your action is one of the most outstanding acts of self-sacrifice and bravery I know, and it shall always remain as the greatest example of personal sacrifice to a comrade-at-arms on our records."

It was at Ibu that the Fijians first met another hero, one who would later become the best friend they ever had. He was a *talatala*, a missionary, but when they first saw him, they nearly shot him!

The Reverend Usaia Sotutu has spent more than 20 years in Bougainville as a pioneer Methodist missionary before the Japanese invaded the island. During the early years, he'd coped with cannibals. Now, it was the Japanese.

The Rev. was persuaded to join the Australian Coastwatchers. He was given a uniform, machine-gun, and the rank of sergeant.

He watched as members of the 1st Battalion struggled up the trail to Ibu. They were almost on him before they looked up and saw him. "They thought I was a devil, a *tevoro*" the Rev. said. "I hadn't cut my hair or beard for two years, the Japanese were hunting me to kill me, and I looked frightening."

"One of their Solomon guides said I was a spirit, and he said "Siutim long lek, na sapos i go daun, em man, tasol sapos i no go daun, em tamoran'. (Shoot him in the leg and if he falls down, he is a man, but if he doesn't, he's a spirit.)

"All the soldiers cried out 'siutim, siutim' . . . and then I said 'Bula, sergeant' and they said 'you're the *talatala*."

The 'bearded prophet' gained their instant respect. He held services on Sundays and patrolled with troops on weekdays, a reverend with a tommy gun. Gradually, Ibu became a refuge for several hundred Bougainvilleans, the wives and families of men working with the Americans at Torokina, all of them under Rev. Sotutu's care.

Before the battalion arrived, the missionary had saved the Coastwatchers on several occasions when their position was betrayed by hostile islanders. Once, he had dragged a fallen officer under a hail of machinegun fire, until he realised it was too late. In two years of dodging the Japanese, there'd been several close encounters: bursts of machinegun fire, but when they looked again, he was gone.

And there was the time, patrolling with four Papua New Guinea scouts, when they walked straight into three Japanese soldiers. The Papuans dived for cover behind a tree, and one of the Japanese soldiers raised a gun to shoot the missionary, still in mid-trail.

A Papuan shot the Japanese soldier, and then one of the other soldiers threw a hand-grenade at the Papuans, but it bounced off the tree, right back into the middle of them. The Japanese were all killed and the talatala was saved.

He seemed to have a charmed life, and that was to prove ever so fortunate for the 1st Battalion.

The Fiji troops had strengthened the mountain outposts until there were four companies, more than 600 men, camped at Kameli, Sisivie, and Tokuo.

They were relatively safe: they had two escape paths — one leading to Torokina along the Laruma River; the other along the Sisivie trail to the west coast.

But then, in mid-February, the Japanese moved in for the kill. Headquarters at Torokina reported the enemy were in great strength, and said the US 37th Division with two Fijian platoons could not keep the Laruma trail open.

The Japanese closed in on Sisivie and Tokuo, and they outnumbered the Fijians 10-to-one.

At Tokuo, a Fijian platoon under Corporal Malokai Mo managed to kill 30 of the enemy before withdrawing.

At Ibu, Major Upton listened to the reports of air reconnaissance and then ordered a complete withdrawal. He hoped to gather all the forces at Sisivie, and then make a break for it. Four platoons with the 200 Bougainvilleans from the camp, began moving toward Sisivie after destroying everything that would be useful to the enemy.

Unfortunately, the enemy was already at Sisivie.

The Japanese were 800 yards from the outpost when they ran into an ambush from Corporal Manoa Roko's platoon, and at least 20 of the enemy were killed before the Bren gunner ran out of ammunition. As the platoon withdrew, Corporal Manoa held the enemy at bay with a tommy gun, then single-handedly repelled two assaults with hand-grenades while his men made their escape. He and a rifleman named Metuisela Vuli, at the last second, fled too.

They encountered more Japanese in the bush and shot their way out. Manoa's gun jammed, and as he stopped to repair it, a Japanese officer stepped from behind a tree and levelled a revolver at him. Manoa pointed the useless weapon at him and the officer disappeared. So did Manoa.

At dusk, still crawling towards where he supposed his platoon to be, a shadow moved behind a tree. Both man and shadow played hide and seek, trying to move into positions to kill the other, until they realised they were both Fijians. It was Metuisela.

When at last they reached Sisivie and found it deserted, they spent a terrifying night, surrounded by Japanese.

All the others had moved from Sisivie, back towards Ibu again, until they met Major Upton's force moving down. Except for two sections of A Company and Roko and Metuisela, presumed dead, the force was complete. But the questions was, where to go now?

The Rev. Usaia Sotutu.

Manoa Roko.

That was when Rev Sotutu stepped forward and said he knew the way out. Almost in disbelief, the major told him to lead the way.

Sotutu asked the men to 'lotu' first. "Yea, though I walk through the valley of death . . ."

Then, the Fijians slowly began to vanish into the thick jungle, the 200 women and children in the middle of the line. Where they left the main track, they painstakingly camouflaged it, praying the enemy wouldn't find it. It was pitch-black: each man held the equipment of the man in front.

With unerring accuracy, Sotutu picked his way through the jungle.

Finally, the force halted. Even then, the end of the column was a mere 100 yards from the Japanese-infested Sisivie trail.

During the second night, Corporal Manoa and Metuisela caught up with the battalion. They had noticed leaves on a shrub were upside-down and when they investigated the obvious camouflage, they discovered an American chewing gum label. They had found the 'gate' leading to their own force!

That night, the two sections of A Company, cut off at Sisivie, also found their way back. Led by Sgt. Semisi Belo, they had sprayed a river crossing with machinegun fire, broken through the Japanese circle, and joined the strange parade through the bush.

The march lasted four days. At some points, they were crossing mountains 5000 feet high. Behind them lay 180 enemy dead at a cost of one Fijian killed and one wounded.

Ahead of them, the landing barges of the 37th US Division Reconnaissance Troop waited, as requested over Rev Sotutu's radio. As the hungry and weary 1st Battalion reached the coast at Kiape, the Americans cheered.

The 1st had cheated death. Within hours, they were back inside the Allied perimeter at Torokina.

Safely aboard the landing craft, First Battalion men are on their way home from Ibu.

First Battalion troops being inspected in the Solomons by Fiji's Governor, Major-General Sir Philip and Major G.T. Upton.

Insert — Fiji's only Victoria Cross winner, Corporal Sefanaia Sukanaivalu.

46   ONE WAS A V.C. WINNER, ONE A CANNIBAL

The Fijians proved themselves such excellent soldiers in the Solomons that the 3rd Battalion was ordered to Bougainville, as well.

It landed at Empress Augusta Bay in late March, 1944 — right at the height of the battle for Torokina beach-head.

The battle raged for two months, and it was so intense that thousands of lives were lost among both Japanese and Allied forces.

It was a hellish beginning for an untried troop, but like any battalion of fighting men, some were to become heroes and some gained notoriety in other ways.

Among them were Fiji's only Victoria Cross winner . . . and a man who was probably the very, very last recorded Fijian cannibal!

* * *

224

A month before the 3rd Battalion arrived, the American Intelligence Service intercepted a secret coded message to the Japanese Supreme Commander in the Pacific. The message ordered an attack on Torokina on March 7. Bombing was to begin three days before, and on D-Day, 300 'zeros' and 'betsy' bombers were to carry out a dawn raid on the American base before the Japanese troops moved in.

The Allies began making preparations for the attack, and they decided the 1st Battalion would operate as a mobile reserve force, ready to move wherever the need was greatest.

March 7th was ominously quiet, but air patrols noted enemy troops moving up to the perimeter.

The next day, artillery began shelling Torokina, and the Japanese pushed in with suicidal determination. When the Japanese broke through the perimeter and gained a few hundred yards, the Americans, just as determined, pushed them back again. Much of the fighting was hand-to-hand, a war of point-blank firing, flamethrower bursts and bayonet thrusts.

By the 15th, 700 of the enemy were dead and the perimeter was still intact. But the Americans had suffered heavily as well; one entire company had been almost completely wiped out.

During this time, the 1st Battalion was patrolling outside the perimeter. There were frequent skirmishes with the enemy, and the Fiji battalion reported the area was littered with enemy dead.

Masters of the bush, the Fijians were once again escaping with light casualties. But then, on March 25th, a patrol ran into a nest of Japanese machine gun posts imbedded on a low hill. There was a swamp on one side and a mine-field on the other. That left little alternative . . .there wasn't any way to outflank it, so the patrol charged straight in. The hill was taken, but the costs were high: a lieutenant was killed and 14 others were wounded.

The following day, more enemy positions were uncovered and the Japanese fought fanatically. Four more Fijians were killed and 9 wounded.

It was to be the same story, day after day, outside the perimeter, the enemy were so firmly entrenched that each day, the patrols came under fire. Just when they thought an area was cleared, snipers would begin their deadly work.

As one of the patrols moved toward Numa Numa, they found Private Asivosori Kete. Asivorosi had been reported killed three days earlier, but when someone noticed a body lying at the bottom of a foxhole, they did a double-take: it moved.

He had been hit by rifle fire, and the bullet entered under his right ear and came out under his left eye.

The Japanese found him and, to make sure, they bayoneted him twice through the chest and once more in the arm. They took the boots off the 'body' and stole the food ration clipped to his belt.

He lay there for three days. The Allied forces had pinpointed the enemy camp and each day, they blasted it with an artillery barrage. Asivorosi either climbed into a foxhole or was blown into it by one of the exploding artillery shells which were landing all around him.

When he was found, he was carried to hospital, but the American medics shook their heads; it almost seemed like a waste of time to try to patch him up. There was no way, they said, he would survive. They worked on him anyway . . . and Asivorosi fooled them. He lived. The man who refused to die went back to his village in Kadavu, fit and well.

Meanwhile, the 3rd Battalion had arrived. They reached Torokina at midnight on March 23rd, just as the Japanese launched their final desperate drive.

At first, they were held in reserve, greenhorns kept out of the action, although their officers went out with 1st Battalion patrols. But the fifth day after their arrival, a reconnaissance patrol moved out beyond the perimeter for "mopping up" operations, and during three days in the jungle, they killed 7 of the enemy. One of the patrol members was Viliame Lomasalato, and he had made a promise to himself. Fijian pride in warfare is deeply engraved, and in Viliame, so was a custom that in Fiji had been a common practice 100 years earlier.

Viliame promised himself that the first Japanese he encountered would be cut into portions and devoured!

In the dense bush, Viliame found his victims and dragged two dead Japanese back to the patrol's camp, intent on sharing them with his *yavusa*, his co-warriors in battle. It took several officers and a wrestling match to prevent him from dismembering the two.

A few weeks later, his unit was at Mawaraka and the fighting was fierce. The platoon was pinned down by enemy fire, and nobody was moving anywhere.

And then Viliame spotted a fallen Japanese soldier. Dashing toward him, he swooped low with a pocket knife, and in one instant had fulfilled his promise. As if filled with a sudden mana, he stood up, firing at the enemy with his tommy gun and lobbing grenades as far as he could throw them.

He called for more and his platoon members, all lying low, kept a continuous chain of them coming. The enemy, those that were still alive, withdrew.

Viliame was almost certainly Fiji's last cannibal, but his curious custom was overlooked in light of his gallantry; he was awarded the Military Medal.

In the patrols that followed, both the 1st and 3rd Battalions delved beyond the perimeter. They captured weapons, including 70 and 75mm guns, and exchanged fire with the enemy, but one thing was now certain: Torokina was not to be taken.

The Japanese attack on the airfield, one of the most vital Allied bases in the Pacific, had failed and the enemy were in full retreat. Allied losses were heavy, but they were small in comparison with the Japanese, who lost 6000 men during March and April.

Back in the perimeter, both battalions had a couple weeks of rest. They played cricket, challenged each other to boxing matches, and even rode homemade surfboards on Torokina's surf. Enemy air bases had taken such a pounding that the nights after April were free of raids. There was a movie every night.

The holiday ended in May, when an effort was made to push the Japanese away from mid-island blockades which prevented the Allies from reaching the east coast. But even this was relatively uneventful. At Jaba and the Mawaraka road, the enemy retreated ahead of them. They found empty pillboxes and abandoned camps. Patrols met opposition in only a few spots, and casualties were light.

For one brief morning in May, the Fijians almost could have believed they were home. In a ceremony which was almost like the *bolebole* (bragging) ritual of old, the Fijians pledged their loyalty to the American Major-General Griswold an the XIV Corps. Dressed in leaves and glistening with oil, they presented yaqona and a tabua while hundreds of American soldiers watched.

General Griswold said he believed no greater compliment had been received by any soldier.

The 1st Battalion had been in the Solomons for 16 months and in almost continuous action for the last six, when it was informed in mid-June that it was going home. The 3rd Battalion was to follow a month later.

As the 1st Battalion set about packing, the 3rd prepared for a second trip to Mawaraka. Word had been received that a number of Boungainvilleans there had collected abandoned weapons and, in about six villages along the Jaba River, were trying to drive out the Japanese.

The Allies decided to give them a hand. About 100 villagers from the Jaba area who had escaped the enemy cordon had been brought safely into Torokina, and they had given valuable information about the enemy defences.

At dawn on June 23rd, five companies moved silently toward Mawaraka following an amphibious landing on a nearby beach. A barrage of shells burst in the tree-tops behind them, but the supporting US artillery quickly located the source and soon after, the barrage ceased.

'D' Company was half-way across an exposed part of beach before the Japanese opened fire from pillboxes on Mawaraka Point, and with big guns hidden in the hills above. The company withdrew temporarily, waited until American gunboats and artillery softened the beachhead a little, and moved back in with grenades.

When the fire lifted, 'D' Company was back in position, and 'E' Company began to wade through the swamp to Mawaraka road.

They were only 100 yards from the road when they were hit with intense fire from machine guns and mortars. Two of the leading scouts were hit and one was killed outright. As men tried to get the injured out of the swamp, there were more casualties.

That is how Corporal Sefanaia Sukanaivalu won his Victoria Cross.

He had already helped recover two of the wounded, and he volunteered to go in and try to rescue more. There was a staccato burst of machine gun fire and then Sefanaia was on the ground, hit twice and so seriously wounded that he was unable to move.

The official account of the citation when he was posthumously awarded the Victoria Cross tells the rest of the story:

"Several attempts were made to rescue Corporal Sefanaia but without success owing to heavy firing encountered on each occasion and further casualties were caused. This gallant NCO then called to his men not to try to get him as he was in a very exposed position, but they replied they would never leave him to fall into the hands of the enemy.

"Realizing his men would not leave him as long as they could see he was alive and knowing that they were all in danger of being killed or captured as long as they remained where they were, Corporal Sefanaia, well aware of the consequences, raised himself up in front of the Japanese machine guns and was riddled with bullets."

Mawaraka was not taken that month. Documents captured later showed that the Japanese had two infantry battalions and an artillery detachment stationed there when the 3rd Battalion went in.

The Australians eventually took the position, and they recovered the body of Corporal Sefanaia, which was buried with full military honours at Cape Moeltke, about 20 miles northwest of Torokina.

On July 25th, the USS Altnitah sailed into Empress Augusta Bay to take the 1st Battalion home. It sailed to Guadalcanal, and then directly to Fiji. Sixteen months earlier, when the battalion had first gone to war, four destroyers and an aircraft carrier had guarded them as they crossed the Pacific. This time, a tiny Corvette stayed with the ship for 24 hours, and then turned back as the Altnitah sailed on, alone.

Few men slept as the ship approached Suva. The first light they saw was Cape Washington on Kadavu, and then, hours later, a blinking Aldis lamp from Suva answered their signal.

Lieutenant-Colonel Ratu Sir Lala Sukuna, along with the Governor and Brigadier Dittmer, stood on the wharf to welcome the troops home. It was August 4, 1944.

As the troops climbed down the ladder and filed past the officials, the crowds behind the barriers watched in quiet respect, solemn and subdued.

But not for long. The *magitis* and the grog parties and the wailing of women for sons who hadn't returned were still going on when the Altnitah slipped her mooring lines and turned back to bring the 3rd Battalion home, too.

The campaign in the Solomons claimed 57 men from the Fiji troops, including those who died of wounds or sickness overseas. But the Fijian's appetite for war was undaunted, and the veterans of the Solomons were energetically training for promised operations in a new theatre of war, Burma, when atomic bombs fell on Hiroshima and Nagasaki, and Japan surrendered.

Fijians on patrol at Batu Pahat.

47   MALAYA: THE SNAKE-IN-THE-GRASS-CAMPAIGN

Two days after the battalion moved into Batu Pahat — the stronghold of the communist terrorists in Malaya — a patrol went out to survey likely ambush positions.

The men were just climbing down from the truck when terrorists opened fire on them, but in a lightning turnabout, the Fijians attacked, led by Sgt. Inoke Tabua. Three of the communists were killed.

Soon after the patrol returned to camp, they received a message from General Templar, Commanding General, Malaya: "Congratulations on try in the first 30 seconds. Convert quickly."

For anyone used to rugby, the message was simple enough, and two days later, another 'A' Company patrol, under 2/Lt Masi, ran into four more armed rebels. Two of the Fiji troops were slightly wounded, but two of the communists were killed.

The battalion's commanding officer, Col. Tinker, sent a message back to the general: "Have converted, score now 5-nil."

The Fijians were pretty good in sports, and their four-year contest in Malaya was to prove no exception.

★ ★ ★

The Emergency, as it was called in Malaya, actually began in 1948. The British-Malayan negotiations to form a Federation of Malaya were bitterly opposed by the Chinese, and armed communist guerillas, operating from jungle hideouts, began making raids to destroy the new Government.

When Britain began assembling colonial forces to combat the threat, it wanted forces proven in jungle warfare. That's how units such as the Kings African Rifles, the Rhodesian African Rifles, the Gurkhas, and the Fijians got there.

On January, 8, 1952, more than 800 men of the 1st Battalion Fiji Infantry Regiment, boarded the troopship Asturias for Malaya. The Fiji Times recorded an "unprecedented display of emotion" as thousands of people lined the streets and wharf to see them off.

Training was brief — a few days in Singapore and a few more at an interim-camp called Nee Soon, — then the battalion was moved to the centre of the Malay Peninsula, Bahau.

Solomone Momoivalu remembers their "baptism by fire":

"We went straight from training camp to the jungle. The battalion received word that CTs (communist terrorists) would be making a ration collection, and Charley Company was sent to prepare an ambush.

"We moved in about 10 at night, 20 men in a half-mile long chain and waited for dawn; Korovulavula was in command, Malakai Mo was platoon sergeant.

"At dawn, nothing had happened and I was having problems keeping my eyes open. Men were throwing stones at each other to keep awake. Suddenly, I heard machinegun fire and Mo and Isireli calling to me . . . the CTs had gone past and I was the nearest man to pursue them.

"I had a Bren gun and everybody was shooting wildly. I could hear the whistle of crossfire from all our positions. Two of the terrorists were dead and I went after the third . . ."

It was the battalion's first kill. The RFMF war diary noted briefly: "Small party of men from C Coy. arrived with bodies of three bandits."

The patrols around Bahau were a proving ground, and the men of the 1st Bn. proved they had what it takes.

General Templar, head of all the operations in Malaya, sent the battalion's commander a special directive: "Am sending your battalion to Batu Pahat in the Young Peng area of Johore under command of the 17th Gurkha Division. I wish to tell all ranks that in selecting your Bn for this task, they are moving to the most troublesome area in Malaya."

It was a compliment, of sorts. For the rest of their stay in Malaya, Yong Peng would be home. Batu Pahat was a heavily indoctrinated area with a large Chinese population and few Malays. The terrain was swampy and difficult most of the time, and during the moonsoon rains, almost impossible.

To make matters worse, the war was a strange, snake-in-the-grass type of conflict. Men hid in the grass and lay in ambush until someone came into their gun sights, a war of ambush and counter-ambush on both sides. Most patrols consisted of only seven or eight men.

Roads weren't any safer than the bush, since small troop carriers were a favourite target for snipers. But the bush hid other hazards as well, including crocodiles, wild pigs and an occasional leopard.

On one patrol, Lt. Paul Manueli came face-to-face with a rogue elephant. It had recently been shot and it was angry. The elephant reached Manueli while he was telling his men to take cover, and it threw him in the air, picked him up again and smashed him down to the ground.

As it nudged him with its foot, the lieutenant played dead — which wasn't far from the truth. He confided later that he thought he was finished.

The communist guerillas were well armed. In fact, they had weapons almost identical to those used by the Fiji troops, including modern rifles, grenades and light machineguns. Some of their ranks were women — but there was nothing delicate about a woman armed with a Sten gun.

In patrol after patrol, contact was made with 'bandits' and by November, 1953, the commanding officer was offering a special prize for the man directly responsible for the battalion's 100th kill.

Among the men responsible for the battalion's success was Sgt. Naikava Lagi. He was awarded the Military Medal after he spearheaded a particularly daring raid on a well-guarded camp, annihilating all of its occupants. He followed it up with four more successful operations, accounting for seven more enemy dead.

Another was Lt. Masi. When a Malayan police patrol was ambushed Lt. Masi heard the firing from a nearby camp and quickly organised a force. The only problem was the riflemen were out on patrol, so the lieutenant's force was composed of cooks, clerks and drivers — none of them combat trained.

Lt. Masi moved straight into the centre of fire and the communists were routed. One of Lt. Masi's "commandos" was a cook named Apeti who, being slightly overweight, fell behind and finally sat down in the road to rest.

Apeti looked up just as two armed guerillas stepped out onto the road . . . and he shot them both with a single (and very lucky?) shot which went right through both of them!

Lt Masi got the honours as leader of the attack force, but the cook must have been the hero in the camp that night.

In the battalion's main camp at Batu Pahat, life was almost normal. It was considered so secure that, by April, 1954, the first eight Fijian families moved in, including Adi Laisa Ganilau. The camp boasted of a school, and Fijian mekes entertained nearby villages.

When the men weren't on patrol, they seemed to be on the sports field, and the Fijian forces mopped up all the trophies and honours for almost all of the international forces in Malaya. A battalion soccer team smashed New Zealand 57 to 0; the Scottish Cameronians 108 to 3, and the football team went to Hong Kong to beat Combined Services 43-0.

So it wasn't surprising that the rifle companies discussed the enemy in terms of a score, a competition which was to get more intense towards war's end.

Some of the action is best described by actual entries in the Royal Fiji Military Forces war diary:

August 6, 1954 — 3rd Platoon, A. Coy, under command of Lt.

Momoivalu contacted 2 CTs, killing 1. Platoon about to move into position when Bren gunner spotted CTs just as CT scout saw him. Both fired simultaneously. Bren gunner responsible for elimination of 150th bandit is L/Cpl Toganivalu . . .

August 19 — Point section under command of Sgt. Lagi spotted tracks crossing river. CTs opened fire. Sgt. O'Brien wounded Sgt. Lagi immediately charged with his section and killed both CTs. During engagement, CT attempted to throw grenade but was shot in hand and grenade fell in river, killing fish. Section enjoyed fish.

September 7 — Maj George Mate informed by acting CO (Major P.K. Ganilau) that he had been awarded Military Cross . . . Major led his Coy. over a period of 14 days through most difficult country to eliminate 7 CTs and destroy numerous camps . . .

September 13 — Conference held in CO's office to discuss possible methods of eliminating Goh Peng Tuan . . .

Goh Peng Tuan was the area's leading terrorist, and in the days that followed, he was to become even more hated by the battalion as the man responsible for its two most serious reverses.

The first of them happened two months later, when 11 men of B Company were returning from a patrol. They were ambushed by about 30 Chinese, and five Fijians were killed. Six more were wounded, including Capt. Rokoca, who was shot twice as he dashed two miles to Yong Peng police station for reinforcements.

Late in the afternoon of Feb. 21, 1955, Goh Peng struck again.

Major Robert Genge, 'A' Company's commanding officer, the 21C, Lt. Julian Toganivalu, along with a Bren gunner, Pte. Josaia Kobiti and a driver, Pte. Timoci Semo, were returning to their base from a conference at headquarters, Batu Pahat.

As they came around a turn, they found the road blocked by concertina wire, and as they slowed, they came under intense fire from about 25 guerillas.

They tried to ram their way through the wire, but then Maj. Genge was shot dead and he fell across the driver. As the jeep lurched out of control and climbed an embankment, a grenade exploded underneath and the vehicle overturned and caught fire.

Lt. Toganivalu, already shot in the leg, was pinned beneath the burning vehicle.

Josaia Kobiti carried Maj. Genge to the side of the road, then freed Lt. Toganivalu and carried him over, as well, still firing as he did it. Timoci Semo ran out of ammunition, and then he was knocked unconscious by the guerillas.

Pte. Kobiti kept on firing until he, too, was out of ammunition. But when the Chinese attacked, he threw the barrel of his Bren gun at them. Surprised, they dropped to the ground again.

The communists ransacked the Jeep, stripped the pistol and holster from the unconscious Lt. Toganivalu, removed everything of value from Maj. Genge's body, grabbed a $2500 payroll, then made ready to deal with Kobiti.

But before they came at him again, an armoured car from Yong Peng police post arrived and, after a quick gun battle, the communists were chased off.

Pte. Josaia Kobiti was awarded the Military Medal and received a citation for unsurpassed bravery — but it was still a bitter day for the battalion.

For weeks on end, patrols combed the bush looking for Goh Peng, and bombers struck CT camps. It was one of these fighter pilots who stole the battalion's revenge: an air attack on a camp had been successful and 14 bodies of the terrorists were recovered. One of them, still wearing Maj. Genge's watch, was Goh Peng Tuan.

As 1955 drew to an end, there were fewer and fewer successes. Patrols led by Lt. Paul Manueli and by Lt. William Toganivalu were successful and recorded eight enemy killed, but others were continually coming in with little to report except deserted, empty camps.

The communists were quitting the area, and by January, 1956, the Fiji Forces probably wished they could, too. Monsoon rains had once again turned the area into deeply flooded swamp. Some platoons, marooned by flood waters, had to have their supplies airdropped to their hilltop camps.

Two months before the 1st Battalion was to leave Malaya, the rifle companies were nearly tied in their "game" — 'D' Co. had 60 kills, 'A' Co. had 61.

Lt. M.V. Buadromo led his D Company platoon out into the bush, intent on evening the score. During seven wet weeks in January and February, his platoon scoured the bush. Just before they were due to move back to base, they received word that Sapali, a noted terrorist who claimed he could be killed only by a silver bullet, would be collecting rations.

An informer pointed out the supply cache, and Lt. Buadromo and his men climbed into drains and into the thick grass of an abandoned rubber estate and waited.

Six men approached, one of them the rubber tapper who had been the platoon's informer. The tapper was nervously trying to hold back, and it seemed impossible that Sapali couldn't see the platoon. He walked up to the supplies, three yards from Lt. Buadromo, before he looked up — and died.

Pte. Timoci Kaci had opened fire with a Bren gun and two of the CTs fell. A third began to run, but Buadromo had exhausted his ammunition so he ran after the terrorist and clubbed him with a carbine!

It was the last active patrol. D Company had won. From then on, patrols returned daily with nothing to report. The terrorists of Batu Pahat had all but disappeared.

On April 28, the 1st Battalion withdrew from operations. They had killed 208 guerillas at a cost of 25 men, 13 of whom had been killed in action.

There were 25 people aboard the Joyita when she left Apia, Western Samoa, on October 3, 1955, for a two-day run to the Tokelaus.

As days passed and the vessel failed to turn up, searches were organised. Then, 37 days after it had sailed, Joyita — waterlogged and listing but still afloat — was found drifting north of Vanua Levu.

Officials from both Fiji and Western Samoa began to investigate, and the more they investigated, the more mysteries they ran into.

It looked as if someone had deliberately tried to sink her: a seacock had been opened and the decks were scorched as if petrol had been poured on them and set alight. More than four tons of cargo was gone. So was the chronometer and log book.

So were the people — 25 people gone without a trace, including the captain who knew Joyita would not sink . . .

★ ★ ★

Joyita in Spanish means 'little jewel'. When she was built in 1931 for a Los Angeles movie-magnate, that's what she was. The 69-foot, 70-ton motor yacht was luxuriously appointed and, besides its mahogany interior, boasted twin diesels and an automatic pilot.

The US Navy requisitioned her during World War II and took it to Pearl Harbour as a patrol boat, and by the time 'Dusty' Miller got it, the vessel was probably a little less lavish.

But Dusty was proud of it. Financed by his fiancee, who was actually the boat's owner, the ex-navy reserve commander began a series of business ventures in the Pacific. One after another the ventures failed. Dusty was a competent seafarer, but a poor businessman.

In one of his last gambits, Miller tried to ferry frozen fish to island markets. That didn't pay off either, but a positive result was that the hold was lined with 640 cubic feet of thick insulating cork. The cork made Joyita practically unsinkable.

Perhaps that was one reason why Dusty didn't bother to carry a lifeboat aboard. The Joyita left Apia on a Monday, bound for Fakaofo in the Tokelaus, 270 miles away. It was to be a mercy mission of sorts. The Tokelau islands were dangerously short of food, and they had radioed that there was an urgent medical problem as well, a man with a gangrenous arm. The Tokelau District Officer, recently appointed from New Zealand, was in Apia waiting to get out to the islands with food and medical aid.

Western Samoa's government refused to charter Joyita because it was of foreign registry and because its last port, Pago Pago, had been cleared without proper papers. But the government turned a blind eye when the biggest copra merchant in the islands, Coxon's, agreed to hire the boat. There were tons of copra in the Tokelaus awaiting export, and the Joyita would serve several purposes at once.

Five Europeans — the District Officer, a doctor and medical assistant, and two copra buyers — were signed on as crew, since the boat was not licensed to carry passengers.

One of the men from Coxen's, G.K. Williams, was listed on the crew list as 'supercargo' and he was carrying a small fortune with him to buy copra: 1000 pounds Samoan. The rest of the 25 on board were Samoan, Gilbertese, and Tokelau islanders.

On October 6, a wireless message from Fakaofo reported that Joyita had not arrived, and a RNZAF Sunderland from Laucala Bay flew to Apia, then across to Fakaofo and back again without sighting anything.

On November 10, the captain of the Tuvalu, enroute from Suva to Funafuti, saw something drifting a few miles off course, and he directed the helmsman to investigate. It was the Joyita, filled with water, listing heavily to port, and empty. The ship stood by until the Joyita could be taken in tow. An air search of the area for any survivors proved fruitless. The officials began to investigate as soon as she reached Suva and was dried out, and there were a lot of immediate questions.

Joyita left Apia with 44 150-lb bags of flour, 15 70-lb bags of sugar, and 460 empty copra sacks, but there wasn't a trace of cargo in any of the holds. Friends who knew Dusty Miller swore he'd never leave the boat, and that he frequently boasted it was unsinkable . . . particularly if the choice was a raft-like float, which was all the Joyita carried.

And there was the mystery of the opened seacock and the charred decks. Why, if people were abandoning the boat, didn't they leave a message behind?

Within 24 hours after Joyita reached Suva, she was world news. Some papers called it another 'Marie Celeste', the ship found adrift in the Atlantic in 1872 with no signs of damage, meals half-eaten on the tables, and no people.

The world press began offering explanations: seaquakes, explosions, pirates. The local press on November 19 startled everyone with a banner headline reading ALL ABOARD JOYITA MURDERED? It claimed the "official view" of the disaster was that Joyita had been set upon by a Japanese fishing fleet known to be in the area near the Tokelaus, and that the Japanese had killed all aboard as postwar revenge.

Government was horrified, and the Colonial Secretary quickly stated that government held no such view, and further noted that such "wild suggestions can only cause grief to anxious relatives".

When, a week later, the Fiji Guardian reported Japanese knives found aboard, the public's imagination went wild. But they were penknives, not Samurai swords, and besides, police lab tests failed to find any trace of blood.

Soon after it was dry-docked, there were some partial answers. Flooding had been caused by a corroded and broken pipe in the cooling system, a break which would have been difficult to trace by the time the water became noticeable. There had been no distress call because there was a break in the aerial wire. So Joyita had been in trouble . . . that much was certain.

A commission of inquiry at Apia began to turn up other interesting bits of evidence. It was learned that Joyita had loaded more than 2,600 gallons of fuel, enough for a journey of 3000 miles, yet it was only going to Fakaofo, 270 miles away.

Dusty Miller had refused to test the radio at Apia, despite continued requests, because he knew it wasn't working.

The port engine was working poorly, if at all, and immediately after it left Apia, witnesses saw smoke coming from the boat, then watched it drift and wallow toward the reef before it eventually got underway again, apparently under one engine. And the commission heard that Dusty was broke, that he had taken odd jobs to pay bills, that his crew had left after he failed to pay them, and that he was "worried and run down".

A storm blew the night Joyita left, and winds were strong. One of the men who had watched the boat clear harbour had remembered thinking he was glad he wasn't on Joyita that night . . .

The commission built a picture of a depressed and desperate captain, unwilling to turn back because the boat would be declared unfit for that charter, and he would lose what appeared to be a last opportunity to get back on his feet.

Taking the boat to sea without a lifeboat, knowing that the radio was out and only one engine working, reflected on Dusty's duties as captain. But it didn't explain any of the other mysteries, and the commission couldn't find the answers, either.

Robin Maugham, author of The Joyita Mystery, interviewed Commander Peter Plowman, Western Samoa's member for marine in government, who came to Suva to inspect the Joyita. Plowman had discovered two interesting and unreported facts: rubbish in the scuppers included a scalpel, needles and catgut, and stained bandages. And an awning had been rigged on Joyita *after* the mishap, because it was lashed to a broken piece of stanchion.

Maugham reconstructed the ill-fated voyage this way: there had been a fight, perhaps between the officials on their way to the Tokelaus, who rightly could have ordered the vessel to return to port, and Dusty Miller who knew that if he returned, he was washed up. In the fight, Miller was injured. As the boat took water and began to list, passengers and crew took to the floats, assuming the boat would sink at any moment. Those that abandoned ship never made land. Miller died. Later, a fishing fleet happened on the hulk, pirated the cargo and log book, threw the body of Dusty Miller overboard, and opened the seacock to dispose of any evidence of their pilferage.

All very plausible.

Long before the speculation died down, Joyita was back at sea again. A Vanua Levu planter, David Simpson, bought her in July, 1956, but six months later, Joyita was aground on Horseshoe Reef in the Koro Sea. All 13 passengers were safely rescued by the 'Yanawai', and Joyita was towed to Levuka. The Master had his certificate cancelled for incompetency, despite the Fijian master's testimony that the ship was "cursed" and that "there was no holding her, she ran for the reef".

In 1958, Joyita was refitted and began to trade regularly between Suva and Levuka, but she hit the reef at Vatuvula, Makogai passage. That was the end of Joyita's sailing days. Robin Maugham bought her as an inspiration for his book, and then she was sold to Major Casling-Cottle in Levuka, who planned to turn the ill-fated launch into a floating museum and tea-room, where visitors from all over the world could munch scones and ponder her mysteries.

But each day, each passing week and each Ovalau storm stripped the vessel of more of her planking. The 'museum' became a rotting hulk, and then a carcass, and then a few ribs sticking out of the sand, and then nothing.

Ratu Sir Lala Sukuna reviews the troops with Sir Ronald Garvey.

49 RATU SUKUNA: THE MAN WHO GRACED A NATION

The cruise ship Arcadia was off the coast of Ceylon, enroute to England.

In the early hours of the morning, well before dawn, the ship's surgeon woke Arcadia's captain, and soon after, the radio operator was tapping out a message to a wireless operator in Suva.

The message was received in Fiji at 9.45am, May 30, 1958. Ratu Sir Lala Sukuna, Fiji's greatest statesman up to that time, had died.

Some aboard the cruise ship mistakenly referred to him as Fiji's 'King', an understandable mistake, considering his regal bearing. Those who had already met the quiet, elegantly-attired gentleman in the tailored sulu shook their heads and said how sad.

A very few knew that, only a month before, Ratu Sir Lala had retired from public service in Fiji and that the Oxford scholar was paying a sentimental return visit to England.

Fewer still could have realised what his death would mean to the Fijian people.

* * *

Ratu Sir Lala, even before his death, was a folk hero. He had walked away from Oxford in his second year of studies to join the French Foreign Legion (Chapter 37) and his exploits during World War I had earned him the Medaille Militaire, the highest honour which France awards.

He returned to Oxford and, by 1921, had both his Bachelor of Arts degree and an invitation to join the English Bar.

Oxford and the Legion gave him the international perspective he needed to round out his leadership qualities, and he was to become the principal link between government and the Fijians — even though he didn't like "officialdom".

He was a Legislative Council member who didn't like wasting time in Council, and he could be a strong antagonist of the European way when it countered Fijian society and traditions.

One of Ratu Sir Lala's best-known speeches, one he gave at the Defence Club in Suva in 1939, was titled "The Fijian's View of the Europeans". It might have offended the colonialists . . .if they had been able to stop laughing. Some of the choice parts:

"We call Europeans 'Kai Vavalagi' as if they all come from the same country, (but) to whatever place they belong, they have these qualities in common: they are rich and excellent subjects for 'kerekere', if only they had more understanding. They never soil their hands with labour; yet they are continuously urging us to do so from the Governor and the Director of Education downwards . . .

"Of the household goods of the Europeans, there is one they continuously serve and obey from the cradle to the grave, and that curiously enough is the thing they call a clock . . .

"Very few European women are really attractive, being mostly thin and fragile. It is they, though, that rule the roost, the men waiting on them hand and foot . . . in government, since the reorganisation, unless you are entitled to possess one of these tokens of superiority (a wife) it is impossible to rise to higher posts . . ."

Ratu Sukuna went on to describe the Englishman as "cold and aloof", but our respect is due to them as they come direct from the country our fathers regarded as the "Home of Men".

Australians, he said, "swear more than Englishmen . . . in a thin, shrill and toneless voice not pleasing to the ear". It was difficult, he noted, to tell when the swearing was in anger of affection, since the Australian used the same words in both situations.

"The New Zealander," Ratu Sukuna concluded, "lives in a bank counting other people's money" and the Americans "dress badly but eat and drink well". They expect to be waited on hand and foot and carry young ladies around for the purpose, as some of our high chiefs do . . ."

The speech might have alienated him from much of the community, but it didn't, because there was too much wisdom in it.

About the same time, he told another European audience that they had little or nothing in common with the Fijian. "He is of the stone age; you are of the era of increasing speed and high explosives. Pitch-forked into your time, he can be no more than an astounded spectator, squinting and doubting, seeing and not understanding."

That was in 1939.

But an editorial in the Fiji Times on April 2, 1958 — on Ratu Sir Lala Sukuna's 70th birthday — noted that it was Ratu Sukuna himself who had made the biggest contribution to "pitck-forking" the Fijian into the modern era.

The editorial said that Ratu Sukuna was "the best of interpreters of his

people to those in authority, and of the affairs of government and of the outside world to the Fijian villager."

It had been largely due to his efforts that the Fijians had gone overseas during World War II. Ratu Sukuna believed that the Fijians would never be recognised until they had shed blood, and it is probably true that the Fijian forces in the Solomons and later, in Malaya, earned a world identity because of it.

Certainly, Fiji established friendships with allied nations which will never be forgotten.

But the biggest task and easily the most delicate was his role in sorting out problems of Fiji land-ownership. It was to keep him occupied for years, and it also provided him with the constant village contacts which made him so much a man of the people.

Ratu Sukuna's work was done around the *yaqona* bowl, from one end of the colony to the other, and so when news of his death reached Fiji, the nation was stunned.

On June 6, Ratu Sir Lala's body lay in state at Rairaiwaqa, Suva. The Fiji Times' description of the events during that day adequately records the emotions:

"Fijians are not supposed to weep when a chief dies — but many did at dawn yesterday, silently.

They were among a crowd of more than 1000 Fijians who saw Ratu Sir Lala Sukuna's body finally come home to Rairaiwaqa, after its long journey from half-way round the world.

When the flag-draped casket was placed on the specially prepared bier after its night-long road journey from Nadi, women of high rank took up their traditional positions on the floor.

Along one wall, other women attendants fanned continuously, in perfect unison.

For much of the day, Lady Liku sat beside the bier.

In the hall, and outside, there was silence. When people spoke, they spoke in whispers. Ordinary Fijians sat in groups at the rear of the big house and none went close.

No Fijian, except relatives and chiefs of high rank, is permitted by tradition to approach the body. But non-Fijians entered the hall from the east and silently passed the bier . . .

In the grounds, Fijian guards stood rigid, alert.

They watched as groups of Fijians, representing the provinces throughout the Colony, waited for their turn to present their gifts in a specially erected hut outside the house.

Dressed in black, they brought with them tabua and mats and gifts ranging from pigs to armfuls of biscuits in tins, yams, dalo and turtle.

Tongans and Lauans wore the traditional tao-vala mats around their waists, women and men took it in turns to blow the davui (conch shell) continuously.

The shell blowing will end when the Adi Maopa sails from Suva on Monday.

But the mournful tones will be taken up again at Lakeba as soon as the funeral vessel is sighted from the distance."

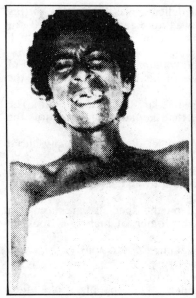
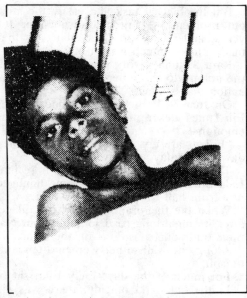

Survivors Nina Rareba and Viliame Qelo were found on a raft near Nasoata Island.

50   TRAGEDY AT SEA

Ten people clung desperately to the sides of a make-shift raft, aware of other voices crying out somewhere in the darkness around them.

The cries were soon drowned out in the wrath of the storm, and those clutching the raft began to sing hymns.

Morning came, and night again. Battered by waves, some began to show signs of weakening. Then, one by one, they began to let go.

Four days after the Kadavulevu sank in the Koro Sea, there were only three survivors . . . out of 90!

The Kadavulevu disaster stood without parallel in Fiji's modern maritime history until, nearly ten years later, the Uluilakeba was hit with the full fury of Cyclone Lottie as she ran for cover in the Lau Group.

This is the story of those two ill-fated vessels and their unfortunate passengers . . .

The island of Nairai was bursting with activity on Easter Sunday in 1964. A big *solevu* at Waitoga village had lasted for two days and the exchange of food and gifts between those at Nairai and about 80 visitors from Suva had left everyone in good spirits.

On that Easter Sunday afternoon, the visitors began carrying their newly-acquired mats, masi and dalo down to the beach as the Waitoga people gathered to farewell them.

Most of those boarding the auxilliary-schooner Kadavulevu, the boat they had chartered from Suva, were women and children: a few men had come along to help carry the presents and the make the ceremonial presentations.

The seas were rough, but it wasn't raining. Viti Levu had been deluged with rain, and serious flooding in Nadi, the Rewa delta and Wainimala valley had marred the holiday for thousands. But at Nairai, there was too much gaiety to cast any gloom on the departure.

Kadavulevu tossed and rolled in the small inlet, pulling on her anchor chains. She wasn't a new boat by any means, but the cutter was one of the best of the inter-island traders, a strong, 45-foot hulled vessel that had seen plenty of rough weather.

She was licensed to carry 29 people. Counting the crew, there were almost 90 aboard, which is to say she had the usual number of passengers for an inter-island run.

The cutter had been at sea less than two hours before it ran into gale conditions, but a bright moon that evening helped ease the discomfort of those aboard. Almost all of the passengers were huddled or rolled-up into any available space, trying to sleep off the effects of sea-sickness.

One elderly couple couldn't sleep. The weather was frightening and their only grandson had been left in their charge. They asked the captain if they could pull into Gau and shelter until the weather improved.

Nina Rareba, a passenger standing in the wheel-house, was also hoping that the boat would head for safe anchorage. But Nina heard the captain tell the old couple that "everything is all right. We will get to Suva."

Moments later, the Kadavulevu smashed broadside into a giant wave, shuddered, heeled onto her side for a brief second — and turned over.

The passengers huddling together out on deck were thrown into the sea immediately. Others somehow managed to clamber out from inside, against the rush of water coming in. They clung to the side of the overturned boat. But then there was a muffled explosion and flames began consuming the hull. They were forced to swim away from the heat.

Debris from the wreck — bits of timber pushed out by the explosion, deck cargo, kerosene tins and anything else that floated — was the only refuge offered to the swimmers. They began making rafts.

To one of those make-shift rafts, 43-year-old Seini Wakesa clutched with all her life. She could hear people thrashing in the water, screaming out names. Some of them she knew, must be holding on to bits of wreckage, too.

As dawn broke on Easter Monday, Seini and five others, including her grandchild, still held on. That afternoon, two of them were swept away. The child disappeared on Tuesday morning.

On Wednesday morning, only Seini and another woman were left. About noon that day, the raft was broken on Nasilai Reef. Seini began swimming with all the strength she had left.

Hours later, she was washed up on Nasoata Island, semi-conscious.

Some boys from Korovou village found her, sprawled on the sand.

Two and a half days after the Kadavulevu foundered, the first survivor had reached land. She blurted out a story of disaster before lapsing into sleep at a Nausori nursing station.

As word of the tragedy spread, the pilot of the RNZAF Sunderland flying boat recalled that, just southwest of Beqa, he had seen something which he had assumed was the wreckage of a house washed down the Rewa River by the recent floods . . . could it have been the Kadavulevu?

Authorities were certain it was, and, since the cutter was licensed to carry 29, they predicted a loss of life "of at least 20."

The search began. A fleet of Rewa punts headed for Nasilai while volunteers combed the coastline from Navua to Rewa. An armada of boats moved out to search the open sea: the pilot boat Seniceva, the Malawai, Yacomai, Inez, Tanoa, Maroro, two RNZAF patrol boats, Union Steam Ship company's launch Ranadi, and even some PWD tugs.

On Thursday afternoon about 2:30, the Seniceva was nearing Nasoata Island where Seini had been found. As the pilot boat crested a wave, it nearly ran into a raft with two more survivors: 14-year-old Viliame Qelo and Nina Rareba, 49. Viliame managed to smile and tell his rescuers he "felt quite well." Nina Rareba, however, was too weak to talk.

At dusk Thursday, the searchers began to come in. They brought no more survivors — only a pitiful and sad collection of charred and smashed debris. A PWD tug returned with the Kadavulevu's empty dinghy, a pillow, and a box containing two dead chickens. The Ranadi found the vessel's deckhouse, along with a life-raft, near Serua Island between the mainland and Beqa.

Friday, the boats went out again. The Sunderland flew overhead.

There was a brief stir of excitement when the flying boat crew spotted a survivor, but then the aircraft dipped lower and they noted the 'survivor' was face down, below the surface. Boats were directed to the area by radio, but were unable to find the body.

The search ended that night. Except for a bundle of mats and more blackened timber, the search boats had found nothing.

Friday, the same day the police released their list of 90 names, Viliame Qelo and Nina Rareba had recovered enough to tell their heart-rending stories.

Two of Nina's eight daughters were on the Kadavulevu when the boat turned turtle. Lora, 14, was with Nina below, and Vika, 18, was on deck. The boat capsized without warning. Amid the noise and confusion, Nina realised one of the voices she could hear was Lora's. Lora shouted that she and Vika were safe on another raft.

That was the last Nina ever heard or saw of her daughters.

Viliame was also down below. He and his mother, Finau, were both asleep on a bunk; his father, Isikeli, was asleep on the floor.

All he remembered at the time was that he suddenly found himself in the water and that, when he surfaced, he couldn't find his mother and father. He saw people holding to to debris, and he swam toward them.

He shared the raft with 10 others, singing and praying until dawn. The second day, he was so thirsty he drank a little saltwater, but then they found a few coconuts washed out to sea in the floods, and they ate the flesh and drank the milk. But by Wednesday, only Nina and Viliame still clung to life. The raft was big enough to hold their weight, except that every time a big wave hit them, the raft turned over and they were flung back into the sea.

Several times, they saw the lights of Suva, but they could not move the raft that direction. By Thursday, they had nearly given up hope. Both were lying face down on the raft, too weak to even talk.

"Then something told me to look up" Viliame said, "and when I did, I saw the pilot launch only three yards away."

Cyclone Lottie hit Fiji on December 10, 1973. It left five thousand homeless on Kadavu, then it moved off to the east, toward Kabara and Fulaga in the southern Lau group.

Between Vatoa and Ogea, Cyclone Lottie found another victim: the 212-ton ship Uluilakeba with 106 passengers and crew aboard — many of them school children on their way to Suva for the Christmas holidays.

The Uluilakeba had left Ogea hours before. Her master, Capt. Jesoni Kuruyawa, told a crew member they would be "in for a rough trip", but apparently, he felt they could ride out the predicted storm in safety.

The centre of the storm passed almost directly overhead. Waves 40-feet high smashed down on the ship and, despite full power, the captain radioed the ship was moving backwards. Marine officials in Suva received the message just before wind snapped the ship's aerial, ending radio contact. They decided the situation didn't yet call for emergency measures.

Passengers were told to stay inside the saloon. They were not given lifejackets, even though the ship was already listing badly. On deck, cadet officer Apisai Vere watched as the wind tore at the lashings of the boxes containing lifejackets, hurling the boxes over the side.

In the engine room, 2nd Engineer Bernard Smith answered a call from the captain for more speed. He replied the engines were at peak power. He was standing knee-deep in water. The lights went out, and three minutes later, the Uluilakeba capsized.

It was 1:30, Monday afternoon. They were 20 miles north of Vatoa.

That same afternoon, Suva received word that the Marine Department's boat Makogai had foundered at Kabara with the loss of five lives. Concern began to mount for the Uluilakeba in the same area.

At dawn on Tuesday, two Fiji Air Services planes left for Lau. One of them was carrying the Prime Minister, Ratu Sir Kamisese Mara, who wanted to be part of the search because of his knowledge of the area.

A Fiji Times photographer on one of the planes kept the following log of events:

11.23 (am) — Sighted liferaft with 1 person in, 1 person hanging on.
11:45 — Sighted 7 people in water. Refuelled.
2:14 pm — Soochow (a freighter enroute from Suva to Auckland which had diverted to the search area) arrived in pick-up area, confirmed 9 survivors aboard.
3:57 — Soochow confirmed 27 survivors aboard.
4:07 — male and female sighted on large white box.

4:11 — male on large yellow plank.
4:13 — young boy in green shirt on plank . . .

Both Prime Minister and press photographer felt the tension of being in the air, unable to directly assist those below. But as the plane circled, it radioed instructions to rescue craft, which picked up the survivors.

The first to be picked up by the Soochow had been in the water nearly two days. They were 8 miles north of Fulaga, and 25 miles from where the Uluilakeba rested on the bottom of the sea. Soochow stayed in the area until the Vuniwai, Rogovoka, and Tug Rigorous reached the area, and then she returned to Suva with 38 of the 41 known survivors.

Among them was Eramasi Salusalu, the Uluilakeba's night-watchman. He awoke as his bunk tipped almost upside down, and he dashed out on deck and jumped.

He heard a scream and looked up. A young woman was half-way out of a porthole, but she couldn't squeeze through. Seconds later, the ship went down. The woman was still stuck in the porthole.

Eramasi and a small boy were both holding onto a bag of coconuts. Then the suction of the sinking ship dragged them under.

"I lost him" Eramasi said. "I went down, down and down and was just about to give up and gasp for breath when I felt the sack break free and shoot up the surface. When I reached the surface, I was stark naked . . ."

He went on to describe how he and a teacher, who was floating on the ship's dalo box, sighted Kabara and then watched both a search plane and a ship pass them by without seeing them. When the plane finally spotted him and directed the Rigorous to pick him up, the teacher had disappeared beneath the waves.

Survivors began telling stories filled with terror. Mothers described how children had been pulled from their arms by the suction. One told of being followed by a shark, and others related the agony of drifting for up to 44 hours, clutching coconuts or boxes to keep afloat.

Capt. David Elliot, master of the Rigorous and a former master of the Uluilakeba, announced the most disheartening news. He said he had observed sharks in great numbers in the search area.

The Marine Department officially listed 79 persons as missing, presumed drowned, from the Uluilakeba disaster, although later it was thought to be fewer.

A subsequent marine inquiry not only rejuvenated sad memories, but brought to light some unfortunate facts. It found that the crew had never been drilled for an emergency, and that some of the crew didn't even know where lifejackets were stored.

And it heard that a number of officers and crew — incuding the captain — had tried to save themselves by lowering a lifeboat while passengers were still in the cabins and saloons.

They were unsuccessful, and the captain was among those dragged down when the Uluilakeba went under.

But it was difficult to criticise the will to survive, and the stories that circulated around the grog bowls after the tragedy were only of the joyous reunions and celebrations of those that reached shore.